(ISC)²®
CCSP® Certified Cloud Security Professional
Official Practice Tests
Third Edition

(ISC)²®

CCSP® Certified Cloud Security Professional

Official Practice Tests

Third Edition

Mike Chapple, Ph.D., CISSP, CCSP

David Seidl, CISSP

SYBEX®
A Wiley Brand

For Robin, again, for another one

Acknowledgments

The authors would like to thank the many people who made this book possible. Those include Jim Minatel at Wiley Publishing who helped us extend the Sybex certification preparation franchise to include this title and has continued to champion with the International Information Systems Security Certification Consortium (ISC)². Carole Jelen, our agent, tackles all the back-end magic for our writing efforts and worked on both the logistical details and the business side of the book with her usual grace and commitment to excellence. Sharif Nijim, our technical editor, pointed out many opportunities to improve our work and deliver a high-quality final product. John Sleeva served as our project manager and Archana Pragash served as our content refinement specialist. They both made sure everything fit together. Many other people we'll never meet worked behind the scenes to make this book a success, and we really appreciate their time and talents to make this next edition come together.

The authors, publisher and (ISC)² would like to acknowledge and thank the previous edition author Ben Malisow for his dedicated effort to advance the cause of CCSP and cloud security education.

About the Authors

Mike Chapple, Ph.D., CISSP, CCSP is an author of the best-selling *CISSP (ISC)² Certified Information Systems Security Professional Official Study Guide* (Sybex, 2021), now in its ninth edition. He is an information security professional with two decades of experience in higher education, the private sector, and government.

Mike currently serves as Teaching Professor of IT, Analytics, and Operations at the University of Notre Dame's Mendoza College of Business. He previously served as Senior Director for IT Service Delivery at Notre Dame, where he oversaw the information security, data governance, IT architecture, project management, strategic planning, and product management functions for the university.

Before returning to Notre Dame, Mike served as Executive Vice President and Chief Information Officer of the Brand Institute, a Miami-based marketing consultancy. Mike also spent four years in the information security research group at the National Security Agency and served as an active duty intelligence officer in the U.S. Air Force.

Mike has written more than 30 books, including *Cyberwarfare: Information Operations in a Connected World* (Jones & Bartlett, 2021), *CompTIA Security+ SY0-601 Study Guide* (Wiley, 2021), *CompTIA Cybersecurity Analyst+ (CySA+) Study Guide* (Wiley, 2020), and the *(ISC)² Certified Information Systems Security Professional (CISSP) Study Guide* (Wiley, 2021).

Mike earned both his BS and PhD degrees from Notre Dame in computer science and engineering. He also holds an MS in computer science from the University of Idaho and an MBA from Auburn University. His IT certifications include the CISSP, Security+, CySA+, CISA, PenTest+, CIPP/US, CISM, CCSP, and PMP credentials.

Mike provides books, video-based training, and free study groups for a wide variety of IT certifications at his website, `https://CertMike.com`.

David Seidl, CISSP is Vice President for Information Technology and CIO at Miami University. During his IT career, he has served in a variety of technical and information security roles, including serving as the Senior Director for Campus Technology Services at the University of Notre Dame, where he co-led Notre Dame's move to the cloud and oversaw cloud operations, ERP, databases, identity management, and a broad range of other technologies and services. He also served as Notre Dame's Director of Information Security and led Notre Dame's information security program. He has taught information security and networking undergraduate courses as an instructor for Notre Dame's Mendoza College of Business and has written books on security certification and cyberwarfare. including co-authoring the previous editions of *CISSP (ISC)² Official Practice Tests* (Sybex, 2021) as well as *CompTIA CySA+ Study Guide: Exam CS0-002, CompTIA CySA+ Practice Tests: Exam CS0-002, CompTIA Security+ Study Guide: Exam SY0-601,* and *CompTIA Security+ Practice Tests: Exam SY0-601* as well as other certification guides and books on information security.

David holds a bachelor's degree in communication technology and a master's degree in information security from Eastern Michigan University, as well as CISSP, CySA+, PenTest+, GPEN, and GCIH certifications.

About the Technical Editors

Sharif Nijim is an associate teaching professor of IT, Analytics, and Operations in the Mendoza College of Business at the University of Notre Dame, where he teaches undergraduate and graduate business analytics and information technology courses.

Before becoming part of the Mendoza faculty, Sharif served as the Senior Director for IT Service Delivery in the University of Notre Dame's Office of Information Technologies. In this role, he was part of the senior leadership team for the Office of Information Technologies, overseeing data stewardship, information security and compliance, learning platforms, product services, project management, and enterprise architecture. Prior to Notre Dame, Sharif co-founded and was a board member of a customer data integration company catering to the airline industry. Sharif also spent more than a decade building and performance-optimizing enterprise-class transactional and analytical systems for clients in the logistics, telecommunications, energy, manufacturing, insurance, real estate, healthcare, travel and transportation, and hospitality sectors.

Gareth Marchant started his professional career as an electrical engineer and has worked in information technology for over 20 years. He has held systems engineering and senior leadership roles in both private and public sector organizations. The central theme throughout his career has been systems architecture and design, covering a broad range of technical services but always focused on resiliency. Gareth currently lives in Nashville, TN, but has recovered IT operations in Florida following tornado strikes and many hurricanes.

Gareth is an (ISC)² and EC-Council certified instructor and currently holds CISSP, CEH, ECIH, SSCP, GMON, CASP+, Security+, CySA+, Network+, Cybersec First Responder, Cyber Secure Coder, and other certifications, as well as a master's degree in computer information systems. In addition to cybersecurity certification prep, he also teaches information systems and cybersecurity courses as an adjunct instructor and is the author of the Official CompTIA CASP+ Self-Paced Study Guide.

John L. Whiteman is a security researcher for Intel Corporation with over 20 years experience. He is a part-time adjunct cybersecurity instructor for the University of Portland and also teaches the UC Berkeley Extension's Cybersecurity Boot Camp. He holds multiple security certifications including CISSP and CCSP. John holds a MSCS from Georgia Institute of Technology and a BSCS from Portland State University.

Justin Hensley has over 15 years of information technology and cybersecurity administration experience and is currently a cybersecurity architect and project manager for CloudFit Software, a managed service provider serving both federal and commercial customers. Previously, he was the Director of Information Security and Infrastructure at University of the Cumberlands and was responsible for the information security program and all infrastructure services for over 30,000 users at two campuses. Along with his experience in the field, he has also been an academician in the classroom for the last 8 years specializing in the fields of information technology and cybersecurity.

Dr. Hensley holds a BS in Computer Information Systems and Business Administration, a MBA, a MS in Information Systems Security, and PhD in Information Technology with an emphasis in Cybersecurity. He also holds several certifications including Certified Information Systems Security Professional (CISSP), Certified Cloud Security Professional (CCSP), and Certified Ethical Hacker (CEH). He currently serves on the board of Central Virginia Community College and as an adjunct instructor in the Liberty University School of Business.

Contents

Introduction

(ISC)² CCSP® Certified Cloud Security Professional: Official Practice Tests, Third Edition is a companion volume to *(ISC)² CCSP® Certified Cloud Security Professional Official Study Guide, Third Edition*. It includes questions in the formats that appear in the version of the CCSP Certification Exam Outline and exam that became effective on August 1, 2022. If you're looking to test your knowledge before you take the CCSP exam, this book will help you by providing more than 900 questions that cover the CCSP Common Body of Knowledge and easy-to-understand explanations of both right and wrong answers.

If you're just starting to prepare for the CCSP exam, we highly recommend that you use *(ISC)² CCSP® Certified Cloud Security Professional Official Study Guide, Third Edition* to help you learn about each of the domains covered by the CCSP exam. Once you're ready to test your knowledge, use this book to help find places where you may need to study more or to practice for the exam itself.

Since this is a companion to *CCSP Study Guide*, this book is designed to be similar to taking the CCSP exam. It contains multipart scenarios as well as standard multiple-choice questions similar to those you may encounter on the certification exam. The book is broken up into eight chapters: six domain-centric chapters with 100 or more questions about each domain, and two chapters that contain 150-question practice tests to simulate taking the exam.

CCSP Certification

The CCSP certification is offered by the International Information System Security Certification Consortium, or (ISC)², a global nonprofit organization. The mission of (ISC)² is to support and provide members and constituents with credentials, resources, and leadership to address cyber, information, software, and infrastructure security to deliver value to society. (ISC)² achieves this mission by delivering the world's leading information security certification program. The CCSP is the cloud-focused credential in this series and is accompanied by several other (ISC)² programs:

- Certified Information Systems Security Professional (CISSP)
- Systems Security Certified Practitioner (SSCP)
- Certified Authorization Professional (CAP)
- Certified Secure Software Lifecycle Professional (CSSLP)
- HealthCare Information Security and Privacy Practitioner (HCISPP)

The CCSP certification covers six domains of cloud security knowledge. These domains are meant to serve as the broad knowledge foundation required to succeed in cloud security roles:

- Cloud Concepts, Architecture, and Design
- Cloud Data Security
- Cloud Platform and Infrastructure Security
- Cloud Application Security
- Cloud Security Operations
- Legal, Risk, and Compliance

The CCSP domains are periodically updated by (ISC)². The most recent revision in August 2022 slightly modified the weighting for Cloud Data Security from 19% to 20% while changing the focus on Cloud Security Operations from 17% to 16%. It also added or expanded coverage of emerging topics in cloud security.

Complete details on the CCSP Common Body of Knowledge (CBK) are contained in the Exam Outline. It includes a full outline of exam topics and can be found on the (ISC)² website at www.isc2.org.

Taking the CCSP Exam

The CCSP exam is administered in English, Chinese, German, Japanese, Korean, and Spanish using a computer-based testing format. Your exam will contain 150 questions with a four-hour time limit. You will not have the opportunity to skip back and forth as you take the exam; you have only one chance to answer each question correctly, so be careful!

Passing the CCSP requires achieving a score of at least 700 out of 1,000 points. It's important to understand that this is a scaled score, meaning that not every question is worth the same number of points. Questions of differing difficulty may factor into your score more or less heavily, and adaptive exams adjust to the test taker.

That said, as you work through these practice exams, you might want to use 70 percent as a goal to help you get a sense of whether you're ready to sit for the actual exam. When you're ready, you can schedule an exam at a location near you through the (ISC)² website.

Questions on the CCSP exam use a standard multiple choice format where you are presented with a question and four possible answer choices, one of which is correct. Remember to read the full question and *all* of the answer options very carefully. Some of those questions can get tricky!

Computer-Based Testing Environment

The CCSP exam is administered in a computer-based testing (CBT) format. You'll register for the exam through the Pearson Vue website and may take the exam in the language of your choice.

You'll take the exam in a computer-based testing center located near your home or office. The centers administer many different exams, so you may find yourself sitting in the same room as a student taking a school entrance examination and a healthcare professional earning a medical certification. If you'd like to become more familiar with the testing environment, the Pearson Vue website offers a virtual tour of a testing center:

`https://home.pearsonvue.com/test-taker/Pearson-Professional-Center-Tour.aspx`

When you take the exam, you'll be seated at a computer that has the exam software already loaded and running. It's a pretty straightforward interface that allows you to navigate through the exam. You can download a practice exam and tutorial from the Pearson Vue website:

`www.vue.com/athena/athena.asp`

 Exam policies can change from time to time. We highly recommend that you check both the (ISC)[2] and Pearson VUE sites for the most up-to-date information when you begin your preparing, when you register, and again a few days before your scheduled exam date.

Exam Retake Policy

If you don't pass the CCSP exam, you shouldn't panic. Many individuals don't reach the bar on their first attempt but gain valuable experience that helps them succeed the second time around. When you retake the exam, you'll have the benefit of familiarity with the CBT environment and CCSP exam format. You'll also have time to study the areas where you felt less confident.

After your first exam attempt, you must wait 30 days before retaking the computer-based exam. If you're not successful on that attempt, you must then wait 60 days before your third attempt and 90 days before your fourth attempt. You may not take the exam more than four times in any 12-month period.

Work Experience Requirement

Candidates who want to earn the CCSP credential must not only pass the exam but also demonstrate that they have at least five years of work experience in the information technology field. Your work experience must include three years of information security experience and one year of experience in one or more of the six CCSP domains.

Candidates who hold the CISSP certification may substitute that certification for the entire CCSP experience requirement. Candidates with the Cloud Security Alliance (CSA)'s Certificate of Cloud Security Knowledge (CCSK) may substitute that certification for one year of experience in the CCSP domains.

If you haven't yet completed your work experience requirement, you may still attempt the CCSP exam. Individuals who pass the exam are designated Associates of (ISC)² and have six years to complete the work experience requirement.

Recertification Requirements

Once you've earned your CCSP credential, you'll need to maintain your certification by paying maintenance fees and participating in continuing professional education (CPE). As long as you maintain your certification in good standing, you will not need to retake the CCSP exam.

Currently, the annual maintenance fees for the CCSP credential are $125 per year. This fee covers the renewal for all (ISC)² certifications held by an individual.

The CCSP CPE requirement mandates earning at least 90 CPE credits during each three-year renewal cycle. Associates of (ISC)² must earn at least 15 CPE credits each year. (ISC)² provides an online portal where certificate holders may submit CPE completion for review and approval. The portal also tracks annual maintenance fee payments and progress toward recertification.

Using This Book to Practice

This book is composed of eight chapters. Each of the first six chapters covers a domain, with a variety of questions that can help you test your knowledge of real-world, scenario, and best-practice security knowledge. The final two chapters are complete practice exams that can serve as timed practice tests to help determine whether you're ready for the CCSP exam.

We recommend taking the first practice exam to help identify where you may need to spend more study time and then using the domain-specific chapters to test your domain knowledge where it is weak. Once you're ready, take the other practice exams to make sure you've covered all of the material and are ready to attempt the CCSP exam.

Sybex Online Learning Environment

To practice in an online testing setting of the same questions, visit www.wiley.com/go/ sybextestprep and register your book to get access to the Sybex Test Platform. Online, you can mix questions from the domain chapters and practice exams, take timed tests, and have your answers scored.

As you go through the questions in this book, please remember the abbreviation RTFQ, which is short for "read the *full* question." There is no better advice you can possibly receive than this. Read every word of every question. Read every possible answer before selecting the one you like. The exam is 125 questions over three hours. You have more than enough time to consider each question thoroughly. There is no cause for hurry. Make sure you understand what the question is asking before responding.

Good luck on the exam. We hope this book helps you pass.

 Like all exams, the Certified Cloud Security Professional (CCSP) certification from (ISC)[2] is updated periodically and may eventually be retired or replaced. At some point after (ISC)[2] is no longer offering this exam, the old editions of our books and online tools will be retired. If you have purchased this book after the exam was retired, or are attempting to register in the Sybex online learning environment after the exam was retired, please know that we make no guarantees that this exam's online Sybex tools will be available once the exam is no longer available.

How to Contact the Publisher

If you believe you've found a mistake in this book, please bring it to our attention. At John Wiley & Sons, we understand how important it is to provide our customers with accurate content, but even with our best efforts, an error may occur.

To submit your possible errata, please email it to our Customer Service Team at wileysupport@wiley.com with the subject line "Possible Book Errata Submission."

CCSP Certified Cloud Security Professional Objectives

Domain 1 Cloud Concepts, Architecture, and Design

- 1.1. Understand cloud computing concepts
  - 1.1.1 Cloud computing definitions
  - 1.1.2 Cloud computing roles (e.g., cloud service customer, cloud service provider, cloud service partner, cloud service broker, regulator)
  - 1.1.3 Key cloud computing characteristics (e.g., on-demand self-service, broad network access, multitenancy, rapid elasticity and scalability, resource pooling, measured service)
  - 1.1.4 Building block technologies (e.g., virtualization, storage, networking, databases, orchestration)

- 1.2 Describe cloud reference architecture
  - 1.2.1 Cloud computing activities
  - 1.2.2 Cloud service capabilities (e.g., application capability types, platform capability types, infrastructure capability types)
  - 1.2.3 Cloud service categories (e.g., Software as a Service (SaaS), Infrastructure as a Service (IaaS), Platform as a Service (PaaS))
  - 1.2.4 Cloud deployment models (e.g., public, private, hybrid, community, multi-cloud)
  - 1.2.5 Cloud shared considerations (e.g., interoperability, portability, reversibility, availability, security, privacy, resiliency, performance, governance, maintenance and versioning, service levels and Service Level Agreements (SLA), auditability, regulatory, outsourcing)
  - 1.2.6 Impact of related technologies (e.g., data science, machine learning, artificial intelligence (AI), blockchain, Internet of Things (IoT), containers, quantum computing, edge computing, confidential computing, DevSecOps)
- 1.3 Understand security concepts relevant to cloud computing
  - 1.3.1 Cryptography and key management
  - 1.3.2 Identity and access control (e.g., user access, privilege access, service access)
  - 1.3.3 Data and media sanitization (e.g., overwriting, cryptographic erase)
  - 1.3.4 Network security (e.g., network security groups, traffic inspection, geofencing, zero trust network)
  - 1.3.5 Virtualization security (e.g., hypervisor security, container security, ephemeral computing, serverless technology)
  - 1.3.6 Common threats
  - 1.3.7 Security hygiene (e.g., patching, baselining)
- 1.4 Understand design principles of secure cloud computing
  - 1.4.1 Cloud secure data lifecycle
  - 1.4.2 Cloud-based business continuity (BC) and disaster recovery (DR) plan
  - 1.4.3 Business impact analysis (BIA) (e.g., cost-benefit analysis, return on investment (ROI))
  - 1.4.4 Functional security requirements (e.g., portability, interoperability, vendor lock-in)
  - 1.4.5 Security considerations and responsibilities for different cloud categories (e.g., Software as a Service (SaaS), Infrastructure as a Service (IaaS), Platform as a Service (PaaS))
  - 1.4.6 Cloud design patterns (e.g., SANS security principles, Well-Architected Framework, Cloud Security Alliance (CSA) Enterprise Architecture)

- 1.5 Evaluate cloud service providers
    - 1.5.1 Verification against criteria (e.g., International Organization for Standardization/International Electrotechnical Commission (ISO/IEC) 27017, Payment Card Industry Data Security Standard (PCI DSS))
    - 1.5.2 System/subsystem product certifications (e.g., Common Criteria (CC), Federal Information Processing Standard (FIPS) 140-2)

Domain 2 Cloud Data Security

- 2.1 Describe cloud data concepts
    - 2.1.1 Cloud data lifecycle phases
    - 2.1.2 Data dispersion
    - 2.1.3 Data flows
- 2.2 Design and implement cloud data storage architectures
    - 2.2.1 Storage types (e.g. long term, ephemeral, raw storage)
    - 2.2.2 Threats to storage types
- 2.3 Design and apply data security technologies and strategies
    - 2.3.1 Encryption and key management
    - 2.3.2 Hashing
    - 2.3.3 Data obfuscation (e.g., masking, anonymization)
    - 2.3.4 Tokenization
    - 2.3.5 Data Loss Prevention (DLP)
    - 2.3.6 Keys, secrets, and certificates management
- 2.4 Implement data discovery
    - 2.4.1 Structured data
    - 2.4.2 Unstructured data
    - 2.4.3 Semi-structured data
    - 2.4.4 Data location
- 2.5 Plan and implement data classification
    - 2.5.1 Data classification policies
    - 2.5.2 Data mapping
    - 2.5.3 Data labeling
- 2.6 Design and implement Information Rights Management (IRM)
    - 2.6.1 Objectives (e.g., data rights, provisioning, access models)
    - 2.6.2 Appropriate tools (e.g., issuing and revocation of certificates)

- 5.2.7 Availability of clustered hosts (e.g., distributed resource scheduling, dynamic optimization, storage clusters, maintenance mode, high availability (HA))
- 5.2.8 Availability of guest operating system (OS)
- 5.2.9 Performance and capacity monitoring (e.g., network, compute, storage, response time)
- 5.2.10 Hardware monitoring (e.g., disk, central processing unit (CPU), fan speed, temperature)
- 5.2.11 Configuration of host and guest operating system (OS) backup and restore functions
- 5.2.12 Management plane (e.g., scheduling, orchestration, maintenance)

- 5.3 Implement operational controls and standards (e.g., Information Technology Infrastructure Library (ITIL), International Organization for Standardization/International Electrotechnical Commission (ISO/IEC) 20000-1)
  - 5.3.1 Change management
  - 5.3.2 Continuity management
  - 5.3.3 Information security management
  - 5.3.4 Continual service improvement management
  - 5.3.5 Incident management
  - 5.3.6 Problem management
  - 5.3.7 Release management
  - 5.3.8 Deployment management
  - 5.3.9 Configuration management
  - 5.3.10 Service level management
  - 5.3.11 Availability management
  - 5.3.12 Capacity management
- 5.4 Support digital forensics
  - 5.4.1 Forensic data collection methodologies
  - 5.4.2 Evidence management
  - 5.4.3 Collect, acquire, and preserve digital evidence
- 5.5 Manage communication with relevant parties
  - 5.5.1 Vendors
  - 5.5.2 Customers
  - 5.5.3 Partners
  - 5.5.4 Regulators
  - 5.5.5 Other stakeholders

- 6.3.5 Restrictions of audit scope statements (e.g., Statement on Standards for Attestation Engagements (SSAE), International Standard on Assurance Engagements (ISAE))

- 6.3.6 Gap analysis (e.g., control analysis, baselines)

- 6.3.7 Audit planning

- 6.3.8 Internal information security management system

- 6.3.9 Internal information security controls system

- 6.3.10 Policies (e.g., organizational, functional, cloud computing)

- 6.3.11 Identification and involvement of relevant stakeholders

- 6.3.12 Specialized compliance requirements for highly-regulated industries (e.g., North American Electric Reliability Corporation/Critical Infrastructure Protection (NERC/CIP), Health Insurance Portability and Accountability Act (HIPAA), Payment Card Industry (PCI))

- 6.3.13 Impact of distributed information technology (IT) model (e.g., diverse geographical locations and crossing over legal jurisdictions)

- 6.4 Understand implications of cloud to enterprise risk management

  - 6.4.1 Assess providers risk management programs (e.g., controls, methodologies, policies, risk profile, risk appetite)

  - 6.4.2 Difference between data owner/controller vs. data custodian/processor

  - 6.4.3 Regulatory transparency requirements (e.g., breach notification, Sarbanes-Oxley (SOX), General Data Protection Regulation (GDPR))

  - 6.4.4 Risk treatment (i.e., avoid, mitigate, transfer, share, acceptance)

  - 6.4.5 Different risk frameworks

  - 6.4.6 Metrics for risk management

  - 6.4.7 Assessment of risk environment (e.g., service, vendor, infrastructure, business)

- 6.5 Understand outsourcing and cloud contract design

  - 6.5.1 Business requirements (e.g., service level agreement (SLA), master service agreement (MSA), statement of work (SOW))

  - 6.5.2 Vendor management (e.g., vendor assessments, vendor lock-in risks, vendor viability, escrow)

  - 6.5.3 Contract management (e.g., right to audit, metrics, definitions, termination, litigation, assurance, compliance, access to cloud/data, cyber risk insurance)

  - 6.5.4 Supply-chain management (e.g., International Organization for Standardization/International Electrotechnical Commission (ISO/IEC) 27036)

Chapter

1

Domain 1: Cloud Concepts, Architecture, and Design

SUBDOMAINS:

✓ 1.1 Understand cloud computing concepts

✓ 1.2 Describe cloud reference architecture

✓ 1.3 Understand security concepts relevant to cloud computing

✓ 1.4 Understand design principles of cloud computing

✓ 1.5 Evaluate cloud service providers

1. Matthew is reviewing a new cloud service offering that his organization plans to adopt. In this offering, a cloud provider will create virtual server instances under the multitenancy model. Each server instance will be accessible only to Matthew's company. What cloud deployment model is being used?

    A. Hybrid cloud

    B. Public cloud

    C. Private cloud

    D. Community cloud

2. Zeke is responsible for sanitizing a set of solid-state drives (SSDs) removed from servers in his organization's datacenter. The drives will be reused on a different project. Which one of the following sanitization techniques would be most effective?

    A. Cryptographic erasure

    B. Physical destruction

    C. Degaussing

    D. Overwriting

3. Tina would like to use a technology that will allow her to bundle up workloads and easily move them between different operating systems. What technology would best meet this need?

    A. Virtual machines

    B. Serverless computing

    C. Hypervisors

    D. Containers

4. Under the cloud reference architecture, which one of the following activities is not generally part of the responsibilities of a customer?

    A. Monitor services

    B. Prepare systems

    C. Perform business administration

    D. Handle problem reports

5. Seth is helping his organization move their web server cluster to a cloud provider. The goal of this move is to provide the cluster with the ability to grow and shrink based on changing demand. What characteristic of cloud computing is Seth hoping to achieve?

    A. Scalability

    B. On-demand self service

    C. Elasticity

    D. Broad network access

6. Sherry is deploying a zero-trust network architecture for her organization. In this approach, which one of the following characteristics would be least important in validating a login attempt?

A. User identity

B. IP address

C. Geolocation

D. Nature of requested access

7. Which one of the following hypervisor models is the most resistant to attack?

A. Type 1

B. Type 2

C. Type 3

D. Type 4

8. Joe is using a virtual server instance running on a public cloud provider and would like to restrict the ports on that server accessible from the internet. What security control would best allow him to meet this need?

A. Geofencing

B. Traffic inspection

C. Network firewall

D. Network security groups

9. Which one of the following cybersecurity threats is least likely to directly affect an object storage service?

A. Disk failure

B. User error

C. Ransomware

D. Virus

10. Vince would like to be immediately alerted whenever a user with access to a sensitive cloud service leaves a defined physical area. What type of security control should he implement?

A. Intrusion prevention system

B. Geofencing

C. Firewall rule

D. Geotagging

11. Which one of the following characteristics is not a component of the standard definition of cloud computing?

A. Broad network access

B. Rapid provisioning

C. Multitenancy

D. On-demand self service

12. Which one of the following sources provides a set of vendor-neutral design patterns for cloud security?

- **A.** Cloud Security Alliance
- **B.** Amazon Web Services
- **C.** Microsoft
- **D.** (ISC)²

13. Lori is using an API to access sensitive information stored in a cloud service. What cloud secure data lifecycle activity is Lori engaged in?

- **A.** Store
- **B.** Use
- **C.** Destroy
- **D.** Create

14. Helen would like to provision a disk volume in the cloud that is mountable from a server. What cloud capability does she want?

- **A.** Virtualized server
- **B.** Object storage
- **C.** Network capacity
- **D.** Block storage

15. Ben is using the sudo command to carry out operations on a Linux server. What type of access is he using?

- **A.** Service access
- **B.** Unauthorized access
- **C.** User access
- **D.** Privileged access

16. Which one of the following cryptographic goals protects against the risks posed when a device is lost or stolen?

- **A.** Nonrepudiation
- **B.** Authentication
- **C.** Integrity
- **D.** Confidentiality

17. Which type of business impact assessment tool is most appropriate when attempting to evaluate the impact of a failure on customer confidence?

- **A.** Quantitative
- **B.** Qualitative
- **C.** Annualized loss expectancy
- **D.** Single loss expectancy

18. Robert is reviewing a system that has been assigned the EAL2 evaluation assurance level under the Common Criteria. What is the highest level of assurance that he may have about the system?

   A. It has been functionally tested.

   B. It has been structurally tested.

   C. It has been formally verified, designed, and tested.

   D. It has been semi-formally designed and tested.

19. Jake would like to use a third-party platform to automatically move workloads between cloud service providers. What type of tool would best meet this need?

   A. Cloud access service broker

   B. Database

   C. Virtualization

   D. Orchestration

20. Robert is responsible for securing systems used to process credit card information. What security control framework should guide his actions?

   A. HIPAA

   B. PCI DSS

   C. SOX

   D. GLBA

21. What type of effort attempts to bring all of an organization's cloud activities under more centralized control?

   A. Cloud access service broker

   B. Cloud orchestration

   C. Cloud governance

   D. Cloud migration

22. Chris is designing a cryptographic system for use within his company. The company has 1,000 employees, and they plan to use an asymmetric encryption system. They would like the system to be set up so that any pair of arbitrary users may communicate privately. How many total keys will they need?

   A. 500

   B. 1,000

   C. 2,000

   D. 4,950

23. Erin is concerned about the risk that a cloud provider used by her organization will fail, so she is creating a strategy that will combine resources from multiple public cloud providers. What term best describes this strategy?

A. Community cloud

B. Multicloud

C. Private cloud

D. Hybrid cloud

24. Which one of the following would normally be considered an application capability of a cloud service provider?

A. Network capacity

B. Hosted email

C. Block storage

D. Serverless computing

25. What activity are cloud providers able to engage in because not all users will access the full capacity of their service offering simultaneously?

A. Oversubscription

B. Overprovisioning

C. Underprovisioning

D. Undersubscription

26. Brian recently joined an organization that runs the majority of its services on a virtualization platform located in its own datacenter but also leverages an IaaS provider for hosting its web services and an SaaS email system. What term best describes the type of cloud environment this organization uses?

A. Public cloud

B. Dedicated cloud

C. Private cloud

D. Hybrid cloud

27. In an infrastructure as a service (IaaS) environment where a vendor supplies a customer with access to storage services, who is normally responsible for removing sensitive data from drives that are taken out of service?

A. Customer's security team

B. Customer's storage team

C. Customer's vendor management team

D. Vendor

28. Lucca is reviewing his organization's disaster recovery process data and notes that the MTD for the business's main website is two hours. What does he know about the RTO for the site when he does testing and validation?

    A. It needs to be less than two hours.

    B. It needs to be at least two hours.

    C. The MTD is too short and needs to be longer.

    D. The RTO is too short and needs to be longer.

29. Alice and Bob would like to use an asymmetric cryptosystem to communicate with each other. They are located in different parts of the country but have exchanged encryption keys by using digital certificates signed by a mutually trusted certificate authority.

When Bob receives an encrypted message from Alice, what key does he use to decrypt the plaintext message's contents?

    A. Alice's public key

    B. Alice's private key

    C. Bob's public key

    D. Bob's private key

30. Jen works for an organization that assists other companies in moving their operations from on-premises datacenters to the cloud. Jen's company does not operate their own cloud services but assists in the use of services offered by other organizations. What term best describes the role of Jen's company?

    A. Cloud service customer

    B. Cloud service partner

    C. Cloud service provider

    D. Cloud service broker

31. Carla is selecting a hardware security module (HSM) for use by her organization. She is employed by an agency of the U.S. federal government and must ensure that the technology she chooses meets applicable federal standards for cryptographic systems. What publication would best help her determine these requirements?

    A. NIST 800-53

    B. NIST 800-171

    C. Common Criteria

    D. FIPS 140-2

32. Ryan is reviewing the design of a new service that will use several offerings from a cloud service provider. The design depends on some unique features offered only by that provider. What should concern Ryan the most about the fact that these service features are not available from other providers?

    A. Vendor lock-in

    B. Interoperability

    C. Auditability

    D. Confidentiality

33. Colin is reviewing a system that has been assigned the EAL7 evaluation assurance level under the Common Criteria. What is the highest level of assurance that he may have about the system?

    A. It has been functionally tested.

    B. It has been methodically tested and checked.

    C. It has been methodically designed, tested, and reviewed.

    D. It has been formally verified, designed, and tested.

34. Which one of the following technologies provides the capability of creating a distributed, immutable ledger?

    A. Quantum computing

    B. Blockchain

    C. Edge computing

    D. Confidential computing

35. Which one of the following systems assurance processes provides an independent third-party evaluation of a system's controls that may be trusted by many different organizations?

    A. Planning

    B. Definition

    C. Verification

    D. Accreditation

36. Which one of the following would be considered an example of infrastructure as a service cloud computing?

    A. Payroll system managed by a vendor and delivered over the web

    B. Application platform managed by a vendor that runs customer code

    C. Servers provisioned by customers on a vendor-managed virtualization platform

    D. Web-based email service provided by a vendor

37. Which of the following is *not* a factor an organization might use in the cost–benefit analysis when deciding whether to migrate to a cloud environment?

    A. Pooled resources in the cloud

    B. Shifting from IT investment as capital expenditures to operational expenditures

    C. The time savings and efficiencies offered by the cloud service

    D. Branding associated with which cloud provider might be selected

38. Barry has a temporary need for massive computing power and is planning to use virtual server instances from a cloud provider for a short period of time. What term best describes the characteristic of Barry's workload?

    A. Quantum computing

    B. Confidential computing

    C. Ephemeral computing

    D. Parallel computing

39. You are reviewing a service-level agreement (SLA) and find a provision that guarantees 99.99% uptime for a service you plan to use. What term best describes this type of provision?

   A. Availability

   B. Security

   C. Privacy

   D. Resiliency

40. Carlton is selecting a cloud environment for an application run by his organization. He needs an environment where he will have the most control over the application's performance. What service category would be best suited for his needs?

   A. SaaS

   B. FaaS

   C. IaaS

   D. PaaS

41. Gavin is looking for guidance on how his organization should approach the evaluation of cloud service providers. What ISO document can help him with this work?

   A. ISO 27001

   B. ISO 27701

   C. ISO 27017

   D. ISO 17789

42. Ed has a question about the applicability of PCI DSS requirements to his organization's credit card processing environment. What organization is the regulator in this case?

   A. SEC

   B. FDA

   C. FTC

   D. PCI SSC

43. Rick is an application developer who works primarily in Python. He recently decided to evaluate a new service where he provides his Python code to a vendor who then executes it on their server environment. What cloud service category includes this service?

   A. SaaS

   B. PaaS

   C. IaaS

   D. CaaS

44. Gordon is developing a business continuity plan for a manufacturing company's IT operations. The company is located in North Dakota and currently evaluating the risk of earthquake. They choose to pursue a risk acceptance strategy. Which one of the following actions is consistent with that strategy?

   A. Purchasing earthquake insurance

   B. Relocating the datacenter to a safer area

   C. Documenting the decision-making process

   D. Reengineering the facility to withstand the shock of an earthquake

45. Matthew is a data scientist looking to apply machine learning and artificial intelligence techniques in his organization. He is developing an application that will analyze a potential customer and develop an estimate of how likely it is that they will make a purchase. What type of analytic technique is he using?

A. Optimal analytics

B. Descriptive analytics

C. Prescriptive analytics

D. Predictive analytics

46. Which one of the following statements correctly describes resource pooling?

A. Resource pooling allows customers to add computing resources as needed.

B. Resource pooling allows the cloud provider to achieve economies of scale.

C. Resource pooling allows customers to remove computing resources as needed.

D. Resource pooling allows customers to provision resources without service provider interaction.

47. The Domer Industries risk assessment team recently conducted a qualitative risk assessment and developed a matrix similar to the one shown here. Which quadrant contains the risks that require the most immediate attention?

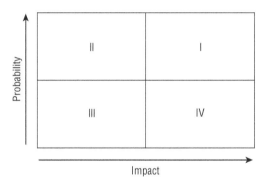

A. I

B. II

C. III

D. IV

48. Which one of the following types of agreements is the most formal document that contains expectations about availability and other performance parameters between a service provider and a customer?

A. Service-level agreement (SLA)

B. Operational-level agreement (OLA)

C. Memorandum of understanding (MOU)

D. Statement of work (SOW)

49. Bianca is preparing for her organization's move to a cloud computing environment. She is concerned that issues may arise during the change and would like to ensure that they can revert back to their on-premises environment in the case of a problem. What consideration is Bianca concerned about?

A. Reversibility

B. Portability

C. Regulatory

D. Resiliency

50. Which one of the following organizations is not known for producing cloud security guidance?

A. SANS Institute

B. FBI

C. Cloud Security Alliance

D. Microsoft

51. Vince is using a new cloud service provider and is charged for each CPU that he uses, every bit of data transferred over the network, and every GB of disk space allocated. What characteristic of cloud services does this describe?

A. Elasticity

B. On-demand self service

C. Scalability

D. Measured service

52. Who is responsible for performing scheduled maintenance of server operating systems in a PaaS environment?

A. The customer.

B. Both the customer and the service provider.

C. No operating system maintenance is necessary in a PaaS environment.

D. The service provider.

53. When considering a move from a traditional on-premises environment to the cloud, organizations often calculate a return on investment. Which one of the following factors should you expect to contribute the most to this calculation?

A. Utility costs

B. Licensing fees

C. Security expenses

D. Executive compensation

54. Devon is using an IaaS environment and would like to provision storage that will be used as a disk attached to a server instance. What type of storage should he use?

   A. Archival storage

   B. Block storage

   C. Object storage

   D. Database storage

55. During a system audit, Casey notices that the private key for her organization's web server has been stored in a public Amazon S3 storage bucket for more than a year. What should she do?

   A. Remove the key from the bucket.

   B. Notify all customers that their data may have been exposed.

   C. Request a new certificate using a new key.

   D. Nothing, because the private key should be accessible for validation.

56. Glenda would like to conduct a disaster recovery test and is seeking a test that will allow a review of the plan with no disruption to normal information system activities and as minimal a commitment of time as possible. What type of test should she choose?

   A. Tabletop exercise

   B. Parallel test

   C. Full interruption test

   D. Checklist review

57. Mark is considering replacing his organization's customer relationship management (CRM) solution with a new product that is available in the cloud. This new solution is completely managed by the vendor, and Mark's company will not have to write any code or manage any physical resources. What type of cloud solution is Mark considering?

   A. IaaS

   B. CaaS

   C. PaaS

   D. SaaS

58. Ben has been tasked with identifying security controls for systems covered by his organization's information classification system. Why might Ben choose to use a security baseline?

   A. They apply in all circumstances, allowing consistent security controls.

   B. They are approved by industry standards bodies, preventing liability.

   C. They provide a good starting point that can be tailored to organizational needs.

   D. They ensure that systems are always in a secure state.

59. What approach to technology management integrates the three components of technology management shown in this illustration?

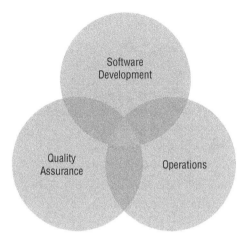

A. Agile

B. Lean

C. DevOps

D. ITIL

60. Stacey is configuring a PaaS service for use in her organization. She would like to get SSH access to the servers that will be executing her code and contacts the vendor to request this access. What response should she expect?

A. Immediate approval of the request.

B. Immediate denial of the request.

C. The vendor will likely request more information before granting the request.

D. The vendor will likely ask for executive-level approval of the request.

61. Tom enables an application firewall provided by his cloud infrastructure as a service provider that is designed to block many types of application attacks. When viewed from a risk management perspective, what metric is Tom attempting to lower by implementing this countermeasure?

A. Impact

B. RPO

C. MTO

D. Likelihood

62. Lisa wants to integrate with a cloud identity provider that uses OAuth 2.0, and she wants to select an appropriate authentication framework. Which of the following best suits her needs?

A. OpenID Connect

B. SAML

C. RADIUS

D. Kerberos

63. Elise is helping her organization prepare to evaluate and adopt a new cloud-based human resource management (HRM) system vendor. What would be the most appropriate minimum security standard for her to require of possible vendors?

A. Compliance with all laws and regulations

B. Handling information in the same manner the organization would

C. Elimination of all identified security risks

D. Compliance with the vendor's own policies

64. Fran's company is considering purchasing a web-based email service from a vendor and eliminating its own email server environment as a cost-saving measure. What type of cloud computing environment is Fran's company considering?

A. SaaS

B. IaaS

C. CaaS

D. PaaS

65. Carl is deploying a set of video sensors that will be placed in remote locations as part of a research project. Due to connectivity limitations, he would like to perform as much image processing and computation as possible on the device itself before sending results back to the cloud for further analysis. What computing model would best meet his needs?

A. Serverless computing

B. Edge computing

C. IaaS computing

D. SaaS computing

66. Ben is working on integrating a federated identity management system and needs to exchange authentication and authorization information for browser-based single sign-on. What technology is his best option?

A. HTML

B. XACML

C. SAML

D. SPML

67. Bert is considering the use of an infrastructure as a service cloud computing partner to provide virtual servers. Which one of the following would be a vendor responsibility in this scenario?

   A. Maintaining the hypervisor

   B. Managing operating system security settings

   C. Maintaining the host firewall

   D. Configuring server access control

68. Nuno's company is outsourcing its email system to a cloud service provider who will provide web-based email access to employees of Nuno's company. What cloud service category is being used?

   A. PaaS

   B. IaaS

   C. SaaS

   D. FaaS

69. What software development methodology is most closely linked to the DevSecOps approach?

   A. Waterfall

   B. Spiral

   C. Agile

   D. Modified waterfall

70. Bailey is concerned that users around her organization are using a variety of cloud services and would like to enforce security policies consistently across those services. What security control would be best suited for her needs?

   A. DRM

   B. IPS

   C. CASB

   D. DLP

71. Roger recently accepted a new position as a security professional at a company that runs its entire IT infrastructure within an IaaS environment. Which one of the following would most likely be the responsibility of Roger's firm?

   A. Configuring accessible network ports

   B. Applying hypervisor updates

   C. Patching operating systems

   D. Wiping drives prior to disposal

72. In which cloud computing model does a customer share computing infrastructure with other customers of the cloud vendor where one customer may not know the other's identity?

   A. Public cloud

   B. Private cloud

   C. Community cloud

   D. Shared cloud

73. Kristen wants to use multiple processing sites for her data, but does not want to pay for a full datacenter. Which of the following options would you recommend as her best option if she wants to be able to quickly migrate portions of her custom application environment to the facilities in multiple countries without having to wait to ship or acquire hardware?

   A. A cloud PaaS vendor

   B. A hosted datacenter provider

   C. A cloud IaaS vendor

   D. A datacenter vendor that provides rack, power, and remote hands services

74. Which one of the following statements about cloud networking is *not* correct?

   A. Security groups are the equivalent of network firewall rules.

   B. IaaS networking is not configurable.

   C. PaaS and SaaS networking are managed by the cloud service provider.

   D. Customers may connect to cloud service provider networks using a VPN.

75. Darcy's organization is deploying serverless computing technology to better meet the needs of developers and users. In a serverless model, who is normally responsible for configuring operating system security controls?

   A. Software developer

   B. Cybersecurity professional

   C. Cloud architect

   D. Vendor

76. What is the international standard that provides guidance for the creation of an organizational information security management system (ISMS)?

   A. NIST SP 800-53

   B. PCI DSS

   C. ISO 27001

   D. NIST SP 800-37

77. You are the security subject matter expert (SME) for an organization considering a transition from a traditional IT enterprise environment into a hosted cloud provider's datacenter. One of the challenges you're facing is whether your current applications in the on-premises environment will function properly with the provider's hosted systems and tools. This is a(n) _____ issue.

   A. Interoperability

   B. Portability

   C. Stability

   D. Security

78. Mike is conducting a business impact assessment of his organization's potential move to the cloud. He is concerned about the ability to shift workloads between cloud vendors as needs change. What term best describes Mike's concern?

   A. Resiliency

   B. Regulatory

   C. Reversibility

   D. Portability

79. Which one of the following statements is correct?

   A. Services that are scalable are also elastic.

   B. There is no relationship between elasticity and scalability.

   C. Services that are elastic are also scalable.

   D. Services that are either elastic or scalable are both elastic and scalable.

80. From a customer perspective, all of the following are benefits of infrastructure as a service (IaaS) cloud services *except* _____.

   A. Reduced cost of ownership

   B. Reduced energy costs

   C. Metered usage

   D. Reduced overhead of administering the operating system (OS) in the cloud environment

81. Encryption is an essential tool for affording security to cloud-based operations. While it is possible to encrypt every system, piece of data, and transaction that takes place on the cloud, why might that not be the optimum choice for an organization?

   A. Key length variances don't provide any actual additional security.

   B. It would cause additional processing overhead and time delay.

   C. It might result in vendor lockout.

   D. The data subjects might be upset by this.

82. _____ is an example of due care, and _____ is an example of due diligence.

    A. Privacy data security policy; auditing the controls dictated by the privacy data security policy

    B. The European Union General Data Protection Regulation (GDPR); the Gramm–Leach–Bliley Act (GLBA)

    C. Locks on doors; turnstiles

    D. Perimeter defenses; internal defenses

83. Which one of the following is a critical component for confidential computing environments?

    A. TEE

    B. TPM

    C. HSM

    D. PKI

84. Which one of the following programs provides a general certification process for computing hardware that might be used in a government environment?

    A. FedRAMP

    B. NIST 800-53

    C. Common Criteria

    D. FIPS 140-2

85. In a Lightweight Directory Access Protocol (LDAP) environment, each entry in a directory server is identified by a _____.

    A. Domain name (DN)

    B. Distinguished name (DN)

    C. Directory name (DN)

    D. Default name (DN)

86. Which one of the following cloud building block technologies is best suited for storing data that is structured into related tables?

    A. Storage

    B. Networking

    C. Databases

    D. Virtualization

87. You are concerned about protecting sensitive data while it is stored in memory on a server. What emerging technology is designed to assist with this work?

    A. Quantum computing

    B. Confidential computing

    C. Edge computing

    D. Fog computing

88. Your organization has migrated into a platform as a service (PaaS) configuration. A network administrator within the cloud provider has accessed your data and sold a list of your users to a competitor. Who is required to make data breach notifications in accordance with all applicable laws?

    A. The network admin responsible

    B. The cloud provider

    C. The regulators overseeing your deployment

    D. Your organization

89. If an organization wants to retain the *most* control of their assets in the cloud, which service and deployment model combination should they choose?

    A. Platform as a service (PaaS), community

    B. Infrastructure as a service (IaaS), hybrid

    C. Software as a service (SaaS), public

    D. Infrastructure as a service (IaaS), private

90. Henry's company has deployed an extensive IoT infrastructure for building monitoring that includes environmental controls, occupancy sensors, and a variety of other sensors and controllers that help manage the building. Which of the following security concerns should Henry report as the most critical in his analysis of the IoT deployment?

    A. There is a lack of local storage space for security logs, which is common to IoT devices.

    B. The IoT devices may not have a separate administrative interface, allowing anybody on the same network to attempt to log in to them and making brute-force attacks possible.

    C. The IoT devices may not support strong encryption for communications, exposing the log and sensor data to interception on the network.

    D. The long-term support and patching model for the IoT devices may create security and operational risk for the organization.

91. In what cloud computing model does the customer build a cloud computing environment in their own datacenter or build an environment in another datacenter that is for the customer's exclusive use?

    A. Public cloud

    B. Private cloud

    C. Hybrid cloud

    D. Shared cloud

92. What cloud computing component is most susceptible to an escape attack?

    A. Hypervisor

    B. Hardware security module

    C. Trusted platform module

    D. Database

93. Steve is concerned that users of his organization's cloud environment may be sending sensitive information over HTTPS connections. What technology would best help him detect this activity?

   A. Traffic inspection

   B. Port blocking

   C. Patching

   D. Geofencing

94. Which one of the following disaster recovery approaches is generally the most cost-effective for an organization?

   A. Hot site

   B. Cloud site

   C. Cold site

   D. Warm site

95. An essential element of access management, _____ is the practice of confirming that an individual is who they claim to be.

   A. Authentication

   B. Authorization

   C. Nonrepudiation

   D. Regression

96. Which one of the following cloud service categories places the most security responsibility with the cloud service provider?

   A. SaaS

   B. PaaS

   C. FaaS

   D. IaaS

97. Alice and Bob are using a symmetric encryption algorithm to exchange sensitive information. How many total encryption keys are necessary for this communication?

   A. 1

   B. 2

   C. 3

   D. 4

98. Mike and Renee would like to use an asymmetric cryptosystem to communicate with each other. They are located in different parts of the country but have exchanged encryption keys by using digital certificates signed by a mutually trusted certificate authority.

   When Mike receives Renee's digital certificate, what key does he use to verify the authenticity of the certificate?

   A. Renee's public key

   B. Renee's private key

    C. CA's public key

    D. CA's private key

99. What computing technology, if fully developed, has the potential to undermine the security of modern encryption algorithms?

    A. Confidential computing

    B. Ephemeral computing

    C. Quantum computing

    D. Parallel computing

100. What is usually considered the difference between business continuity (BC) efforts and disaster recovery (DR) efforts?

    A. BC involves a recovery time objective (RTO), and DR involves a recovery point objective (RPO).

    B. BC is for events caused by humans (like arson or theft), whereas DR is for natural disasters.

    C. BC is about maintaining critical functions during a disruption of normal operations, and DR is about recovering to normal operations after a disruption.

    D. BC involves protecting human assets (personnel, staff, users), whereas DR is about protecting property (assets, data).

Chapter

2

Domain 2: Architecture and Design

SUBDOMAINS:

✓ 2.1 Describe cloud data concepts

✓ 2.2 Design and implement cloud data storage architectures

✓ 2.3 Design and apply data security technologies and strategies

✓ 2.4 Implement data discovery

✓ 2.5 Plan and implement data classification

✓ 2.6 Design and implement Information Rights Management (IRM)

1. An email is an example of what type of data?

    A. Structured data

    B. Semi-structured data

    C. RFC-defined data

    D. Unstructured data

2. Nick wants to ensure that data is properly handled once it is classified. He knows that data labeling is important to the process and will help his data loss prevention tool in its job of preventing data leakage and exposure. When should data be labeled in his data lifecycle?

    A. Creation

    B. Storage

    C. Use

    D. Destruction

3. Jacinda is planning to deploy a data loss prevention (DLP) system in her cloud environment. Which of the following challenges is most likely to impact the ability of her DLP system to determine whether sensitive data is being transmitted outside of her organization?

    A. Lack of data labeling

    B. Use of encryption for data in transit

    C. Improper data labeling

    D. Use of encryption for data at rest

4. Susan wants to ensure that super user access in her cloud environment can be properly audited. Which of the following is not a common item required for auditing of privileged user access?

    A. The remote IP address

    B. The account used

    C. The password used

    D. The local IP address

5. Ben's organization uses the same data deletion procedure for their on-site systems and their third-party-provided, cloud-hosted systems. Ben believes there is a problem with the process currently in use, which involves performing a single-pass zero-wipe of the disks and volumes in use before they are reused. What problem with this approach should Ben highlight for the cloud environment?

    A. Crypto-shredding is a secure option for third-party-hosted cloud platforms.

    B. Zero-wiping alone is not sufficient, and random patterns should also be used.

    C. Zero- wiping requires multiple passes to ensure that there will be no remnant data.

    D. Drives should be degaussed instead of wiped or crypto-shredded to ensure that data is fully destroyed at the physical level.

6. Jason has been informed that his organization needs to place a legal hold on information related to pending litigation. What action should he take to place the hold?

    A. Restore the files from backups so that they match the dates for the hold request.

    B. Search for all files related to the litigation and provide them immediately to opposing counsel.

    C. Delete all the files named in the legal hold to limit the scope of litigation.

    D. Identify scope files and preserve them until they need to be produced.

7. Murali is reviewing a customer's file inside of his organization's customer relationship management tool and sees the customer's Social Security number listed as XXX-XX-8945. What data obfuscation technique has been used?

    A. Anonymization

    B. Masking

    C. Randomization

    D. Hashing

8. An XML file is considered what type of data?

    A. Unstructured data

    B. Restructured data

    C. Semi-structured data

    D. Structured data

9. Lucca wants to implement logging in an infrastructure as a service cloud service provider's environment for his Linux instances. He wants to capture events like creation and destruction of systems, as part of scaling requirements for performance. What logging tool or service should he use to have the most insight into these events?

    A. Syslog from the Linux systems

    B. The cloud service provider's built-in logging function

    C. Syslog-NG from the Linux systems

    D. Logs from both the local event log and application log from the Linux systems

10. Joanna's company uses a load balancer to distribute traffic between multiple web servers. What data point is often lost when traffic passes through load balancers to local web servers in a cloud environment?

    A. The source IP address

    B. The destination port

    C. The query string

    D. The destination IP address

11. Isaac is using a hash function for both integrity checking and to allow address data to be referenced without the actual data being exposed. Which of the following attributes of the data will be not be lost when the data is hashed?

    A. Its ability to be uniquely identified

    B. The length of the data

    C. The formatting of the data

    D. The ability to sort the data based on street number

12. Amanda's operating procedures for secure data storage require her to ensure that she is using data dispersion techniques. What does Amanda need to do to be compliant with this requirement?

    A. Delete all data not in secure storage.

    B. Store data in more than one location or service.

    C. Avoid storing data in intact form, requiring data from more than one location to use a data set.

    D. Geographically separate data by at least 15 miles to ensure that a single natural disaster cannot destroy it.

13. Lisa runs Windows instances in her cloud-hosted environment. Each Windows instance is created with a C: drive that houses the operating system and application files. What type of storage best describes the C: drive for these Windows instances?

    A. Long-term storage

    B. Ephemeral storage

    C. Raw storage

    D. Volume-based storage

14. Steve is working to classify data based on his organization's data classification policies. Which of the following is not a common type of classification?

    A. Size of the data

    B. Sensitivity of the data

    C. Jurisdiction covering the data

    D. Criticality of the data

15. Chris is reviewing his data lifecycle and wants to take actions in the data creation stage that can help his data loss prevention system be more effective. Which of the following actions should he take to improve the success rate of his DLP controls?

    A. Data labeling

    B. Data classification

    C. Hashing

    D. Geolocation tagging

16. Gary is gathering data to support a legal case on behalf of his company. Why might he digitally sign files as they are collected and preserve them along with the data in a documented, validated way?

    A. To allow for data dispersion

    B. To ensure the files are not copied

    C. To keep the files secure by encrypting them

    D. To support nonrepudiation

17. Valerie is performing a risk assessment for her cloud environment and wants to identify risks to her organization's ephemeral volume-based storage used for system drives in a scalable, virtual machine–based environment. Which of the following is not a threat to ephemeral storage?

    A. Inadvertent exposure

    B. Malicious access due to credential theft

    C. Poor performance due to its ephemeral nature

    D. Loss of forensic artifacts

18. Which storage type is most likely to have remnant data issues in an environment in which the storage is reused for other customers after it is reallocated if it is not crypto-shredded when it is deallocated and instead is zero-wiped?

    A. Ephemeral storage

    B. Raw storage

    C. Long-term storage

    D. Magneto-optical storage

19. Kathleen wants to perform data discovery across a large data set and knows that some data types are more difficult to perform discovery on than others. Which of the following data types is the hardest to perform discovery actions on?

    A. Unstructured data

    B. Semi-structured data

    C. Rigidly structured data

    D. Structured data

20. Isaac wants to filter events based on the country of origin for authentications. What log information should he use to perform a best-effort match for logins?

    A. userID

    B. IP address

    C. Geolocation

    D. MAC address

21. Charleen wants to use a data obfuscation method that allows realistic data to be used without the data being actual data associated with specific users or individuals. What data obfucation method should she use?

    A. Hashing

    B. Shuffling

    C. Randomization

    D. Masking

22. Michelle wants to track deletion of files in an object storage bucket. What potential issue should she be aware of if her organization makes heavy use of object-based storage for storage of ephemeral files?

    A. The logging may not be accurate.

    B. Logging may be automatically disabled if too many events occur.

    C. Creation and deletion events cannot be logged in filesystems.

    D. The high volume of logging may increase operational costs.

23. Diana is outlining the labeling scheme her organization will use for their data. Which of the following is not a common data label?

    A. Creation date

    B. Data monetary value

    C. Date of scheduled destruction

    D. Confidentiality level

24. Susan wants to be prepared for legal holds. What organizational policy often accounts for legal holds?

    A. Data classification policy

    B. Retention policy

    C. Acceptable use policy

    D. Data breach response policy

25. Henry wants to follow the OWASP guidelines for key storage. Which of the following is not a best practice for key storage?

    A. Keys must be stored in plaintext to allow for access.

    B. Keys must be protected in both volatile and persistent memory.

    C. Keys stored in databases should be encrypted using key encryption keys.

    D. Keys should be protected in storage to ensure that they are not modified or changed inadvertently.

26. Marco wants to implement an information rights management tool. What phase of the data lifecycle relies heavily on IRM to ensure the organization retains control of its data?

    A. Create

    B. Store

    C. Share

    D. Destroy

27. JSON is an example of what type of data?

    A. Structured data

    B. Semi-structured data

    C. Unstructured data

    D. Labeled data

28. Charleen wants to perform data discovery on her organization's data, which is stored in archival storage hosted by her organization's cloud service provider. What issue should she point out about this discovery plan?

    A. It may be slow and costly due to how archival storage is designed and priced.

    B. The data may not exist because it has been archived.

    C. The discovery process cannot be run against archival storage because it is not online under normal circumstances.

    D. The data will need to be decrypted before being scanned for discovery purposes.

29. Ujama's manager has asked him to perform data mapping to prepare for his next task. What will Ujama be doing?

    A. Adding data labels to unstructured data

    B. Matching fields in one database to fields in another database

    C. Identifying the storage locations for files of specific types on system drives

    D. Building a file and folder structure for data storage

30. Lin wants to ensure that her organization's data labels remain with the data. How should she label her data to give it the best chance of retaining its labels?

    A. Embed the labels in the filename.

    B. Add the labels to the file's content at the beginning of the file.

    C. Add labels to the file metadata.

    D. Add the labels to the file's content at the end of the file.

31. Nina's organization has lost the cryptographic keys associated with one of their cloud-based servers. What can Nina do to recover the data the keys were used to protect?

    A. Generate new keys to recover the data.

    B. Use the passphrase for the keys to recover the keys.

    C. Reverse the hash that was used to encrypt the data.

    D. The data is lost and Nina cannot recover it.

32. Madani is planning to perform data discovery on various data sets and files his organization has. On which type of data will discovery be most easily performed?

A. Unstructured data

B. Semi-structured data

C. Encrypted data

D. Structured data

33. Ashley tracks the handling of a forensic image, including recording who handles it, when it was collected and when each transfer occurs, and why the transfer occurred. What practice is Ashley performing?

A. Documenting chain of custody

B. Ensuring repudiation

C. A legal hold

D. Forensic accounting

34. Which of the following is not a common goal of data classification policies?

A. Identifying classification levels

B. Assigning responsibilities

C. Defining roles

D. Mapping data

35. Hiroyuki wants to optimize his organization's data labeling process. How and when should he implement data labeling to be most efficient and effective?

A. Manual labeling at the data creation stage

B. Automated labeling at the data creation stage

C. Automated labeling at the data use stage

D. Manual labeling at the data use stage

36. Jen wants to ensure that keys used by individuals in her organization can be handled properly. Which of the following is not a best practice for handling long-term keys in use by humans?

A. Anonymize access using the key

B. Identify the key user

C. Identify when the key is used

D. Uniquely tag the keys

37. Danielle wants to ensure that the data stored in her cloud-hosted datacenter is properly destroyed when it is no longer needed. Which of the following options should she choose?

A. Physical destruction of the media

B. Crypto-shredding

C. Degaussing

D. Overwriting

38. Charles wants to use tokenization as a security practice for his organization's data. What technical requirement will he have to meet to accomplish this?

   A. He will need to encrypt his data.

   B. He will need two distinct databases.

   C. He will need to use a FIPS 140-2 capable cryptographic engine to create tokens.

   D. He will need to deidentify the data.

39. Once Charles has his two databases ready, what step comes next in the tokenization process?

   A. Data discovery to identify sensitive data

   B. Tokenization of the index values

   C. Hashing each item in the database

   D. Randomization of data in the database to prepare for tokenization

40. Jack wants to understand how data is used in his organization. What tool is often used to help IT professionals understand where and how data is used and moved through an organization?

   A. Data classification

   B. Data mapping

   C. Dataflow diagrams

   D. Data policies

41. Annie has a database with a field titled "chosen name" and she has another database with a field titled "name." She knows that these fields are used for the same purpose in her organization and wants to use data from both databases. What process could she use to match these and other fields to allow her to do so more easily?

   A. Data mapping

   B. Column consolidation

   C. Data labeling

   D. Columnar aggregation

42. Which of the following items is not commonly included in dataflow diagrams?

   A. Data types or fields

   B. Services

   C. Systems

   D. Data lifespan information

43. Jim's organization wants to implement cryptographic erasure as their primary means of destroying data when they are done with it. What first step is required to support this through the data's lifecycle?

   A. Hash all of the data at creation.

   B. Zero-wipe drives before they are used to ensure no previous data is resident.

   C. Encrypt the drive or volume at creation.

   D. All of the above.

44. Charles wants to store data in a relational database, which uses columns and tables that describe the data. Which of the following types of data cannot be easily stored in a relational database other than as a text blob?

   A. Structured data

   B. Semi-structured data

   C. Unstructured data

   D. All of the above

45. Olivia wants to write a data retention policy for her organization. Which list best describes common components of a retention policy?

   A. Retention periods, regulatory compliance requirements, data classification, data deletion and lifespan, and archiving and retrieval procedures

   B. Retention periods, logging, data classification, data deletion processes, and compliance requirements

   C. Data classification requirements, regulatory compliance requirements, data creation and tagging requirements, and data retrieval procedures

   D. Regulatory and compliance requirements and mapping to retention periods for the organization, legal hold processes, and data deletion requirements

46. Hui wants to revoke a certificate issued by her information rights management (IRM) system. How can she verify that the certificate has been revoked?

   A. Issue a new certificate using the same information as the original certificate.

   B. Attempt to access the data using her own certificate.

   C. Check the IRM's certificate revocation list.

   D. Delete the private keys for the original certificate.

47. Frank's organization is preparing to adopt an information rights management tool. What IRM capability focuses on providing rights to individuals based on their roles to ensure appropriate data access?

   A. Tagging

   B. Data labeling

   C. Encryption

   D. Provisioning

48. Randy is following his organization's data classification policy and tags data that was identified in the organization's business impact analysis. What type of classification is Randy performing?

   A. Criticality

   B. Jurisdiction

   C. Security

   D. Sensitivity

49. Susan is concerned that her organization doesn't understand how a critical application works in their cloud environment. Recent issues indicate that her organization's developers and cloud architects have different ideas about how systems and services work together. What should Susan prepare to help document and explain how systems and services work together?

    A. Data classification

    B. A business impact analysis

    C. A dataflow diagram

    D. Data mapping

50. Jane is considering data dispersion as a security and availability strategy for her organization. What risk should she highlight as the most significant potential problem if her organization does adopt a multivendor approach to dispersion?

    A. Data dispersion makes it difficult to encrypt data.

    B. Geographic dispersion may impact performance.

    C. An outage at a provider may result in data not being available.

    D. Most cloud vendors do not offer support for dispersion.

51. Selah is implementing an information rights management system. What requirement will she encounter if she wants to control files on workstations and laptops?

    A. The need to deploy a cloud-native server

    B. The need to install an agent on endpoint devices

    C. The need to deploy an on-site server

    D. The need to install an agent on cloud-based systems

52. Audio and video files are examples of what type of data?

    A. Unstructured data

    B. Sensitive data

    C. Labeled data

    D. Structured data

53. Wayne wants to perform data discovery on a very large data set stored in a cloud service using a tool that is hosted in a different cloud service, which will require copying the data to the cloud where the tool resides. What is the primary cost concern he should consider when evaluating an option like this?

    A. The cost of the storage tier the data is currently in

    B. Ingress and egress fees for moving the data between cloud services

    C. The cost of logs generated by the discovery process in the cloud where it is hosted

    D. The cost of logs generated by the discovery process in the cloud where the data resides

54. Amanda's organization uses a chain of custody process for forensic data and has captured a drive image from a compromised system hosted in their cloud environment. Amanda wants to analyze the drive without causing issues that might result in repudiation of the drive image or an issue with the chain of custody of the image. What actions should she take to analyze the drive?

   A. Analyze the drive while connected to a forensic write-protect device.

   B. Analyze the drive using only approved forensic software.

   C. Make a copy of the original image, validate it, and then analyze the copy.

   D. Log all actions taken on the original copy of the drive to maintain a chain of custody.

55. Which of the following is not a common information rights management tool control capability?

   A. Preventing taking a screenshot or photo of the displayed text

   B. Disabling copying of text

   C. Preventing local copies from being saved

   D. Disallowing printing

56. Felix operates his organization's cloud resources in multiple countries, including member states of the European Union. What is the most significant concern Felix should express about conducting data discovery across data sets contained in their cloud storage?

   A. Costs may vary across difference regions, making it difficult to estimate the price for the discovery.

   B. Regulatory requirements will vary across different locations and may make compliance difficult during discovery.

   C. Structured data will be harder to process than unstructured data, making inter-region discovery challenging.

   D. Encryption may not be allowed between regions, making the discovery less secure.

57. Jason wants to lower the ongoing cost of using storage in his cloud infrastructure as a service environment for logs and other data that is infrequently accessed. What should he consider doing with the data?

   A. Delete the data to save costs.

   B. Archive the data to a lower cost storage tier.

   C. Move the data to a third-party service provider to reduce costs.

   D. Archive the data to a higher performance storage tier.

58. Frank knows that his organization adds data labels for data during its creation. What additional phase of the cloud data lifecycle often includes data labels as data is combined or modified?

   A. Store

   B. Use

   C. Sharing

   D. Deletion

59. Chris wants to send data from his web application to client systems securely. What encryption protocol should he use?

   A. SSL

   B. MD5

   C. SHA-1

   D. TLS

60. Kathleen's organization uses a technique known as bit-splitting that breaks up encrypted information across multiple cloud services to make it more difficult to acquire and recover the data. What cloud data concept best describes activities like this?

   A. Data dispersion

   B. Data mapping

   C. Business continuity

   D. Dataflows

61. Gurleen's organization has preserved data due to a legal hold, but the data has hit the end of its retention timeframe due to statutory requirements. What should Gurleen do?

   A. Contact the appropriate government agency about the statute to inquire about the legal hold.

   B. Delete the data based on the statutory requirements.

   C. Continue to preserve the data to meet the legal hold requirements.

   D. Make a copy of the data for the legal hold and delete the original data.

62. Quentin's organization uses ephemeral storage that is attached to systems when they are instantiated in the organization's cloud-hosted environment. What will happen when the instances are terminated?

   A. The volume will be retained to be used with a future instance.

   B. The volume will be wiped and reused for the next instance owned by Quentin's organization that is instantiated.

   C. The data will be moved to a long-term storage tier until it is manually deleted.

   D. The storage will be wiped and reclaimed by the provider to be allocated elsewhere.

63. Renee wants to set a retention period for log files in her data retention policy that minimizes the ongoing cost of retention. What retention period should she select for ephemeral logs that do not have a contractual or legal requirement for retention?

   A. 45 days

   B. 6 months

   C. 3 years

   D. 7 years

64. Brian has been tasked with performing a cryptographic erasure process on an encrypted drive. What steps does he need to take to ensure that the data is securely destroyed?

   A. Destroy all copies of the encryption key.

   B. Encrypt, then decrypt the drive.

   C. Decrypt, then re-encrypt the drive with a new key.

   D. Degauss the drive, then zero-wipe it.

65. Lincoln wants to identify threats to the availability of data stored in a long-term storage service like Amazon's Glacier. Which of the following threats should he identify as impacting availability?

   A. Service outages

   B. Credential theft

   C. Improper permissions

   D. Lack of encryption

66. Theresa wants to identify endpoint systems rather than users for her information rights management system. What is typically used to identify a system to an IRM?

   A. A system name

   B. An IP address

   C. A user ID and password

   D. A certificate

67. Derek's organization uses a cryptographic one-way function applied to data in a database to allow it to be referenced without using the actual data. What anonymization technique are they using?

   A. Anonymization

   B. Masking

   C. Hashing

   D. Shuffling

68. Henry stores his cloud environment's log files in a filesystem designed for durability and performance for logs. What type of storage is he using?

   A. Long-term storage

   B. Ephemeral storage

   C. Raw storage

   D. Volume-based storage

69. Alaina's organization uses a secrets management service provided by their cloud service provider. Alaina knows that the secrets are critical to the operations of the service and wants to implement a "break-glass" emergency procedure in case the service is unavailable. Which of the following is not a common best practice for this type of secrets recovery capability?

A. Build an automated backup system for secrets.

B. Test the restore process for secrets regularly.

C. Use a second instance in the original provider's cloud for the backup system.

D. Encrypt backups and place them on secure storage.

70. Alaina wants to implement secrets detection to help identify issues with secrets exposure. Which of the following techniques will most easily help her organization detect poor practices in internal test environments without undue risk?

A. Use a secrets manager for development, test, and production to keep secrets secure.

B. Use standard test secrets and search for them.

C. Use multiple detection utilities to reduce the chance of missing a secret.

D. Use high entropy secrets to limit the possibility of guessed secrets.

71. Angie wants to move 100 terabytes of her organization's data to archival class storage in her cloud provider's environment. Which of the following decision points will be most impactful when deciding on cost of the new solution?

A. The amount of data to be archived

B. The type of data

C. The sensitivity of the data

D. Retrieval time

72. What process is shown in the following figure?

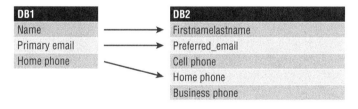

A. Field hashing

B. Table matching

C. String comparison

D. Data mapping

73. Wei's organization is implementing an information rights management system. What IRM process ensures that users receive the rights and privileges they need to access files protected by the IRM?

    A. Tagging

    B. Provisioning

    C. Labeling

    D. Data mapping

74. Dana is preparing to move her organization's data to cloud archival storage. Which of the following is the most important consideration related to performance for archival storage?

    A. The cost of the storage

    B. Data access patterns

    C. The volume or amount of data

    D. The amount of time the data will be stored for

75. What role defined by a data classification policy holds the overall responsibility for data and is typically a member of senior management?

    A. The data custodian

    B. The data owner

    C. The data processor

    D. The data user

76. Elaine's organization has suffered a data breach, and tokenized data has been exposed. What concern should Elaine express about the tokenized data?

    A. It can be un-hashed to reveal the original data.

    B. Tokenized data does not create a data breach concern.

    C. Tokenized data is only a concern if the database it is matched with is also exposed.

    D. Tokenized data could be decrypted if the encryption key for the tokens was also stolen.

77. Asha wants to be able to easily restore files in her cloud service environment if a change is accidentally made. What feature could she use to allow easy restoration?

    A. Enable versioning.

    B. Use a daily backup process.

    C. Set up recurring snapshots.

    D. Enable automatic archiving.

78. Brian is reviewing his organization's secrets management policies and practices. Which of the following is not a practice that they should use?

    A. Reduce the number of people with administrative access to the secret store.

    B. Regularly rotate secrets.

    C. Maximize the rights of important secrets to reduce the total number of secrets required.

    D. Enable logging and alerting on secrets access and usage.

79. Chris wants to audit access to highly sensitive data stored in his cloud provider's block storage service. What type of logging should he enable to monitor for use of privileged accounts to access specific buckets?

   A. Enable authentication logging.

   B. Enable access logging.

   C. Enable bandwidth monitoring.

   D. Enable timestamps.

80. Jaime is performing data discovery and wants to search for a specific term in the unstructured data she's working with. What type of discovery is she performing?

   A. Label-based discovery

   B. Metadata-based discovery

   C. Content-based discovery

   D. Structure-based discovery

81. Mike has become aware of a certificate's private key that has been exposed as part of an incident. What should Mike do first to limit the potential impact of the exposure?

   A. Immediately issue a new certificate and securely transmit it to the user.

   B. Immediately revoke the certificate and add it to the certificate revocation list.

   C. Search for all locations of the certificate to understand what impact its exposure may have.

   D. Interview the user or owner to identify why the certificate was exposed.

82. Dan's DLP deployment has been experiencing false positives when keying on pattern matching, resulting in extra work for his organization's security team. What can he do to best improve the DLP's performance if the DLP is currently relying on pattern matching as the primary means of identifying sensitive information?

   A. Tag data with its sensitivity level.

   B. Apply a data lifecycle and delete unneeded data to reduce the data being monitored.

   C. Classify data based on a classification scheme.

   D. Use regular expressions to improve the pattern matching algorithm's success rate.

83. Olivia's cloud environment uses ephemeral machines that are instantiated and shut down as utilization grows and shrinks. She is concerned about the ability to determine what system an event occurred on. What key data element should she ensure is recorded when each machine sends log data?

   A. The system's IP address

   B. An administrative user associated with the system

   C. A unique tag for each system instance

   D. The system's deletion time

84. Valerie's organization is legally allowed to dispose of specific operational data after 7 years and has an automated disposal process that removes the data based on lifecycle tags. Valerie has recently been informed that the data from one customer has been placed on a legal hold. What should she do?

A. Delete the data; the law allows disposal at 7 years, regardless of legal holds.

B. Preserve the data requested until the legal hold is over.

C. Retain the full data set until the legal hold is over.

D. Make a copy of all of the data, move it to alternate storage, and delete the original to meet both legal requirements.

85. Heikki is preparing to deploy a data loss prevention system. He has prioritized, categorized, and labeled his data. What will he need to do to ensure that the system can help secure his organization's data?

A. Establish DLP policies.

B. Perform data matching.

C. Define the data lifecycle.

D. Train users.

86. Kara is performing data discovery on a large number of pictures and uses the data embedded in the photos, including the time it was taken, the camera, and similar data. What type of discovery is she performing?

A. Metadata-based discovery

B. Content-based discovery

C. Tag-based discovery

D. Label-based discovery

87. Rick is informed that the development team for one of his organization's applications is using tokenized data for customer information. What does Rick know based on this information?

A. The actual customer information is stored in the tokenized database.

B. The customer data is secure because tokens cannot be breached.

C. A breach of the token database would result in a customer data breach.

D. The tokenized data can be looked up against a database that contains customer data.

88. As part of an incident response process, Jack wants to validate the integrity of system instances running in his cloud environment. What can he do to quickly and efficiently check that the virtual machine images have not been modified?

A. Check the cloud provider's logs for modifications to the machine.

B. Check hashes of machine instances against a hash of the original.

C. Check timestamps and dates for files on the machine against the original.

D. Rebuild the machine and manually compare it against the original.

89. Tara has backups for her cloud service stored in the long-term storage service her cloud service provider provides and in a separate third-party long-term backup environment. What concept has Tara implemented?

   A. Deduplication

   B. Dispersion

   C. Protected supply chain

   D. Lifecycle management

90. Christina's organization operates branches in multiple countries but wants to archive its data in the organization's primary cloud-hosting environment in North America. What is the most important concern she should raise about centralizing data in this scenario?

   A. The need to ensure regulatory compliance

   B. The potential for exposure as the data is moved

   C. Transfer speeds from international locations

   D. The fact that permissions may need to be remapped due to the move

91. What cloud data lifecycle phase occurs at the question mark shown in the following figure?

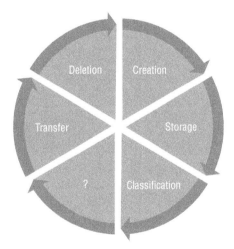

   A. Archive

   B. Distribute

   C. Encrypt

   D. Use

92. Ben has used a hashing algorithm on a file. Which of the following is not something he will know about the output?

   A. It will be of fixed length.

   B. It will be nonreversible.

   C. Identical files will generate identical output.

   D. Two different files can be hashed to the same output.

93. Jacinda wants to implement an information rights management solution. What phase of the cloud data lifecycle will rely heavily on the IRM to ensure that privileges are appropriately managed?

   A. Create

   B. Store

   C. Share

   D. Destroy

94. What cloud data lifecycle stage occurs at the question mark shown in the following image?

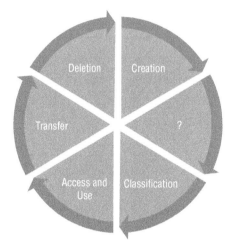

   A. Storage

   B. Encryption

   C. Labeling

   D. Provisioning

95. Naomi's organization has removed addresses, names, and phone numbers from data sets while retaining customer information like orders and website activity. What data obfuscation technique has she used?

   A. Anonymization

   B. Hashing

   C. Shuffling

   D. Tokenization

96. Melissa is designing her organization's data retention policy. Which of the following is not a common component of a data retention policy?

   A. Retention periods

   B. Data value

   C. Regulatory compliance

   D. Data classification

97. Gary's cloud provider gives him direct access to actual drives in servers as part of his hosting plan. What type of storage is Gary using when he installs operating systems and applications on those drives?

   A. Long-term storage

   B. Ephemeral storage

   C. Raw storage

   D. Volume-based storage

98. Maria has implemented an information rights management tool for her cloud-hosted Share-Point site. What requirement will her organization's SharePoint users need to meet to access controlled files?

   A. They will need to access the files only via local fileshares.

   B. They will need to use multifactor authentication for all file access.

   C. They will need to open the files using tools that support IRM.

   D. They will need to request access to each file before opening it.

99. Angelo is implementing a data discovery process. Which of the following steps should he begin with to help speed up the discovery process?

   A. Map data to compliance requirements.

   B. Extract and catalog metadata.

   C. Scan for sensitive data.

   D. Classify data.

100. Bob has contracted with his cloud service provider to allow his organization to directly access SSDs in his environment due to specialized requirements and to certify that the drives have been physically destroyed after they are removed from use by his organization. What type of storage is Bob using?

   A. Long-term

   B. Raw storage

   C. Ephemeral storage

   D. Block storage

Chapter

3

Domain 3: Cloud Platform and Infrastructure Security

SUBDOMAINS:

✓ 3.1 Comprehend cloud infrastructure and platform components

✓ 3.2 Design a secure datacenter

✓ 3.3 Analyze risks associated with cloud infrastructure and platforms

✓ 3.4 Plan and implementation of security controls

✓ 3.5 Plan business continuity (BC) and disaster recovery (DR)

1. Barry is the CIO of an organization that recently suffered a serious operational issue that required activation of the disaster recovery plan. He would like to conduct a lessons learned session to review the incident. Who would be the best facilitator for this session?

   A. Barry, as chief information officer

   B. Chief information security officer

   C. Disaster recovery team leader

   D. External consultant

2. If the cloud is used for BC/DR purposes, the loss of _____ could gravely affect your organization's RTO.

   A. Any cloud administrator

   B. A specific VM

   C. Your policy and contract documentation

   D. ISP connectivity

3. Brent is reviewing the controls that will protect his organization in the event of a sustained period of power loss at his on-premises datacenter. Which one of the following solutions would best meet his needs?

   A. Redundant servers

   B. Uninterruptible power supply (UPS)

   C. Generator

   D. RAID

4. Carolyn is concerned that users on her network may be storing sensitive information, such as Social Security numbers, on their hard drives without proper authorization or security controls. What third-party security service can she implement to best detect this activity?

   A. IDS

   B. IPS

   C. DLP

   D. TLS

5. What individuals should have access to the management plane of a cloud datacenter?

   A. Service provider engineers

   B. Customer engineers

   C. End users

   D. Both A and B

6. Roland is a physical security specialist in an organization that has a large amount of expensive lab equipment that often moves around the facility. Which one of the following technologies would provide the most automation of an inventory control process in a cost-effective manner?

A. IPS

B. Wi-Fi

C. RFID

D. Ethernet

7. Becka recently signed a contract with an alternate data processing facility that will provide her company with space in the event of a disaster. The facility includes HVAC, power, and communications circuits but no hardware. What type of facility is Becka using?

A. Cold site

B. Warm site

C. Hot site

D. Mobile site

8. Your organization has its production environment hosted in a cloud environment. You are considering using cloud backup services for your BC/DR purposes as well. What would probably be the best strategy for this approach, in terms of redundancy and resiliency?

A. Have your cloud provider also provide BC/DR backup.

B. Keep a BC/DR backup on the premises of your corporate headquarters.

C. Use another cloud provider for the BC/DR backup.

D. Move your production environment back into your corporate premises, and use your cloud provider to host your BC/DR backup.

9. Philip is developing a new security tool that will be used by individuals in many different subsidiaries of his organization. He chooses to use Docker to deploy the tool to simplify configuration. What term best describes this approach?

A. Virtualization

B. Abstraction

C. Simplification

D. Containerization

10. What is the *most* important asset to protect in cloud BC/DR activities?

A. Intellectual property

B. Hardware at the cloud datacenter

C. Personnel

D. Data on portable media

11. Carla is developing the design of a cloud infrastructure service offering that she will be reselling to a number of customers. What component of her stack is most directly responsible for performing tenant partitioning of the virtual machines belonging to different customers?

    A. Access control lists

    B. Network security group

    C. Firewall

    D. Hypervisor

12. Carlos is planning a design for a datacenter that will be constructed within a new four-story corporate headquarters. The building consists of a basement and three above-ground floors. What is the best location for the datacenter?

    A. Basement

    B. First floor

    C. Second floor

    D. Third floor

13. Chris is an information security professional for a major corporation and, as he is walking into the building, he notices that the door to a secure area has been left ajar. Physical security does not fall under his responsibility, but he takes immediate action by closing the door and informing the physical security team of his action. What principle is Chris demonstrating?

    A. Due care

    B. Due diligence

    C. Separation of duties

    D. Informed consent

14. Roger recently accepted a new position as a security professional at a company that runs its entire IT infrastructure within an IaaS environment. Which one of the following would most likely be the responsibility of Roger's firm?

    A. Configuring the network firewall

    B. Applying hypervisor updates

    C. Patching operating systems

    D. Wiping drives prior to disposal

15. Candace is designing a backup strategy for her organization's file server. She would like to perform a backup every weekday that has the smallest possible storage footprint. What type of backup should she perform?

    A. Incremental backup

    B. Full backup

    C. Differential backup

    D. Transaction log backup

16. Alyssa's team recently implemented a new system that gathers information from a variety of log sources, analyzes that information, and then triggers automated playbooks in response to security events. What term best describes this technology?

A. SIEM

B. Log repositories

C. IPS

D. SOAR

17. Nick is evaluating options for his organization's future datacenters. Which one of the following options normally incurs the largest up-front cost?

A. Colocation facilities

B. Cloud datacenters

C. On-premises datacenters

D. SaaS offerings

18. Ben is an IT auditor and would like to ensure that the organization has mechanisms in place to create an appropriate audit trail for systems and applications. Which one of the following technologies aggregates and correlates log entries?

A. SIEM

B. IPS

C. EDR

D. CASB

19. In addition to the security controls implemented by the cloud provider, a cloud customer must consider the security controls implemented by _____.

A. The respective regulator

B. The end user(s)

C. Any vendor the cloud customer previously used in the on-premises environment

D. Any third parties the provider depends on

20. Brittney is reviewing her organization's disaster recovery process data and notes that the MTD for the business's database server is 30 minutes. What does she know about the RTO for the server?

A. It needs to be less than 30 minutes.

B. It needs to be at least 30 minutes.

C. The MTD is too short and needs to be longer.

D. The RTO is too short and needs to be longer.

21. Cameron is worried about distributed denial-of-service (DDoS) attacks against his company's primary web application. Which of the following options will provide the most resilience against large-scale DDoS attacks?

   A. Implement a CDN.

   B. Increase the number of servers in the web application server cluster.

   C. Contract for DDoS mitigation services via the company's ISP.

   D. Increase the amount of bandwidth available from one or more ISPs.

22. John's network begins to experience symptoms of slowness. He launches a packet capture tool and realizes that the network is being bombarded with TCP SYN packets and believes that his organization is the victim of a denial-of-service attack. What principle of information security is being violated?

   A. Availability

   B. Integrity

   C. Confidentiality

   D. Denial

23. Mike recently implemented an intrusion prevention system designed to block common network attacks from affecting his organization. What type of risk management strategy is Mike pursuing?

   A. Risk acceptance

   B. Risk avoidance

   C. Risk mitigation

   D. Risk transference

24. You are trying to determine the critical assets that your organization must protect in your BC/DR activities. Which one of the following artifacts would be most useful in your work?

   A. Quantitative risk analysis

   B. Qualitative risk analysis

   C. Business impact analysis

   D. Risk appetite

25. A component failure in the primary HVAC system leads to a high temperature alarm in the datacenter that Kim manages. After resolving the issue, what should Kim consider to prevent future issues like this?

   A. A closed loop chiller

   B. Redundant cooling systems

   C. Swamp coolers

   D. Relocating the datacenter to a colder climate

26. Joe is the security administrator for a cloud-based ERP system. He is preparing to create accounts for several new employees. What default access should he give to all of the new employees as he creates the accounts?

    A. Read only

    B. Editor

    C. Administrator

    D. No access

27. Jason operates a cloud datacenter and would like to improve the ability of administrators to interact programmatically with backend solutions on the management plane. What technology can he use to best allow this type of automation?

    A. CASB

    B. API

    C. Hypervisor

    D. Python

28. Which of the following is a device specially designed to handle the management of cryptographic keys?

    A. Key management box (KMB)

    B. Hardware security module (HSM)

    C. Ticket-granting ticket (TGT)

    D. Trusted computing base (TCB)

29. What individual in an organization bears ultimate responsibility for the success of the disaster recovery plan?

    A. End users

    B. BC/DR team leader

    C. CISO

    D. CEO

30. Michael is responsible for forensic investigations and is investigating a security incident that involved the defacement of a corporate website. The web server in question ran on a virtualization platform, and the marketing team would like to get the website up and running as quickly as possible. What would be the most reasonable next step for Michael to take?

    A. Keep the website offline until the investigation is complete.

    B. Take the virtualization platform offline as evidence.

    C. Take a snapshot of the compromised system and use that for the investigation.

    D. Ignore the incident and focus on quickly restoring the website.

31. In a virtualized computing environment, what component is responsible for enforcing separation between guest machines?

   A. Guest operating system

   B. Hypervisor

   C. Kernel

   D. Protection manager

32. Best practice for planning the physical resiliency for a cloud datacenter facility includes _____.

   A. Having one point of egress for personnel

   B. Ensuring that redundant cabling/connectivity enters the facility from different sides of the building/property

   C. Ensuring that all parking areas are near generators so that personnel in high-traffic areas are always illuminated by emergency lighting, even when utility power is not available

   D. Ensuring that the foundation of the facility is rated to withstand earthquake tremors

33. Jen is designing a datacenter that will be used to offer cloud services to her organization's customers. She is concerned about separating systems that process information that belongs to different customers from each other. What networking technology would best allow her to enforce this separation?

   A. BGP

   B. LAN

   C. VLAN

   D. VPN

34. Risk should always be considered from a business perspective. When a risk is accepted, it should be balanced by a corresponding _____.

   A. Profit

   B. Performance

   C. Cost

   D. Opportunity

35. You are designing a cloud datacenter that is expected to meet Tier 2 status according to the Uptime Institute standards. What level of availability must you achieve to meet this standard?

   A. 99.422%

   B. 99.671%

   C. 99.741%

   D. 99.995%

36. Ursula is examining several virtual servers that her organization runs in an IaaS service. She discovers that the servers are all running a scheduling service that is no longer used by the organization. What action should she take?

   A. Ensure the service is fully patched.

   B. Remove the service.

   C. Leave the service alone unless it is causing issues.

   D. Contact the vendor for instructions.

37. When discussing the cloud, we often segregate the datacenter into the terms *compute, storage,* and *networking. Compute* is made up of _____ and _____.

    A. Routers; hosts

    B. Application programming interfaces (APIs); northbound interfaces (NBIs)

    C. Central processing units (CPUs); random access memory (RAM)

    D. Virtualized; actual hardware devices

38. What type of IaaS storage is typically used to provide disk volumes that are mountable on virtual server instances?

    A. Dedicated disks

    B. Block

    C. Encrypted

    D. Object

39. Which one of the following statements about file storage security in the cloud is correct?

    A. File stores are always kept in plaintext in the cloud.

    B. There is no way to sanitize file storage space in the cloud.

    C. Virtualization prevents the use of application-based security controls.

    D. Virtual machines are stored as snapshotted files when not in use.

40. Javier is assisting with the implementation of a cloud-based SaaS solution. He is concerned about the ability of remote users to interact directly with the database supporting the application by exploiting a web application vulnerability. What type of vulnerability would permit this access?

    A. SQL injection

    B. Cross-site scripting

    C. Cross-site request forgery

    D. Server-side request forgery

41. When considering cloud data backup strategies (i.e., whether you are making backups at the block, file, or database level), which element of your organization's BC/DR plan will be *most* affected by your choice?

    A. Recovery time objective

    B. Recovery point objective

    C. Maximum allowable downtime

    D. Mean time to failure

42. Which of the following technologies is commonly implemented by websites to encrypt data being sent between the web server and an end user?

    A. VPN

    B. TLS

    C. VLANs

    D. IPsec

43. "Return to normal operations" is a phase in BC/DR activity when the emergency is over and regular production can resume. Which of the following can sometimes be the result when the organization uses two different cloud providers for the production and BC/DR environments?

A. Both providers are affected by the emergency, extending the time before return to normal can occur.

B. The BC/DR provider becomes the new normal production environment.

C. Regulators will find the organization in violation of compliance guidance.

D. All data is lost irretrievably.

For questions 44–48, refer to the following scenario:

Gary was recently hired as the first chief information security officer (CISO) for a local government agency that makes heavy use of cloud computing resources. The agency recently suffered a security breach and is attempting to build a new information security program. Gary would like to apply some best practices for security operations as he is designing this program.

44. As Gary decides what access permissions he should grant to each user, what principle should guide his decisions about default permissions?

A. Separation of duties

B. Least privilege

C. Aggregation

D. Separation of privileges

45. As Gary designs the program, he uses the matrix shown here. What principle of information security does this matrix most directly help enforce?

Roles/Tasks	Application Programmer	Security Administrator	Database Administrator	Database Server Administrator	Budget Analyst	Accounts Receivable	Accounts Payable	Deploy Patches	Verify Patches
Application Programmer		X	X	X					
Security Administrator	X		X	X	X	X	X	X	
Database Administrator	X	X		X					
Database Server Administrator	X	X	X						
Budget Analyst		X				X	X		
Accounts Receivable		X			X		X		
Accounts Payable		X			X	X			
Deploy Patches		X							X
Verify Patches								X	
	Potential Areas of Conflict								

    A. Separation of duties

    B. Aggregation

    C. Two-person control

    D. Defense in depth

46. Gary is preparing to create an account for a new user in a federal government agency. He is working to assign privileges to the HR database. What two elements of information must Gary verify before granting this access?

    A. Credentials and need to know

    B. Clearance and need to know

    C. Password and clearance

    D. Password and biometric scan

47. Gary is preparing to develop controls around access to root encryption keys and would like to apply a principle of security designed specifically for very sensitive operations. Which principle should he apply?

    A. Least privilege

    B. Defense in depth

    C. Security through obscurity

    D. Two-person control

48. How often should Gary and his team conduct a review of the privileged access that a user has to sensitive systems? (Select all that apply.)

    A. On a periodic basis

    B. When a user leaves the organization

    C. When a user changes roles

    D. On a daily basis

49. Which one of the following hypervisor types is generally considered to offer the greatest level of security?

    A. Type 1

    B. Type 2

    C. Type 3

    D. Type 4

50. Yolanda is helping her organization decide whether to build their own datacenters or lease space from a colocation provider. What would be the major benefit of using a colocation provider?

    A. Reduced cost

    B. Increased security

    C. Reduced complexity

    D. Increased capability

51. Which one of the following components is not necessary in a Tier 1 datacenter?

    A. Uninterruptible power supplies

    B. Dual-power supplies in systems

    C. Backup generator

    D. Cooling

52. Fred is working to design security controls for a cloud environment where remote systems will need to gain command-line access to Linux servers in an automated fashion. Which one of the following authentication approaches will provide the strongest security in this scenario?

    A. Multifactor authentication

    B. Digital certificates

    C. Biometric authentication

    D. Strong passwords

53. In software-defined networking (SDN), the northbound interface (NBI) usually handles traffic between the _____ and the _____.

    A. Cloud customer; ISP

    B. SDN controllers; SDN applications

    C. Cloud provider; ISP

    D. Router; host

54. A user signs on to a cloud-based social media platform. In another browser tab, the user finds an article worth posting to the social media platform. The user clicks on the platform's icon listed on the article's website, and the article is automatically posted to the user's account on the social media platform. This is an example of what?

    A. Single sign-on

    B. Insecure direct identifiers

    C. Identity federation

    D. Cross-site scripting

55. Which of the following is a device specially purposed to handle the issuance, distribution, and storage of cryptographic keys?

    A. Key management box (KMB)

    B. Hardware security module (HSM)

    C. Ticket-granting ticket (TGT)

    D. Trusted computing base (TCB)

56. Sprawl is mainly a(n) _____ problem.

    A. Technical

    B. External

    C. Management

    D. Logical

57. You are in charge of creating the business continuity and disaster recovery (BC/DR) plan and procedures for your organization. You decide to have a tabletop test of the BC/DR activity. Which of the following will offer the best value during the test?

    A. Have all participants conduct their individual activities via remote meeting technology.

    B. Task a moderator well versed in BC/DR actions to supervise and present scenarios to the participants, including randomized special events.

    C. Provide copies of the BC/DR policy to all participants.

    D. Allow all users in your organization to participate.

58. What can be revealed by an audit of a baseline virtual image, used in a cloud environment?

    A. Adequate physical protections in the datacenter

    B. Potential criminal activity before it occurs

    C. Whether necessary security controls are in place and functioning properly

    D. Lack of user training and awareness

59. You are in charge of creating the business continuity and disaster recovery (BC/DR) plan and procedures for your organization. Your organization has its production environment hosted by a cloud provider, and you have appropriate protections in place. Which of the following is a significant consideration for your BC/DR backup?

    A. Enough personnel at the BC/DR recovery site to ensure proper operations

    B. Good cryptographic key management

    C. Access to the servers where the BC/DR backup is stored

    D. Forensic analysis capabilities

60. The minimum essential characteristics of a cloud datacenter are often referred to as "ping, power, pipe." What does this term mean?

    A. Remote access for a customer to racked devices in the datacenter; electrical utilities; connectivity to an internet service provider (ISP)/the internet

    B. Application suitability; availability; connectivity

    C. Infrastructure as a service (IaaS); software as a service (SaaS); platform as a service (PaaS)

    D. Antimalware tools; controls against distributed denial-of-service (DDoS) attacks; physical/environmental security controls, including fire suppression

61. Which of the following poses a *new* risk in the cloud, not affecting the traditional, on-premises IT environment?

    A. Internal threats

    B. Multitenancy

    C. Natural disasters

    D. Distributed denial-of-service (DDoS) attacks

62. Software-defined networking (SDN) allows network administrators and architects to perform all the following functions *except* _____.

  A. Reroute traffic based on current customer demand

  B. Create logical subnets without having to change any actual physical connections

  C. Filter access to resources based on specific rules or settings

  D. Deliver streaming media content in an efficient manner by placing it closer to the end user

63. Mary is reviewing the availability controls for the system architecture shown here. What technology is shown that provides fault tolerance for the database servers?

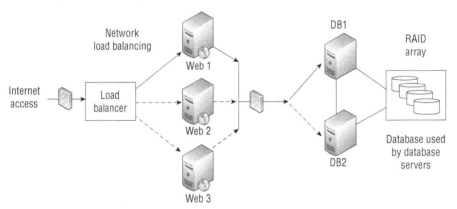

  A. Failover cluster

  B. UPS

  C. Tape backup

  D. Cold site

64. Using one cloud provider for your operational environment and another for your BC/DR backup will give you the additional benefit of _____.

  A. Allowing any custom VM builds you use to be instantly ported to another environment

  B. Avoiding vendor lock-in/lockout

  C. Increased performance

  D. Lower cost

65. The cloud customer will usually not have physical access to the cloud datacenter. This enhances security by _____.

  A. Reducing the need for qualified personnel

  B. Limiting access to sensitive information

  C. Reducing jurisdictional exposure

  D. Ensuring statutory compliance

66. Which one of the following services would be least likely described as providing computing capability?

    A. Virtual server instances

    B. FaaS

    C. Object storage

    D. Containers

67. What is the main reason virtualization is used in the cloud?

    A. Virtual machines (VMs) are easier to administer.

    B. If a VM is infected with malware, it can be easily replaced.

    C. With VMs, the cloud provider does not have to deploy an entire hardware device for every new customer.

    D. VMs are easier to operate than actual devices.

68. Which one of the following test types is most likely to have an impact on production operations?

    A. Full test

    B. Parallel test

    C. Walkthrough test

    D. Simulation test

Questions 69 and 70 refer to the following scenario:

Brendan is analyzing the symptoms of a cloud attack that took place in his organization's IaaS offering. In this attack, one customer was able to access resources on a virtual machine belonging to another customer by launching an attack from their own virtual machine.

69. What term best describes this attack?

    A. Escape

    B. Overflow

    C. Injection

    D. Scripting

70. What component of Brendan's service offering was most directly responsible for allowing this attack?

    A. Compute

    B. Hypervisor

    C. Management plane

    D. Storage

71. Melissa uses the snapshot capabilities of her cloud service provider to make backup copies of the disk volumes that support her virtual machines. What type of storage is most likely used to store these backups?

A. Dedicated disks

B. Block

C. Encrypted

D. Object

72. If you use the cloud for BC/DR purposes, even if you don't operate your production environment in the cloud, you can cut costs by eliminating your _____.

A. Security personnel

B. BC/DR policy

C. Old access credentials

D. Need for a physical hot site/warm site

73. Using a virtual machine baseline image could be very useful for which of the following options?

A. Physical security

B. Auditing

C. Training

D. Customization

74. Which one of the following audit mechanisms would be able to provide the most accurate reconstruction of user activity?

A. Application logs

B. Security logs

C. Netflow records

D. Packet capture

75. You are in charge of creating the business continuity and disaster recovery (BC/DR) plan and procedures for your organization. Your organization has its production environment hosted in a cloud environment and no longer operates secure on-premises datacenters. You are considering using cloud backup services for your BC/DR purposes as well. What would probably be the best strategy for this approach, in terms of redundancy and resiliency?

A. Have your cloud provider also provide BC/DR backup.

B. Keep a BC/DR backup on the premises of your corporate headquarters.

C. Use another cloud provider for the BC/DR backup.

D. Move your production environment back into your corporate premises, and use your cloud provider to host your BC/DR backup.

76. The BC/DR plan/policy should include all of the following *except* _____.

A. Tasking for the office responsible for maintaining/enforcing the plan

B. Contact information for essential entities, including BC/DR personnel and emergency services agencies

C. Copies of the laws/regulations/standards governing specific elements of the plan

D. Checklists for BC/DR personnel to follow

77. A Security Assertion Markup Language (SAML) identity assertion token uses the
_____ protocol.

   A. Extensible Markup Language (XML)

   B. Hypertext Transfer Protocol (HTTP)

   C. Hypertext Markup Language (HTML)

   D. American Standard Code for Information Interchange (ASCII)

78. Anita's IaaS provider allows her to choose the region of the world where she will operate her primary server instances and a different region where she will operate her backup instances. Which one of the following is the most important concern that Anita should consider?

   A. Regulatory compliance.

   B. Physical security.

   C. Environmental factors such as humidity.

   D. It doesn't matter. Data can be saved anywhere without consequence.

79. There are many ways to handle risk. However, the usual methods for addressing risk are not all possible in the cloud because _____.

   A. Cloud data risks cannot be mitigated

   B. Migrating into a cloud environment necessarily means you are accepting all risks

   C. Some risks cannot be transferred to a cloud provider

   D. Cloud providers cannot avoid risk

80. To support all aspects of the CIA triad (confidentiality, integrity, availability), all of the following aspects of a cloud datacenter need to be engineered with redundancies *except*
_____.

   A. Power supply

   B. HVAC

   C. Administrative offices

   D. Internet service provider (ISP)/connectivity lines

81. You are reviewing the requirements for a new datacenter with leaders from functional teams. The discussions are centering on the amount of data that may be lost if an outage occurs. What metric is most directly related to this discussion?

   A. Recovery time objective

   B. Recovery point objective

   C. Maximum allowable downtime

   D. Mean time to failure

82. What term describes the process of granting users access to resources?

   A. Identification

   B. Authentication

   C. Authorization

   D. Federation

83. Which of the following risks is probably *most* significant when choosing to use one cloud provider for your operational environment and another for BC/DR backup/archive?

   A. Physical intrusion

   B. Proprietary formats/lack of interoperability

   C. Vendor lock-in/lockout

   D. Natural disasters

84. In which cloud service model does the customer lose the *most* control over configuration of services?

   A. Infrastructure as a service (IaaS)

   B. Platform as a service (PaaS)

   C. Software as a service (SaaS)

   D. Function as a service (FaaS)

85. Warren is working with a cloud service provider on the terms of a new service that his organization will depend on as a disaster recovery capability. Which one of the following actions will provide Warren with the best assurance that the service will function correctly?

   A. Audit all performance functions.

   B. Audit all security functions.

   C. Perform a full-scale test.

   D. Mandate this capability in the contract.

86. Charles is the BC/DR program manager for a cloud service provider. He is assessing the risks facing his program. He believes that the organization has done adequate BC/DR planning but they have never actually activated the plan. Which of the following would most likely pose the *most* significant risk to the organization?

   A. Not having essential BC/DR personnel available during a contingency

   B. Not including all BC/DR elements in the cloud contract

   C. Returning to normal operations too soon

   D. Telecommunications outages

87. What type of fire suppression system poses the greatest risk to datacenter equipment if it fails?

   A. Dry pipe

   B. Preaction

   C. Wet pipe

   D. Gas

88. Where is isolation failure probably *least* likely to pose a significant risk?

   A. Public cloud

   B. Private cloud

   C. PaaS environment

   D. SaaS environment

89. What can hamper the ability of a cloud customer to protect their assets in a managed services arrangement?

    A. Prohibitions on port scanning and penetration testing

    B. Geographical dispersion

    C. Rules against training users

    D. Laws that prevent them from doing so

90. Which of the following terms describes a means to centralize logical control of all networked nodes in the environment, abstracted from the physical connections to each?

    A. Virtual private network (VPN)

    B. Software-defined network (SDN)

    C. Access control lists (ACLs)

    D. Role-based access control (RBAC)

91. Of the following options, which is a reason cloud datacenter audits are often less easy to verify than traditional audits?

    A. Data in the cloud can't be audited.

    B. Controls in the cloud can't be audited.

    C. Getting physical access can be difficult.

    D. There are no regulators for cloud operations.

92. Which of these most directly determines the critical assets, recovery service level (RSL), recovery time objective (RTO), and recovery point objective (RPO) for BC/DR purposes?

    A. Business drivers

    B. User input

    C. Regulator mandate

    D. Industry standards

93. A cloud provider will probably require all of the following *except* _____ before a customer conducts a penetration test.

    A. Notice

    B. Description of scope of the test

    C. Physical location of the launch point

    D. Test timeframe/duration

94. Glenda would like to conduct a disaster recovery test and is seeking a test that will allow a review of the plan with no disruption to normal information system activities and as minimal a commitment of time as possible. What type of test should she choose?

    A. Tabletop exercise

    B. Parallel test

    C. Full interruption test

    D. Checklist review

95. DDoS attacks do not affect _____ for cloud customers.

    A. Productivity

    B. Availability

    C. Connectivity

    D. Integrity

96. Where should multiple emergency egress points be included?

    A. At the power distribution substation

    B. Within the datacenter

    C. In every building on the campus

    D. In the security operations center

97. Which of the following controls would be useful to build into a virtual machine baseline image for a cloud environment?

    A. GPS tracking/locator

    B. Automated vulnerability scan on system startup

    C. Access control list (ACL) of authorized personnel

    D. Write protection

98. Cloud providers will probably not allow _____ as part of a customer's penetration test.

    A. Network mapping

    B. Vulnerability scanning

    C. Reconnaissance

    D. Social engineering

99. Having your BC/DR backup stored with the same cloud provider as your production environment can help you _____.

    A. Maintain regulatory compliance

    B. Spend less of your budget on traveling

    C. Train your users about security awareness

    D. Recover quickly from minor incidents

100. Virtual machine (VM) configuration management (CM) tools should require that managed systems perform _____.

    A. Biometric recognition

    B. Anti-tampering mechanisms

    C. Log file generation

    D. Hackback capabilities

Chapter

4

Domain 4: Cloud Application Security

SUBDOMAINS:

✓ **4.1 Advocate training and awareness for application security**

✓ **4.2 Describe the software development life cycle (SDLC) process**

✓ **4.3 Apply the secure software development life cycle (SDLC)**

✓ **4.4 Apply cloud software assurance and validation**

✓ **4.5 Use verified secure software**

✓ **4.6 Comprehend the specifics of cloud application software**

✓ **4.7 Design appropriate identity and access management solutions (IAM)**

1. Mikayla wants to validate a component of her software that she has downloaded from GitHub. How can she validate that the underlying software does not have security flaws when it is downloaded and included in her environment as part of her integration process?

   A. Validate the checksum of the file.

   B. Validate the signature of the file.

   C. Validate the hash of the file.

   D. Mikayla cannot ensure that there are no security flaws via the options described.

2. Lin wants to allow her users to use existing credentials provided by a third-party identity provider when they access her service. What element will she have to provide from the following list?

   A. User IDs

   B. Authentication

   C. Authorization

   D. Identity proofing

3. Joanna's software vendor does not provide source code to their clients. In the following list, what is her best option to test the security of the vendor's software package?

   A. Perform static analysis of the software.

   B. Implement pair-programming techniques.

   C. Review the software for hard-coded secrets.

   D. Perform dynamic testing.

4. What SDLC model is most frequently associated with cloud development processes?

   A. Agile

   B. RAD

   C. Spiral

   D. Waterfall

5. Susan wants to avoid common pitfalls in cloud application development. Which of the following pitfalls is frequently associated with cloud environments?

   A. Reliability of applications built in the cloud

   B. Scalability of applications built in the cloud

   C. Redundancy of applications built in the cloud

   D. Security of applications built in the cloud

6. Susan wants to avoid issues with data integration. She is aware that the OWASP Cloud Top 10 includes service and data integration security issues, and is deploying a REST-based API for her customers to use when accessing her service. She is using API keys, but she is concerned about third parties intercepting and accessing the data. What should she include in her implementation to address this concern?

   A. Data tokenization

   B. Ensure encryption at rest

   C. Ensure encryption in transit

   D. Data masking

7. Ben wants to gather business requirements for his software development effort and is using an Agile methodology. Which of the following is not a common means of gathering user requirements in an Agile process?

    A. Brainstorming

    B. Documentation review

    C. User observation

    D. Surveys

8. Encryption at rest is a protective design element included in SDLCs for cloud environments due to what common cloud design motif?

    A. Rapid elasticity

    B. Multitenancy

    C. Measured services

    D. Scalability

9. Nick wants to avoid common pitfalls in his CI/CD pipeline. Which of the following is a common CI/CD pitfall that can harm cloud development efforts?

    A. Automation of processes

    B. Use of metrics

    C. Using multiple deployment paths

    D. Reliance on a version control system

10. Maria wants to integrate her existing identity provider with her cloud provider's services. What common standard is used for most cloud identity provider integration?

    A. IDPL

    B. OpenLDAP

    C. SAML

    D. ConnectID

11. Jack wants to enable his team to develop cloud-native applications. Which of the following is not a common element in a cloud-native application design?

    A. Optimized assembly code

    B. Automated release pipelines

    C. Containers

    D. Microservices

12. At which phase of the software development life cycle (SDLC) is user involvement *most* crucial?

    A. Define

    B. Design

    C. Development

    D. Test

13. Brian wants to ensure that he takes the OWASP Top 10 Cloud risks into account in his development process. He knows that regulatory compliance is on the list, and he wants to include it in the SDLC. During what phase of the SDLC would it make the most sense to consider regulatory compliance?

    A. Analysis and requirements definition

    B. Design

    C. Implementation

    D. Testing

14. The testing process that Angie is using for her organization includes access to the design specifications, source code, and running applications. What type of security testing methodology is she using?

    A. White box

    B. Gray box

    C. Red box

    D. Black box

15. The CWE/SANS Top 25 most dangerous software errors includes the use of hard-coded credentials. What common cloud service component can be used to avoid this problem for cloud-hosted software and applications?

    A. An MFA token

    B. A TPM

    C. A KMS

    D. An API key

16. Dana's organization requires an SBOM for each application it deploys. What OWASP Top 10 item does an SBOM help to avoid?

    A. Vulnerable and outdated components

    B. Broken access control

    C. Injection

    D. Security misconfiguration

17. The company that Yun works for provides API access to customers. Yun wants to rate-limit API access and gather billing information while using a central authorization and access management system. What type of tool should Yun put in place to meet these requirements?

    A. An API gateway

    B. An API proxy

    C. An API firewall

    D. A next-generation API manager

18. What phase of the SDLC is IAST typically associated with?

   A. Design

   B. Testing

   C. Implementation

   D. Deployment

19. Gary's cloud service provides customers with access to APIs. Which of the following is a common security flaw in APIs?

   A. Use of unstructured data

   B. Lack of authentication

   C. Use of semi-structured data

   D. Lack of encryption

20. Dan wants to encrypt data at rest in his cloud environment. What encryption standard should he look for when encrypting data at rest?

   A. TLS

   B. AES-256

   C. SSL

   D. Blowfish

21. Mark wants to ensure that his software vendor is using industry best practices as part of their software validation process. He knows that NIST defines a number of recommended minimums for verification of code by developers. Which of the following is not a NIST recommended minimum standard for vendor or developer verification of code?

   A. Use automated testing.

   B. Perform code-based (static) analysis.

   C. Only check internally developed software.

   D. Conduct threat modeling.

22. Lori wants to ensure that the included software components provided by her vendor are secure. What type of process should she use to conduct an assessment of those packages?

   A. A web application vulnerability scan

   B. A software composition analysis

   C. A vulnerability scan

   D. A version number validation process

23. Christine has documented a software testing user story that states: "As an attacker, I will upload malicious software as part of my form submission which will exploit the parsing software that reads user submissions." What type of testing is Christine preparing for?

   A. Abuse case testing

   B. Static testing

   C. QA testing

   D. SCA testing

24. OWASP'S Application Security Verification Standard (ASVS) has three primary usage models. Which of the following is not an intended usage model based on its design objectives?

A. To be used as a metric

B. To be used for auditing

C. To be used as guidance

D. To be used during procurement

25. Ian wants to use a cloud-specific list of application issues. Which of the following options should he choose?

A. The OWASP Top 10

B. The NIST Dirty Dozen

C. The SANS Top 25

D. The MITRE ATT&CK-RS

26. Nick wants to use a common format for his team's software versioning. What versioning format should he use if he wants to use a common industry practice?

A. Codename.version

B. Major.build.minor.patch

C. RFC number.version.patch

D. Major.minor.patch

27. What term is used to describe the list of all of the software components of a product?

A. Component index

B. SBOM

C. Version catalog

D. SCCM

28. Valerie's company has recently experienced successful SQL injection attacks against a third-party application they use. The vendor has not yet provided a patch for the SQL injection flaw, but Valerie needs to keep the application in production due to business requirements. What type of tool could Valerie put in place to protect against the SQL injection attacks on her web application?

A. A DAM

B. A WAF

C. An XML firewall

D. An API gateway

29. Jackie wants to allow applications to run using the libraries and other dependencies they need without having to have an independent operating system for each application. What technology should she use to allow her to easily move application packages between different operating systems?

A. Packages

B. Containers

C. Virtual machines

D. Hypervisors

30. Charles logs in using his organization's credentials and is able to use that login throughout a variety of systems and applications. What technology is Charles using?

    A. SAML

    B. SSO

    C. OpenID Connect

    D. OTP

31. Henry wants to ensure that only authorized customers are able to use his organization's public-facing APIs. What common security technique is for this purpose?

    A. API keys

    B. Single sign-on

    C. API federation

    D. Complex API passwords

32. Nancy wants to ensure that her organization does not have an issue with licensing for her software, and she knows that the vendor controls access using a licensing server that each installation checks in with. Which of the following should she pay particular attention to in order to ensure that she does not have a service interruption at some point in the future?

    A. The license term

    B. Whether the terms of the license can be disclosed

    C. The license cost

    D. Third party sub-licenses included in the contract

33. Isaac wants to ensure that his cloud service provider is using cryptographic systems that meet widely accepted standards. What U.S. government standard should he expect his provider to comply with their cryptographic systems?

    A. GDPR

    B. FIPS 140-2

    C. SSL

    D. SHA-2

34. Megan wants to increase the auditability of the use of privileges in her infrastructure. Which of the following solutions will have the biggest positive impact on auditability?

    A. Use shared service accounts.

    B. Use multifactor authentication.

    C. Use dynamic secrets.

    D. Use API keys.

35. In the testing phase of the software development life cycle (SDLC), software performance and _____ should both be reviewed.

    A. Version

    B. Complexity

    C. Size

    D. Security

36. Chris wants to use a cloud provider–hosted mechanism to store and manage his organization's secrets. What type of solution should he look for?

   A. KMS

   B. PKI

   C. CA

   D. KCS

37. What entity provides authentication services in a federation?

   A. IdP

   B. RP

   C. SP

   D. SSO

38. Docker is an example of what sort of tool?

   A. Microservices launcher

   B. Cloud application security broker

   C. A containerization platform

   D. A web application firewall

39. Yasmine is working with a software as a service vendor. What part of the environment does Yasmine's company have responsibility for?

   A. Applications and data storage.

   B. The OS, middleware, and runtime.

   C. Storage and networking.

   D. The vendor is responsible for the environment.

40. Jason wants to use multifactor authentication. Which of the following lists a valid multi-factor set?

   A. A username, password, and PIN

   B. A username, password, and app-generated code on a phone

   C. A username, voiceprint, and fingerprint

   D. A username, app-generated code, and token-generated code

41. Kim wants to use version control for her software. What common tool could her organization use to perform this function?

   A. Jenkins

   B. Chef

   C. Git

   D. Puppet

42. Ramon's organization uses Office 365 but relies on their own Active Directory credentials to log into O365. What is this type of configuration called?

    A. Federated identity

    B. Structured identity

    C. Shared identity

    D. Constrained identity

43. Gretchen wants to ensure that her organization is in compliance with their software licenses. Which of the following is the most important step for most organizations in ensuring license compliance?

    A. Using only open source software

    B. Tracking all software versions

    C. Using only commercial software

    D. Software inventory

44. Laura wants to use a threat modeling tool to assess threats in her environment. Which of the following models has been abandoned by Microsoft and replaced with a new model?

    A. DREAD

    B. PASTA

    C. STRIDE

    D. ATASM

45. Aisha's organization has deployed a cloud application security broker. Which of the following is not a typical purpose for a CASB to be deployed?

    A. To control usage-based costs

    B. To limit access based on service categories

    C. To help limit the potential for sensitive data loss

    D. To detect anomalous usage patterns

46. Kathleen wants to test potentially malicious software in a secure way. What cloud application architecture concept can she apply to help her do so?

    A. An IPS

    B. A SIEM

    C. Sandboxing

    D. Antivirus

47. Kieran's team has deployed a CASB and wants to focus on data protection. Which of the following capabilities will most effectively help protect against third parties accessing data while it travels between Kieran's on-premises location and their cloud vendors?

    A. Encryption

    B. Tokenization

    C. Masking

    D. Upload prevention

48. Selah is preparing a container to deploy her application to a cloud service provider's containerization service. Which of the following components will not be included in the container?

   A. The host kernel for the operating system

   B. The libraries needed by the application

   C. The configuration files for the application

   D. The binaries belonging to the application

49. Olivia is preparing to generate API keys and knows that they need to have certain characteristics to be secure. Which of the following best describes an API key that will be considered secure?

   A. Unique, random, and non-guessable

   B. Unique, sequential, and traceable

   C. Repeatable, sequential, and traceable

   D. Repeatable, logged, and traceable

50. Ian is using a CASB to control usage of cloud services. He wants to ensure that users in his organization only use cloud services that are approved for their role. What two elements should he define in his rules to most effectively accomplish this?

   A. Identity and activity

   B. Activity and data

   C. Identity and service

   D. Service and data

51. Jack wants to use the ATASM model. Which of the following is not one of the key elements of an ATASM assessment?

   A. Attacks

   B. Threats

   C. Architecture

   D. Mitigations

52. Testing done on running code is known as what type of testing?

   A. Dynamic

   B. Automatic

   C. Structured

   D. Static

53. A web application firewall (WAF) can understand and act on what type of traffic?

   A. Border Gateway Protocol (BGP)

   B. Simple Mail Transfer Protocol (SMTP)

   C. Internet Control Message Protocol (ICMP)

   D. Hypertext Transfer Protocol (HTTP)

54. Henry wants to design his SDLC to help prevent the most common application security issues. Where in the SDLC should he insert controls to ensure that his application architecture is secure?

A. Analysis and requirements definition

B. Design

C. Deployment

D. Operations and maintenance

55. Jacinda's manager has asked her to set up a sandbox environment to help validate third-party software before it is run. What should Jacinda prepare an environment to handle?

A. Optimizing the production environment by moving processes that are not frequently used into the sandbox

B. Allowing secure remote access for users who need resources in the cloud environment

C. Running malware for analysis purposes

D. Creating secure subnets of the production environment

56. Valerie wants to decouple her application infrastructure from her underlying operating system platforms to allow her to more easily migrate between cloud service providers. What type of solution will best fit her needs?

A. Use custom configured Linux virtual machines to host the application.

B. Use containers configured for the application to host the application.

C. Use the cloud provider's native serverless infrastructures to host the applications.

D. Use default Linux systems with default configurations to host the application.

57. Gary wants to monitor privileged credential use in his Microsoft SQL Server environment, which he hosts with an IaaS provider. What type of tool should Gary select to help with this need?

A. A WAF

B. A database SIEM

C. A DB-IPS

D. A DAM

58. Paula wants to avoid denial-of-service attacks against her APIs. What controls should she select to most effectively provide this type of security?

A. Use an IPS and a scalable architecture.

B. Use a scalable architecture and set throttling limits and quotas.

C. Require authentication and use an IPS.

D. Require authentication and set throttling limits and quotas.

59. Sandboxing can often be used for _____.

A. Testing user awareness and training

B. Testing API security

C. Testing software before putting it into production

D. Testing software to validate its compliance with regulatory requirements

60. Jen wants to ensure that the encryption modules she is using in her application design are secure. What type of validation or certification should she look for?

   A. PCI compliant

   B. AES-cert

   C. FIPS 140-2

   D. GLBA validated

61. Kwame wants to limit the impact of potentially compromised secrets in his environment. What should he do to most effectively limit the issues compromised secrets can cause?

   A. Extend secrets lifecycle.

   B. Rotate secrets.

   C. Replace secrets with tokens.

   D. Implement a secret expiration list.

62. As part of her organization's SDLC, Olivia is testing whether the business logic in a new application generates correct output. What type of testing is Olivia conducting?

   A. Stress testing

   B. Functional testing

   C. Load testing

   D. Nonfunctional testing

63. Olivia's organization wants to adopt multifactor authentication. Which of the following MFA models is considered less secure than the others?

   A. Hardware tokens

   B. Mobile applications

   C. SMS factors

   D. USB tokens

64. Ben wants to validate open source software packages used in his environment. Which of the following is not a valid dynamic testing option?

   A. Use manual security testing of the live application.

   B. Use an application vulnerability scanner.

   C. Use manual security testing of the source code.

   D. Conduct unit and integration testing of the application.

65. Yariv's abuse case testing has identified an issue with their web application that allows bots to conduct automated attacks. What type of protection could he implement to limit the impact of bots performing actions like this?

   A. Filter known SQL injection attacks from web queries.

   B. Use a CAPTCHA before allowing user actions.

   C. Require users to log in before performing actions.

   D. Prevent XSS by limiting special characters in form submissions.

66. Emily logs in to a third-party website using her Google credentials. What role is Google playing in the authentication process?

    A. Google is the service provider.

    B. Google is the storage provider.

    C. Google is the authorization provider.

    D. Google is the identity provider.

67. Software developers designing applications that allow access to protected customer information for the cloud should expect to include options to ensure all of the following capabilities *except* _____.

    A. Encryption of data at rest

    B. Encryption of data in transit

    C. Data masking

    D. Randomizing customer data

68. Kristen wants to filter her SAML traffic for potential attacks, including rate-limiting requests and validating content. Which of the following solutions is purpose-built for this type of security design?

    A. A DAM with OpenID support

    B. A SAML compliant IDS

    C. An XML firewall

    D. A WAF

69. Which of the following is not true about single sign-on (SSO)?

    A. Reduction in password fatigue

    B. Reduces password reuse

    C. Prevents the use of multifactor authentication

    D. Makes end-user credential management easier

70. What does static application security testing (SAST) examine?

    A. Software outcomes

    B. User performance

    C. System durability

    D. Source code

71. Angela wants to deploy multifactor authentication (MFA) for her organization and wants to integrate with her cloud provider. Which of the following MFA options is least likely to be easily supported by a cloud provider?

    A. Hardware tokens

    B. Biometric readers

    C. Mobile applications

    D. SMS factors

72. Christina is following a typical SDLC process and has completed the planning phase. What phase typically follows the Planning phase in most SDLCs?

A. Design

B. Deployment

C. Maintenance

D. Requirements Gathering

73. Annie's organization uses a waterfall methodology for its SDLC. What description best fits a waterfall methodology?

A. Development efforts can move easily between phases to meet organizational needs.

B. The outcome of each phase serves as the input to the next phase.

C. Development efforts repeat in cycles until the development is complete.

D. The outcome of each phase determines whether the process moves forward or backward in the SDLC process.

74. During what phase of the SDLC are business requirements most likely to be mapped to how the software will be built?

A. Requirements Definition

B. Design

C. Testing

D. Secure Operations

75. Stress testing is a form of what type of testing?

A. Black box

B. Functional testing

C. White box

D. Nonfunctional testing

76. Gabriel's organization wants to ensure that their open source software is properly licensed. What should they were do?

A. Contact the authors of each component to request permission to use them.

B. Engage a third-party license management vendor to ensure compliance with the licenses.

C. Pay appropriate licensing fees to the licensing organization for each software component.

D. Review the licenses for each component to ensure they are in compliance.

77. Sofia is preparing a list of the likely attacks against her APIs. Which of the following is not a common attack against APIs?

A. Injection

B. Malware

C. Distributed denial-of-service

D. Credential stuffing

78. The SAFECode Fundamental Practices for Secure Software Development includes a section on handling errors. What common development best practice does it reference?

A. Providing too much information in errors

B. Handling errors in a secure and graceful way

C. Ensuring unanticipated errors are provided only to administrators

D. Ensuring unanticipated errors are provided only to users

79. Jason wants to use TLS to protect his organization's production web traffic. Who should generate the x.509 certificate for his website?

A. Jason should generate it on the web servers.

B. Jason should use his company's internal certificate authority.

C. Jason should use a commercial certificate authority.

D. Jason should generate the certificate on a separate administrative workstation used only for that purpose.

80. Lisa wants to ensure that the open source software package she has downloaded is legitimate. The software download site provides an SHA2 hash, a cryptographic signature, a file size, and a version number. Which of these options provides the greatest level of certainty?

A. The SHA2 hash

B. The cryptographic signature

C. The file size

D. The version number

81. James has created monitoring instrumentation for his application and uses the instrumentation to assess performance as well as function during the QA stage of his SDLC. What type of software validation methodology is he using?

A. IAST

B. Interactive DST

C. SCA

D. Structured DST

82. Michelle is using the SAFECode Fundamental Practices for Secure Software Development as an underlying foundation for her organization's development practices. She wants to develop an encryption strategy and knows that SAFECode describes how to do so. Which of the following is not a best practice for developing an encryption strategy for applications according to SAFECode?

A. Ensuring encryption algorithms cannot be changed easily

B. Defining what to protect

C. Assessing what encryption mechanisms meet the organization's requirements

D. Deciding on a key management solution

83. In a platform as a service (PaaS) model, who should *most* likely be responsible for the security of the applications in the production environment?

    A. Cloud customer

    B. Cloud provider

    C. Regulator

    D. Programmers

84. James wants to test his software for business logic issues that knowledgeable users could use to take advantage of his software. What type of testing should he invest in?

    A. Abuse case testing

    B. Black box testing

    C. Use case testing

    D. White box testing

85. Frankie wants to implement single sign-on for her organization. Which of the following options is not commonly supported for SSO in cloud environments?

    A. Cloud provider native SSO

    B. Active Directory

    C. SAML

    D. LDAP

86. Regardless of which model the organization uses for system development, in which phase of the software development life cycle (SDLC) will user input be requested and considered?

    A. Define

    B. Design

    C. Development

    D. Detect

87. Pete is reviewing his environment based on the OWASP Cloud Native Application Security Top 10. He knows that container configuration is a top concern and has identified that his containers currently run as root. How can he remediate this issue?

    A. Set the operating system to prevent root logins.

    B. Set a non-privileged user as the container owner.

    C. Set a non-privileged user as the process owner.

    D. Use multifactor authentication for the root user.

88. Jessica's quality assurance testing process involves identifying software flaws, including business logic flaws and other coding mistakes. What type of testing should she perform to most effectively identify underlying code quality issues?

    A. Static testing

    B. Black box testing

    C. Dynamic testing

    D. Software composition analysis

89. Which of the following is *not* checked when using the STRIDE threat model?

   A. The ability of users to gain administrative access rights without proper permission

   B. The ability of internal personnel to trigger business continuity/disaster recovery activities

   C. The ability of a participant in a transaction to refute that they've taken part in the transaction

   D. The ability of an unauthorized user to pretend to be an authorized user

90. Kathleen's organization uses a microservices architecture to deliver its major applications. What type of security tool is best suited to providing security for microservices that rely on APIs and service discovery?

   A. CASB

   B. XML firewall

   C. RPC gateway

   D. API gateway

91. At which phase of the software development life cycle (SDLC) should security personnel first be involved?

   A. Define

   B. Design

   C. Develop

   D. Test

92. Tahir configures his organization's QA environment to simulate logins for 25% more users than typically log in at the maximum usage for their major web application. Which term best describes the type of testing Tahir is conducting?

   A. Dynamic, nonfunctional testing

   B. Dynamic, functional testing

   C. Static, functional testing

   D. Static testing, nonfunctional testing

93. When Joanna logs into a service provider that her organization works with, the service provider sends a request to her organization's identity provider to determine if she is already authenticated. If she is, the identity provider sends a token to the service provider confirming that she is authenticated, and her browser will pass a token to the service provider that is validated based on the trust relationship the service provider has with the identity provider. What type of infrastructure is Joanna using?

   A. RDP

   B. SSO

   C. OTP

   D. MFA

94. Ben's team uses the STRIDE model to identify security threats. What security property does tampering impact in the STRIDE model?

    A. Integrity

    B. Confidentiality

    C. Availability

    D. Authorization

95. Carmen's organization wants to provide awareness training using a community-based web application security guide. What community standard is best suited to this type of training?

    A. ASVS

    B. CVE

    C. OWASP

    D. NIST

96. Henry uses an IAST process as part of his SLDC. What SDLC phase is IAST most likely to occur in?

    A. Planning

    B. Building

    C. Deployment

    D. Testing

97. Malika wants to ensure that human error doesn't influence the security of secrets in her organization. Which of the following practices will most effectively prevent human-related issues from influencing her secrets security?

    A. Use a common passphrase word list in an automated CI/CD pipeline.

    B. Require password complexity.

    C. Generate passphrases randomly.

    D. Exclusively use shared passphrases.

98. Frank knows that his organization intends to use federated identities as part of its cloud services environment. What standard should he ensure that his existing on-site identity management system supports to help with this?

    A. SAML

    B. FIPS 140-2

    C. XML

    D. FIM

99. James uses a CI/CD pipeline at the core of his development process. What design pattern should he use to ensure his QA process doesn't impact production?

A. Add software going through QA to his production environment to allow live testing.

B. Create a new environment for QA testing, then promote to production after testing.

C. Replicate the production environment for QA testing, then promote to production after testing.

D. Add software to the QA environment for testing, then allow production users to access QA with instrumentation in place.

100. Tara's organization uses a three-level application security verification standard, and requires that their most secure applications reach level 3 with in-depth validation and testing. What application security standard are they using?

A. ASVS

B. SAFECode

C. OWASP

D. SANS/CWE

Chapter

5

Domain 5: Cloud Security Operations

SUBDOMAINS:

✓ 5.1 Build and implement physical and logical infrastructure for cloud environment

✓ 5.2 Operate and maintain physical and logical infrastructure for cloud environment

✓ 5.3 Implement operational controls and standards [e.g., Information Technology Infrastructure Library (ITIL), International Organization for Standardization/International Electrotechnical Commission (ISO/IEC) 20000-1]

✓ 5.4 Support digital forensics

✓ 5.5 Manage communication with relevant parties

✓ 5.6 Manage security operations

1. What term is used to describe agreements between IT service providers and customers that describe service-level targets and responsibilities of the customer and provider?

   A. OLA

   B. SAC

   C. SLA

   D. SLR

2. Sally is building her organization's communication plans and knows that customers are an important group to include in the plan. What key function does proactive customer communication help with?

   A. Notification of breaches

   B. Regulatory compliance

   C. Managing expectations

   D. Problem management

3. Juanita has discovered unexpected programs running on her freshly installed Linux system that was built using her cloud provider's custom Linux distribution but that did not allow connections from the internet yet. What is the most likely reason for this?

   A. Juanita inadvertently installed additional tools during the installation process.

   B. The version of Linux automatically downloads helper agents when installed.

   C. Cloud vendors often install helper utilities in their own distributions.

   D. Attackers have installed applications.

4. Ben wants to manage operating system and application patches for thousands of machines hosted in an infrastructure as a service vendor's cloud. What should he do?

   A. Use the cloud vendor's native patch management tools.

   B. Use the operating system vendor's patch management tools.

   C. Use manual update processes.

   D. Write custom scripts to manage updates.

5. Jason's organization is required to provide information about its cloud operating environment, including yearly audit information to regulators in his industry. What is he most likely to be able to provide to the regulators when they ask for a security audit of his hosted environment?

   A. A recent audit conducted by staff from Jason's organization

   B. A recent audit conducted by a third-party auditor hired by Jason's organization

   C. Direct audit permissions for the regulators to audit the cloud provider

   D. A copy of the cloud provider's third-party audit results

6. Tracy has set up a cloud hardware security module (HSM) service for her organization in her cloud-hosted environment. What activity is she preparing for?

    A. Securely storing and managing secrets

    B. Ensuring end-to-end encryption between cloud and on-site systems

    C. Managing the security of the underlying hardware in the environment

    D. Detecting attacks against hosted systems

7. Charles wants to be able to create new servers as needed for his environment using variables and configuration files to configure the systems to meet changing needs. What type of solution should he implement to help with this type of orchestration?

    A. A CI/CD pipeline

    B. Infrastructure as code

    C. A check-in/checkout design

    D. An application interface

8. James wants to establish key performance indicators for his service continuity management practice based on ITIL. Which of the following is a useful KPI for service continuity management?

    A. The number of business processes with continuity agreements

    B. The number of vulnerabilities found in installed software per period of time

    C. The number of patches installed per period of time

    D. The number of natural disasters in the local area in a year

9. Zoe wants to speed up her traditional release management process. What modern approach is best suited to an ITIL v4–based rapid-release-oriented organization?

    A. Waterfall

    B. Agile/DevOps

    C. Spiral

    D. RAD

10. ITIL v4 includes a seven-step continual improvement model. What item occurs at the end of the process before it starts again?

    A. Determining the vision

    B. Assessing results

    C. Taking action

    D. Determining the goal

11. Tim puts a server in his virtualization environment into maintenance mode. Which of the following events will occur?

    A. Migrates the running virtual machines to other hardware

    B. Pauses all running VMs immediate

    C. Sends a notification to users, then pauses running VMs

    D. Marks the machine as unavailable for new VMs

12. Kathleen wants to centralize her log capture and analysis capabilities and use automated tools to help her identify likely security issues. What type of tool should she look for?

    A. SIEM

    B. IPS

    C. CASB

    D. MITRE

13. Elaine wants to ensure that traffic is encrypted in transit. What technology is commonly used to secure data in transit?

    A. VLANs

    B. TLS

    C. DNSSEC

    D. DHCP

14. Ujama wants to protect systems in his environment from being accessed via SSH. What should he do if he needs to leave the service available for local connections?

    A. Block inbound connections to TCP port 3389 on his firewall.

    B. Block outbound connections to TCP port 3389 on his firewall.

    C. Block inbound connections to TCP port 22 on his firewall.

    D. Block outbound connections to TCP port 22 on his firewall.

15. Ron wants to use a central system to store information about system and software configurations and their relationships. What tool is often used for this to support standards-based configuration management practices like those found in ITIL v4?

    A. CRM

    B. CMDB

    C. Configuration item

    D. Change catalog

16. Maria's manager is concerned about patching for the underlying cloud environment that her platform as a service (PaaS) vendor provides. What should Maria tell her manager?

    A. Maria's organization is responsible for patching and needs to set up a regular patch cycle.

    B. The vendor is responsible for patching and there is no patching that needs to be done by customers in a PaaS environment.

    C. Negotiations need to be done with the vendor to determine which organization is responsible for patch management.

    D. The contract will determine which organization is responsible for patch management.

17. ITIL v4 describes three subprocesses related to availability management. What are these three subprocesses?

  A. Designing services for availability, disaster recovery testing, determining availability targets

  B. Availability management, availability metrics, and availability improvement

  C. Designing services for availability, availability testing, and availability monitoring and reporting

  D. Availability planning, availability improvement, availability validation

18. Naomi's organization has recently experienced a data breach. Which of the following parties is least likely to require notification based on existing contracts or regulations?

  A. Customers

  B. Vendors

  C. Regulators

  D. Partners

19. Megan is starting her organization's change management practices. She has conducted an asset inventory. What step is typically next in a change management process?

  A. Creating a baseline

  B. Deploying new assets

  C. Establishing a CMB

  D. Documenting deviations from the baseline

20. Dan wants to use clipboard-based drag and drop between his virtualized desktops in a Type 2 hypervisor environment. Which of the following steps is most likely to allow him to access additional features that require virtualization environment integration to work?

  A. Building the virtual machines as containers

  B. Installing guest operating system virtualization tools

  C. Installing virtualization environment orchestration tools

  D. Building the containers as virtual machines

21. Geoff knows that ITIL v4 focuses on four information security management practices. Which of these processes could involve an SOC 2 Type 2 audit?

  A. Design of security controls

  B. Security testing

  C. Management of security incidents

  D. Security review

22. Theresa is building an automated CI/CD pipeline. She wants to ensure that code that passes through the pipeline is secure before it moves from staging to production. What is her best option if she wants to test the running application?

    A. Manual static code review

    B. Automated code review

    C. Using a web application firewall

    D. Using an IPS

23. The Cloud Security Alliance's Cloud Incident Response (CIR) framework documents typical breakdowns for customer versus cloud provider responsibilities in incident response, including pointing to cloud providers as being responsible for almost all risks in an SaaS environment. In an IaaS environment, who is responsible for network risks?

    A. The customer

    B. Both the customer and the service provider

    C. The service provider

    D. Third-party incident responders

24. Eleanor wants to build her organization's change management processes. What is the typical first step for change management efforts?

    A. Policy creation

    B. Baselining

    C. Documentation creation

    D. Vulnerability scanning

25. Juanita is responsible for a web application that is split between an on-site application environment and a cloud-hosted database. Juanita knows the application performs thousands of small database queries for some transactions. What performance monitoring option is most important to her application's performance?

    A. The network routes between the datacenters

    B. Network throughput between the two datacenters

    C. The bandwidth between the two datacenters

    D. Network response time (latency) between the datacenters

26. Kolin needs to collect forensic data from an Azure-hosted VM. What should he do to validate his forensic data after capturing disk snapshots for the VM's OS and data disks?

    A. Compare hashes of the VM's OS and data disks and the snapshots of each.

    B. Make two copies of the snapshots and compare hashes between the snapshot hashes.

    C. Export the VM as a hash, then validate the hash.

    D. Export the VM as a disk image and compare the disk image's digital signature to the original.

27. Ilya wants to use an ITIL v4–based practice for capacity and performance management. Which of the following is not a typical subprocess for capacity and performance management under ITIL?

    A. Customer KPI oversight

    B. Service capacity management

    C. Component capacity management

    D. Capacity management reporting

28. Nick's organization has experienced a data breach of their cloud-hosted environment. Which of the following is most likely to need to be communicated with based on regulations?

    A. Vendors

    B. Customers

    C. Partners

    D. Law enforcement

29. Valerie has created disk images of virtual machines running in her cloud environment. What key digital forensic requirement should she ensure is handled properly if she believes that the information will be used for a legal case in the future?

    A. Legal hold

    B. Chain of custody

    C. Seizure requirements

    D. Disposal requirements

30. Asha wants to take advantage of her cloud provider's ability to schedule instances to match her business practices. What practice will help her handle a large number of instances with different scheduling requirements?

    A. Using a third-party scheduler

    B. Enabling auto-scheduling

    C. Tagging

    D. Disabling unused instances

31. Which of the following is *not* an aspect of host hardening?

    A. Removing all unnecessary software and services

    B. Patching and updating as needed

    C. Adding new hardware to provide increased performance

    D. Installing a host-based firewall and an intrusion detection system (IDS)

32. Isabella has been asked to review her organization's patch management scheme. The current process focuses on manual patch installation on a weekly window. Isabella is interested in moving to an automated patch deployment process on a more frequent basis. What risk is most commonly associated with automated patching systems?

A. The potential to disrupt systems due to a patching issue or bad patch

B. The inability to report on patches that fail installation

C. The inability to report on patches that are not installed

D. The potential to increase patching speed and accuracy

33. In order to enhance virtual environment isolation and security, a best practice is to _____.

A. Ensure that all virtual switches are not connected to the physical network

B. Ensure that management systems are connected to a different physical network than the production systems

C. Never connect a virtual switch to a physical host

D. Connect physical devices only with virtual switches

34. Deployment management is a component of which service management practice in ITIL v4?

A. Problem management

B. Release management

C. Change management

D. IT asset management

35. Carlos wants to monitor CPU load, temperature, and voltages for his virtual machine. What should Carlos do to achieve this?

A. Carlos cannot track temperature and voltages for his virtual system, but he can track load using the underlying hardware.

B. Carlos cannot track load, but he can track temperature and voltages for his virtual system and should use the underlying hardware for the VM.

C. Carlos cannot track temperature and voltages for a virtual CPU, but he can track load via the operating system.

D. Carlos cannot track load and voltages, but he can install a thermal sensor to track his virtual machine's temperature.

36. Megan is responsible for ensuring that her organization's continual service improvement efforts are meeting their goals. What formal role does Megan hold under ITIL?

A. CSI manager

B. Process architect

C. Process owner

D. Customer

37. Felicia wants to apply rules to her Amazon AWS VPC to limit the IPs that can contact her servers. What feature should she use to do this?

A. Honeypots

B. IDS

C. IPS

D. Network security groups

38. Designing system redundancy into a cloud datacenter allows all the following capabilities *except* _____.

A. Incorporating additional hardware into the production environment to support increased redundancy

B. Preventing any chance of service interruption

C. Load-sharing/balancing

D. Planned, controlled failover during contingency operations

39. Raj is required to provide proof of PCI compliance to his acquiring bank. What should he ask for from his cloud service provider?

A. An attestation of compliance

B. An SOC 1 Type 1 audit

C. An SOC 2 Type 2 audit

D. To allow him to conduct a PCI audit of the vendor

40. Naomi wants to conduct a vulnerability scan of her cloud environment. What requirement is she likely to need to meet with her cloud service vendor for an IaaS environment?

A. She can only scan her own internal systems.

B. She will have to use the service provider's scanning tools.

C. She can only scan her own external systems.

D. She will need to schedule a time and date for the scans.

41. Naomi has completed her vulnerability scan and wants to remediate the systems she has discovered vulnerabilities on. What is a typical patching process for IaaS-hosted systems when concerns exist about the potential impact of patching?

A. Use a script to patch each system.

B. Stand up new, patched instances, then replace the unpatched systems using load balancers.

C. Create new instances with the patches installed, shut down the existing instances, and assign new IP addresses for the new systems.

D. Manually patch each system.

42. When putting a system into maintenance mode, it's important to do all of the following
    except _____.

    A. Transfer any live virtual guests off the host

    B. Turn off logging

    C. Lock out the system from accepting any new connections

    D. Notify customers if there are any interruptions

43. The operating system that Jack wants to install in his cloud environment requires a cryp-
    tographic store as part of the boot process to ensure that the hardware has been validated.
    Which of the following tools will allow him to meet this requirement?

    A. Hardware HSM

    B. Cloud TPM

    C. Virtual TPM

    D. Cloud HSM

44. Yarif runs an operating system and then uses a hypervisor running on that operating system
    to run virtual machines. What type of hypervisor is he running?

    A. A classic hypervisor

    B. Type 1

    C. An advanced hypervisor

    D. Type 2

45. What key function is described by ITIL's incident management practice?

    A. Engaging third-party responders based on best practices

    B. Managing problem escalations

    C. Restoring a service as soon as possible after an incident

    D. Identifying incidents to allow response

46. Lucca has experienced an event that interrupts normal service in his organization. How
    would ITIL classify this?

    A. As an incident

    B. As an SLA violation

    C. As a problem

    D. As an MSA violation

47. What description best explains the relationship between problems and incidents?

    A. Every problem is the result of an incident, but not all incidents are problems.

    B. Problems and incidents are distinct and unrelated.

    C. Problems are handled by support desks, and incidents are handled by security
    professionals.

    D. Every incident is the result of a problem, but not all problems are incidents.

48. Olivia wants to establish key performance indicators compatible with ITIL for her availability management practice. Which of the following is not a useful availability KPI?

   A. Availability of the service relative to SLAs for the service

   B. The number of service interruptions

   C. The duration of the service interruptions

   D. The number of individuals impacted by service interruptions

49. What underlies the information security management according to ITIL v4?

   A. Event filtering and correlation rules

   B. Security advisories

   C. Information security policies

   D. Security alerts

50. Emily is in charge of her organization's deployment management as part of a CI/CD pipeline. What process typically needs to occur for a deployment to occur?

   A. A change request must be approved.

   B. The change advisory board must review the change.

   C. Automated testing and validation must complete successfully.

   D. The next version must enter the pipeline.

51. Chris wants to capture forensic data in his cloud environment. What type of capture methodology is most likely to be used for virtual machines in a cloud infrastructure as a service environment?

   A. Forensic image acquisition using a tool like DD

   B. Use of the provider's snapshot tool

   C. Forensic image acquisition using a tool like DBAN

   D. Use of the provider's file copy utilities

52. Tools like Terraform, CloudFormation, Ansible, Chef, and Puppet are often associated with what type of strategy?

   A. Incident response

   B. Agile SDLC

   C. Infrastructure as code

   D. Legal hold

53. Alaina wants to align her organization's service-level management to an ISO standard. Which ISO standard describes service management?

   A. ISO 20000-1

   B. ISO 27001

   C. ITIL v4

   D. COBIT

54. Rene is an SOC manager and wants to centralize incident and log information. What type of tool should she acquire and implement?

    A. NOC

    B. SIEM

    C. IPS

    D. DLP

55. What risk does an IPS pose that an IDS does not?

    A. An IPS cannot use signature-based detection.

    B. An IPS can block legitimate traffic.

    C. An IPS cannot use behavior-based detection.

    D. An IPS can fail open, while an IDS cannot.

56. Amanda wants to use logging from her IaaS cloud environment to determine if an external user is accessing one of her servers. What type of logging should she enable in her cloud provider's environment to do so?

    A. System logging

    B. Performance logging

    C. Flow logging

    D. Storage bucket logging

57. Amanda wants to use her SIEM to detect attacks based on network traffic and behavior baselines that adapt to changes over time using learning techniques. What feature is she most likely to use for this purpose?

    A. AI

    B. Log correlation

    C. Threat intelligence

    D. Reporting

58. Kathleen knows that her cloud provider makes a DHCP service available to systems in their IaaS environment. What does she know that her systems will receive from the DHCP server?

    A. A default gateway, subnet mask, DNS server, and IP address

    B. A default route, a subnet mask, an IP address, and a MAC address

    C. An IP address and a MAC address

    D. An IP address, a subnet mask, a DNS server, and firewall rule definitions for the local network

59. Ben wants to secure his virtualization environment. Which of the following is not a common security practice used to help protect virtualization infrastructure and systems?

    A. Enable secure boot.

    B. Disable cut and paste between the VM and console.

    C. Remove unnecessary hardware.

    D. Use the virtual machine console whenever possible.

60. Chelsea wants to prevent network-based attacks against her cloud-hosted system. Which of the following is not an appropriate solution to stop attacks?

A. Honeypots

B. Firewalls

C. Security groups

D. Intrusion prevention systems

61. Methods for achieving high-availability cloud environments include all of the following *except*

A. Using instances running on alternate CPU architectures

B. Multiple system vendors for the same services

C. Explicitly documented business continuity and disaster recovery (BC/DR) functions in the service-level agreement (SLA) or contract

D. Failover capability back to the customer's on-premises environment

62. Susan's website is unable to be loaded by her customers due to a system outage. What ITIL practice should Susan invest in to ensure that this does not happen again?

A. Availability management

B. Deployment management

C. Change management

D. Capacity management

63. Li's organization uses a software as a service tool for their productivity work. After a recent compromise of user credentials, Li wants to perform digital forensics. What types of information can Li obtain for forensic analysis in an SaaS environment?

A. Logs

B. Disk images

C. VM snapshots

D. Network packet capture data

64. What ISO/IEC 20000-1 capacity management subprocess is most closely aligned with SLAs with customers?

A. Business capacity management

B. Service capacity management

C. Contract capacity management

D. Component capacity management

65. Derek wants to set up a 24×7 team to monitor for and respond to security incidents. What should he implement?

A. SIEM

B. NAS

C. SCCM

D. SOC

66. Hui's organization uses a tool to automate the configuration, deployment, and coordination of hundreds of small IaaS instances that make up her organization's application stack. What term best describes this type of tool?

A. Scheduling

B. Maintenance mode

C. Orchestration

D. Abstraction

67. Megan's organization uses a tool that captures a system and network behavioral baseline, then monitors for changes from that baseline that may indicate compromises. The tool uses the data it captures to update its model and to become more accurate in its detections. What type of tool is Megan using?

A. IPS

B. Artificial intelligence

C. Log analysis

D. Forensic data capture

68. Jim has deployed a system that appears to be a vulnerable host on a network. The system is instrumented to capture attacker commands and tools. What type of network security control has Jim deployed?

A. A honeypot

B. A darknet

C. A honeynet

D. A bastion host

69. Olivia has identified data that she wants to capture as part of a digital forensics effort. What step typically comes after forensic artifacts are identified?

A. Analysis

B. Documentation

C. Presentation

D. Preservation

70. Mike's organization is considering adopting an infrastructure as code (IaC) strategy. What should Mike identify as a potential risk in an IaC environment?

A. IaC decreases consistency.

B. IaC is not easily updated.

C. IaC decreases speed.

D. IaC can cause errors to spread quickly.

71. Keith is preparing to implement a storage cluster for his organization. Which of the following is not a benefit that he can expect to come from using storage clusters?

   A. Lower cost

   B. Higher performance

   C. Greater availability

   D. Increased capacity

72. Lisa wants to maintain a configuration model for her organization that contains all of the information that the organization needs about their CIs (configuration items). What ITIL process should she follow?

   A. Configuration control

   B. Configuration identification

   C. Configuration verification

   D. Configuration audit

73. Dan is considering what key data he should gather about systems in his IaaS environment. He is moving from a traditional on-site datacenter and has the following list of monitoring items he currently tracks. Which of the following will he still be able to track in an IaaS platform?

   A. CPU utilization

   B. Fan speed

   C. System temperature

   D. CPU voltage

74. What term is used to describe a component or service that needs to be managed as part of configuration management efforts in an organization?

   A. Configuration model

   B. Configuration record

   C. Configuration item

   D. Service asset

75. Henry knows that his IaaS provider bills are based on usage for his instances. Which of the following is not usually a billable item for IaaS providers for their typical instances?

   A. Compute usage

   B. Network bandwidth usage

   C. Storage usage

   D. Latency

76. Charles wants to obtain forensic artifacts for his IaaS cloud-hosted systems. Which of the following is not an artifact typically captured for IaaS cloud-hosted systems?

A. The hypervisor's memory state

B. Disk volumes

C. The instance's memory state

D. Logs from the cloud environment

77. Selah wants to conduct a vulnerability scan of her SaaS provider's service as part of her ongoing security operations responsibility. What should she do?

A. Contact the provider and ask about appropriate scan windows.

B. Request vulnerability scan data from the vendor.

C. Scan the provider on a regular basis whenever she wants to.

D. Consider asking the SaaS provider about their own patching and scanning practices.

78. Which of the following has the highest impact in determining whether the business continuity and disaster recovery (BC/DR) effort has a chance of being successful?

A. Perform an integrity check on archived data to ensure that the backup process is not corrupting the data.

B. Encrypt all archived data to ensure that it can't be exposed while at rest in the long term.

C. Periodically restore from backups.

D. Train all personnel on BC/DR actions they should take to preserve health and human safety.

79. Chris wants to use an ISO standard for collecting, preserving, and identifying electronic evidence. What ISO standard should he select?

A. ISO/IEC 27001:2012

B. ISO/IEC 27037:2012

C. ISO/IEC 9000:2016

D. ISO/IEC 27002:2022

80. Melissa is responsible for establishing an SOC in her organization. Which of the following services is not a typical SOC offering?

A. Vulnerability management

B. Threat management

C. Incident response

D. eDiscovery

81. Ryan wants to perform a backup of his GitHub-hosted code repository. What option should he choose to ensure that he has a backup he controls?

A. Use GitHub's built-in backup capability.

B. Use the API to clone the repository.

C. Use GitHub's snapshot tool to clone the repository to another repo.

D. Use a third-party GitHub repository copy.

82. ISO/IEC 20000-1 includes three subprocesses for capacity management. Which of the following lists matches those three subprocesses?

   A. Business capacity management, service capacity management, component capacity management

   B. Staffing capacity management, service capacity management, component capacity management

   C. Business capacity management, service capacity management, organizational capacity management

   D. Staffing capacity management, business capacity management, and component capacity management

83. Maria is planning her organization's ISO/IEC 20000-1–based release management plan. Which of the following elements is not typically part of an RDM plan?

   A. Risk assessment

   B. Build planning

   C. Testing

   D. Decommissioning

84. Hannah wants to align her information security management program to ISO/IEC 20000-1. According to the standard, what must be done with an information security policy?

   A. Establish, approve, and communicate an information security policy.

   B. Create and regularly update an information security policy.

   C. Adopt an ISO/IEC standard template-based information security policy.

   D. Undergo a third-party review of the organization's security policy.

85. Mike's VMWare cluster moves virtual machines from heavily loaded hosts to hosts with lower loads. What technology is Mike using?

   A. Automatic instance management

   B. Distributed resource scheduling

   C. Round-robin load balancing

   D. Instance segregation

86. Which of the following is not commonly measured as part of a disk's hardware monitoring?

   A. Powered-on time

   B. Drive temperature

   C. Drive health

   D. Used capacity

87. ITIL v4 defines four subprocesses for service-level management. Which of the following is not one of the four subprocesses?

   A. Maintenance of the service-level management framework

   B. Identification of service requirements

   C. Pricing structures and penalties

   D. Service-level monitoring and reporting

88. Michelle wants to run an application from low-trust devices. What type of cloud-based solution could help her run the application in a secure way?

    A. Use a local virtual machine.

    B. Use a bastion host.

    C. Use a jumpbox.

    D. Use a virtual client.

89. Because most cloud environments rely heavily on virtualization, it is important to lock down or harden the virtualization software, or any software involved in virtualization. Which of the following is *not* an element of hardening software?

    A. Removing unused services and libraries

    B. Maintaining a strict license catalog

    C. Patching and updating as necessary

    D. Removing default accounts

90. What key document in business continuity management practices ensures that organizations can return to a known consistent state as well as to a working state?

    A. The business continuity strategy

    B. The recovery plan

    C. The IT service continuity report

    D. The disaster recovery invocation guideline

91. Jason's company operates their small business in a cloud-hosted environment. After a recent breach, Jason wants to conduct forensics. What should Jason do to ensure his organization conducts proper forensic capture in a cloud environment if he is not a forensic practitioner?

    A. Follow ISO standards to identify and preserve the data.

    B. Engage third-party forensic professionals.

    C. Follow his cloud provider's best practices to identify and preserve the data.

    D. Request that his cloud provider perform the forensic efforts.

92. Which of the following factors would probably most affect the design of a cloud datacenter?

    A. Geographic location

    B. Proximity to population centers

    C. Cost

    D. Security requirements

93. Rick is creating a policy defining his organization's change management process. Which of the following is not a common change management policy element?

    A. Defining the composition of the change management board

    B. The change management process itself

    C. A requirement to prevent deviation from the baselines established in the policy

    D. Enforcement measures

94. Which of the following cloud datacenter functions do *not* have to be performed on isolated networks?

A. Customer access provision

B. Management system control interface

C. Storage controller access

D. Customer production activities

95. When cloud computing professionals use the phrase *ping, power, pipe*, which of the following characteristics is *not* being described?

A. Logical connectivity

B. Human interaction

C. Electricity

D. Facility space

96. You are the security manager for a small retail business involved mainly in direct e-commerce transactions with individual customers (members of the public). The bulk of your market is in Asia, but you do fulfill orders globally. Your company has its own datacenter located within its headquarters building in Hong Kong, but it also uses a public cloud environment for contingency backup and archiving purposes. Your cloud provider is changing its business model at the end of your contract term, and you have to find a new provider. In choosing providers, which tier of the Uptime Institute rating system should you be looking for, if minimizing cost is your ultimate goal?

A. 1

B. 3

C. 4

D. 8

97. Isaac is the IT manager for a small surgical center. His organization is reviewing upgrade options for its current, on-premises datacenter. The organization wants to increase its disaster recovery and business continuity capabilities without making significant investments in staffing or technology. Which of the following options should Isaac recommend?

A. Building a completely new datacenter

B. Adding additional DR/BC capabilities to the existing datacenter

C. Moving to a cloud-hosted datacenter

D. Staying with the current datacenter

98. What does chain-of-custody documentation and tracking help with?

A. Nonrepudiation

B. Plausible deniability

C. Data tampering by investigators

D. Engaging with law enforcement

99. Ben wants to provide logical separation between two network segments. What technology is often used to define networks for this purpose?

    A. DHCP

    B. VLANs

    C. VPNs

    D. STP

100. When designing a cloud datacenter, which of the following aspects is *not* necessary to ensure continuity of operations during contingency operations?

    A. Access to clean water

    B. Broadband data connection

    C. Extended battery backup

    D. Physical access to the datacenter

Chapter 6

Domain 6: Legal, Risk, and Compliance

SUBDOMAINS:

✓ 6.1 Articulate legal requirements and unique risks within the cloud environment

✓ 6.2 Understand privacy issues

✓ 6.3 Understand audit process, methodologies, and required adaptations for a cloud environment

✓ 6.4 Understand implications of cloud to enterprise risk management

✓ 6.5 Understand outsourcing and cloud contract design

1. Your company is considering migrating its production environment to the cloud. In reviewing the proposed contract, you notice that it includes a clause that requires an additional fee, equal to six monthly payments (equal to half the term of the contract) for ending the contract at any point prior to the scheduled date. This is best described as an example of _____.

    A. Favorable contract terms

    B. Strong negotiation

    C. Infrastructure as a service (IaaS)

    D. Vendor lock-in

2. Cathy is developing an eDiscovery program to help her organization formalize its compliance with legal hold obligations. She would like to use an industry standard to guide her toward best practices. What standard should she consider using for this work?

    A. ISO 27001

    B. ISO 27002

    C. ISO 27050

    D. ISO 27701

3. In regard to most privacy guidance, the data processor is _____.

    A. The individual described by the personally identifiable information (PII)

    B. The entity that collects or creates the personally identifiable information (PII)

    C. The entity that uses personally identifiable information (PII) on behalf of the controller

    D. The entity that regulates personally identifiable information (PII)

4. Your company is defending itself during a civil trial for a breach of contract case. Personnel from your IT department have performed forensic analysis on event logs that reflect the circumstances related to the case.

    In order for your personnel to present the evidence they collected during forensic analysis as expert witnesses, you should ensure that _____.

    A. Their testimony is scripted, and they do not deviate from the script

    B. They present only evidence that is favorable to your side of the case

    C. They are trained and certified in the tools they used

    D. They are paid for their time while they are appearing in the courtroom

5. After conducting a qualitative risk assessment of her organization, Prisha decides to recommend adding a new module to the firewall that will filter out inbound malware. What type of risk response behavior is she recommending?

    A. Accept

    B. Transfer

    C. Reduce

    D. Reject

6. Nora is an employee of Acme Widgets and works on a team of auditors who examine the organization's financial controls. She is currently working on a project to evaluate whether payments to cloud providers are proper and will be reporting her results to management. What term best describes Nora's role in this project?

  A. Internal assessment

  B. External audit

  C. Internal audit

  D. External assessment

7. Carla is assigned to manage her organization's privacy program and is working to communicate to customers about a change in the organization's privacy practices. She plans to send an email notifying customers of the change and allowing them to opt out of the use of their data. Which GAPP principle is *not* described in this scenario?

  A. Notice

  B. Management

  C. Access

  D. Choice and Consent

8. You're a medical student at a private research university in the midwestern United States; you make your tuition payments directly from your bank account via a debit card. Which of the following laws and standards will *not* be applicable to you, your personal data, or the data you work with as a student?

  A. Sarbanes–Oxley Act (SOX)

  B. Health Information Portability and Accountability Act (HIPAA)

  C. Payment Card Industry Data Security Standards (PCI DSS)

  D. Family Educational Rights and Privacy Act (FERPA)

9. Rolando is a risk manager with a large-scale cloud service provider. The firm recently evaluated the risk of California mudslides on its operations in the region and determined that the cost of responding outweighed the benefits of any controls it could implement. The company chose to take no action at this time. What risk management strategy did Rolando's organization pursue?

  A. Risk avoidance

  B. Risk mitigation

  C. Risk transference

  D. Risk acceptance

10. Yolanda is the chief privacy officer for a financial institution and is researching privacy requirements related to customer checking accounts. Which one of the following laws is most likely to apply to this situation?

  A. GLBA

  B. SOX

  C. HIPAA

  D. FERPA

11. Bill is conducting an audit of a cloud provider under SSAE and ISAE standards. During the audit, he discovers that some records required to complete one of his tests were accidentally destroyed and are not recoverable. There are no alternative tests available for this control objective. What action should Bill take?

    A. Describe the limitation in the audit scope statement.

    B. Postpone the audit for one year until adequate records are available.

    C. Issue a failing audit report.

    D. Remove this test from the audit and test a different control objective instead.

12. Which of the following is *not* a way in which an entity located outside the European Union (EU) can be allowed to gather and process privacy data belonging to EU citizens?

    A. Be located in a country with a nationwide law that complies with the EU laws.

    B. Appeal to the EU High Court for permission.

    C. Create binding contractual language that complies with the EU laws.

    D. Join the Privacy Shield program in its own country.

13. Which type of business impact assessment tool is most appropriate when attempting to evaluate the impact of a failure on customer confidence?

    A. Quantitative

    B. Qualitative

    C. Annualized loss expectancy

    D. Reduction

14. An audit against the _____ will demonstrate that an organization has a holistic, comprehensive program of internal security controls.

    A. Statement on Auditing Standards (SAS) 70 standard

    B. Statement on Standards for Attestation Engagements (SSAE) 18 standard

    C. Service Organization Control (SOC) 2, Type 2 report matrix

    D. ISO 27001 certification requirements

15. An IT security audit is designed to reveal all of the following *except* _____.

    A. Financial fraud

    B. Malfunctioning controls

    C. Inadequate controls

    D. Failure to meet target standards and guidelines

16. During an IT audit, the CEO of a cloud provider demands regular updates on the testing process. How should auditors respond to this demand?

    A. Refuse to provide the CEO with any information until the conclusion of the audit.

    B. Refer the matter to the client's Board of Directors.

    C. Provide the CEO with regular updates.

    D. Refer the matter to the audit firm's partnership review board.

17. Which of the following is a U.S. audit standard often used to evaluate cloud providers?

    A. ISO 27001

    B. SOX

    C. SSAE 18

    D. IEC 43770

18. Digital forensics investigators perform all of the following actions routinely except for securely _____ data.

    A. Collecting

    B. Creating

    C. Analyzing

    D. Presenting

19. A(n) _____ includes reviewing the organization's current position/performance as revealed by an audit against a given standard.

    A. Service Organization Control (SOC) report

    B. Gap analysis

    C. Audit scoping statement

    D. Federal guideline

20. Belinda is auditing the financial controls of a manufacturing company and learns that the financial systems are run on a major IaaS platform. She would like to gain assurance that the platform has appropriate security controls in place to assure the accuracy of her client's financial statements. What action should she take?

    A. Perform an IT audit of the cloud provider.

    B. Obtain a SOC 1 report.

    C. Obtain a SOC 2 report.

    D. Continue testing only controls at the client and note the use of the cloud provider in her report.

21. Tony is developing a business continuity plan and is having trouble prioritizing resources because of the difficulty of combining information about tangible and intangible assets. What would be the most effective risk assessment approach for him to use?

    A. Quantitative risk assessment

    B. Qualitative risk assessment

    C. Neither quantitative nor qualitative risk assessment

    D. Combination of quantitative and qualitative risk assessment

22. What was the first international privacy standard specifically for cloud providers?

    A. National Institute of Standards and Technology (NIST) Special Publication (SP) 800-37

    B. Personal Information Protection and Electronic Documents Act

    C. Payment Card Industry

    D. ISO 27018

23. Which one of the following elements of information is not considered a direct identifier that would trigger most United States (U.S.) state data breach laws?

A. Student identification number

B. Social Security number

C. Driver's license number

D. Credit card number

24. Which of the following items, included in the contract between a cloud customer and cloud provider, can best aid in reducing vendor lock-in?

A. Data format type and structure

B. Availability

C. Storage space

D. List of available OSs

25. Which of the following contract terms *most* incentivizes the cloud provider to meet the requirements listed in the service-level agreement (SLA)?

A. Regulatory oversight

B. Financial penalties

C. Performance details

D. Desire to maintain customer satisfaction

26. Fran recently conducted a review of the risk management program in her organization and developed an analysis of all of the risks facing the organization and their quantitative impact. What term best describes this analysis?

A. Risk appetite

B. Risk tolerance

C. Risk controls

D. Risk profile

27. Which of the following was the first international standard addressing the privacy aspects of cloud computing for consumers?

A. ISO 27001

B. ISO 27018

C. ISO 27002

D. GDPR

28. You are the security manager for a software company that uses platform as a service (PaaS) in a public cloud service. Your company's general counsel informs you that they have received a letter from a former employee who is filing a lawsuit against your company. You should immediately issue a(n) _____ to all personnel and offices within your company.

   A. Litigation hold notice

   B. Audit scoping letter

   C. Statement of work

   D. Memorandum of agreement

29. Gwen is a cybersecurity professional for a financial services firm that maintains records of their customers. These records include personal information about each customer, including the customer's name, Social Security number, date and place of birth, and mother's maiden name. What category best describes these records?

   A. PHI

   B. Proprietary data

   C. PII

   D. EDI

30. Aaron is concerned about the possibility that a cloud vendor that his organization relies on may go out of business. What term best describes this risk?

   A. Vendor lock-in

   B. Vendor viability

   C. Vendor lockout

   D. Vendor diversity

31. Mike recently implemented an intrusion prevention system designed to block common network attacks from affecting his organization. What type of risk management strategy is Mike pursuing?

   A. Risk acceptance

   B. Risk avoidance

   C. Risk mitigation

   D. Risk transference

32. Viola is planning a user account audit to determine whether accounts have the appropriate level of permissions and that all permissions were approved through a formal process. The organization has approximately 50,000 user accounts and an annual employee turnover rate of 24 percent. Which one of the following sampling approaches would be the most effective use of her time when choosing records for manual review?

   A. Select all records that have been modified during the past month.

   B. Ask access administrators to identify the accounts most likely to have issues and audit those.

   C. Select a random sample of records, either from the entire population or from the population of records that have changed during the audit period.

   D. Sampling is not effective in this situation, and all accounts should be audited.

33. Which one of the following issues is not normally addressed in a service-level agreement (SLA)?

    A. Confidentiality of customer information

    B. Failover time

    C. Uptime

    D. Maximum consecutive downtime

34. Elise is helping her organization prepare to evaluate and adopt a new cloud-based human resource management (HRM) system vendor. What would be the most appropriate minimum security standard for her to require of possible vendors?

    A. Compliance with all laws and regulations

    B. Handling information in the same manner the organization would

    C. Elimination of all identified security risks

    D. Compliance with the vendor's own policies

35. HAL Systems recently decided to stop offering public NTP services because of a fear that its NTP servers would be used in amplification DDoS attacks. What type of risk management strategy did HAL pursue with respect to its NTP services?

    A. Risk mitigation

    B. Risk acceptance

    C. Risk transference

    D. Risk avoidance

36. Who would normally conduct a review of security controls under SSAE 18?

    A. Security team

    B. External auditor

    C. Government regulator

    D. IT leadership

37. Tom enables an application firewall provided by his cloud infrastructure as a service provider that is designed to block many types of application attacks. When viewed from a risk management perspective, what metric is Tom attempting to lower by implementing this countermeasure?

    A. Impact

    B. RPO

    C. MTO

    D. Likelihood

38. Which of the following statements about SSAE-18 is not correct?

    A. It mandates a specific control set.

    B. It is an attestation standard.

    C. It is used for external audits.

    D. It uses a framework, including SOC 1, SOC 2, and SOC 3 reports.

39. Matt works for a telecommunications firm and was approached by a federal agent seeking assistance with wiretapping one of Matt's clients pursuant to a search warrant. Which one of the following laws requires that communications service providers cooperate with law enforcement requests?

    A. ECPA

    B. CALEA

    C. Privacy Act

    D. HITECH Act

40. Tim's organization recently received a contract to conduct sponsored research as a government contractor. What law now likely applies to the information systems involved in this contract?

    A. FISMA

    B. PCI DSS

    C. HIPAA

    D. GISRA

41. Katie is conducting a thorough review of all of the personally identifiable information (PII) used by her organization. What term best describes this assessment?

    A. BIA

    B. BPA

    C. PPA

    D. PIA

42. Kevin is reviewing and updating the security documentation used by his organization. He would like to document some best practices for securing cloud computing services that his team has implemented over the past year. The practices are generalized in nature and do not cover specific services. What type of document would be best for this purpose?

    A. Policy

    B. Standard

    C. Guideline

    D. Procedure

43. Colin is conducting an audit of the internal information security management system (ISMS) of a cloud service provider. Which one of the following items would normally be outside the scope of this audit?

    A. Uses of customer data

    B. Accuracy of financial statements

    C. Network firewall protections

    D. Endpoint security

44. Which of the following is *not* an enforceable governmental request?

    A. Warrant

    B. Subpoena

    C. Court order

    D. Affidavit

45. Helen is assessing a cloud provider's risk management methodology. Which one of the following documents would be least helpful to her in this effort?

    A. ISO 31000

    B. NIST 800-37

    C. COBIT

    D. PCI DSS

46. Vincent is responsible for a privacy program that spans international borders. Of the following countries where his organization operates, which does not have a comprehensive national privacy law?

    A. United States

    B. France

    C. Canada

    D. Germany

47. Nitesh is conducting a global audit of a multinational cloud service provider and has a question about appropriate testing procedures. Which one of the following documents would be most applicable to his situation?

    A. ISAE 3402

    B. ISAE 3410

    C. SSAE 16

    D. SSAE 18

48. Which of the following represents the legislation enacted to protect shareholders and the public from enterprise accounting errors and fraudulent practices?

    A. PCI

    B. Gramm–Leach–Bliley Act (GLBA)

    C. Sarbanes–Oxley Act (SOX)

    D. HIPAA

49. Joe's organization is considering expanding the geographic footprint of its datacenters to include facilities located in other countries. What is likely going to be the most serious complication introduced by this expansion?

    A. Multiple jurisdictions

    B. Different electric standards

    C. Internet connectivity and bandwidth

    D. Operating system compatibility

50. FlyAway Travel has offices in both the European Union (EU) and the United States and transfers personal information between those offices regularly. They have recently received a request from an EU customer requesting that their account be terminated. Under the General Data Protection Regulation (GDPR), which requirement for processing personal information states that individuals may request that their data no longer be disseminated or processed?

    A. The right to access

    B. Privacy by design

    C. The right to be forgotten

    D. The right of data portability

51. In most privacy-regulation situations, which entity is *most* responsible for deciding how a particular privacy-related data set will be used or processed?

    A. The data subject

    B. The data controller

    C. The data steward

    D. The data custodian

52. Which of the following is probably the *most* volatile form of data that might serve a forensic purpose in a virtualized environment?

    A. Virtual instance RAM

    B. Hardware RAM

    C. Hypervisor logs

    D. Drive storage

53. Wanda is working with one of her organization's European Union business partners to facilitate the exchange of customer information. Wanda's organization is located in the United States. What would be the best method for Wanda to use to ensure GDPR compliance?

    A. Binding corporate rules

    B. Privacy Shield

    C. Standard contractual clauses

    D. Safe harbor

54. You are the chief information officer (CIO) for an IT hardware manufacturer. Your company uses cloud-based software as a service (SaaS) services, including email. You receive a legal request for data pertinent to a case. Your eDiscovery efforts will largely be dependent on _____.

    A. The cloud provider

    B. Regulators

    C. The cloud customer

    D. Internal IT personnel

55. Ben is responsible for the security of payment card information stored in a database. Policy directs that he remove the information from the database, but he cannot do this for operational reasons. He obtained an exception to the policy and is seeking an appropriate compensating control to mitigate the risk. What would be his best option?

    A. Purchasing insurance

    B. Encrypting the database contents

    C. Removing the data

    D. Objecting to the exception

56. James has been asked to lead a review of his organization's compliance with GAPP principles. What area will most directly fall into the scope of his assessment?

    A. Accounting

    B. Privacy

    C. Cybersecurity

    D. eDiscovery

57. Brad recently learned that his organization will be subject to a new legal requirement due to an expansion of their work into a new industry. What type of analysis should Brad perform first?

    A. Business impact analysis

    B. Privacy impact analysis

    C. Gap analysis

    D. Baseline development

58. Which one of the following organizations would not be automatically subject to the privacy and security requirements of HIPAA if they engage in electronic transactions?

    A. Healthcare provider

    B. Health and fitness application developer

    C. Health information clearinghouse

    D. Health insurance plan

59. Bella is working to develop a long-term relationship with a consulting firm that will assist in her organization's cloud migration. She would like to create a contract that may govern the terms of many different projects. What type of document should she create?

A. MSA

B. BPA

C. SOW

D. MOU

60. What best describes the Cloud Security Alliance Cloud Controls Matrix?

A. A set of regulatory requirements for cloud service providers

B. A set of software development life cycle requirements for cloud service providers

C. A security controls framework that provides mapping/cross relationships with the main industry-accepted security standards, regulations, and controls frameworks such as the ISO 27001/27002, ISACA's COBIT, and PCI-DSS

D. An inventory of cloud service security controls that are arranged into separate security domains

61. Gordon's organization is considering using a new cloud vendor to handle their backups. He is conducting a risk assessment to determine the amount of damage that lost backups at the provider should be expected to cause each year. What metric has Gordon identified?

A. ALE

B. ARO

C. SLE

D. EF

62. Greg's company operates only in the United States. They recently experienced a significant data breach involving the personal data of many of their customers. Which breach laws should they review to ensure that they are taking appropriate action?

A. The breach laws of the jurisdiction where they are headquartered.

B. The breach laws of all jurisdictions where they do business.

C. The breach laws of the federal government only because this involves interstate commerce.

D. No breach laws would apply to this situation.

63. _____ is the legal concept whereby a cloud customer is held to a reasonable expectation for providing security of its users' and clients' privacy data.

A. Due care

B. Due diligence

C. Liability

D. Reciprocity

64. Robert is responsible for securing systems used to process credit card information. What security control framework should guide his actions?

    A. NERC/CIP

    B. PCI DSS

    C. HITECH

    D. GLBA

65. You are considering adding a web application firewall to your public-facing applications to reduce the risk of an attack. If you implement the firewall, what risk treatment action are you taking?

    A. Risk avoidance

    B. Risk acceptance

    C. Risk mitigation

    D. Risk transference

66. You are conducting a risk assessment for a cloud service provider that will be operating infrastructure for an electric utility. What regulatory framework is most relevant to this organization?

    A. HIPAA

    B. HITECH

    C. NERC/CIP

    D. PCI DSS

67. You are concerned that different virtual machines in your organization have different security configurations and would like to apply a standard configuration at the time they are built. What term describes this approach?

    A. Scanning

    B. Baselining

    C. Operationalizing

    D. Customizing

68. You are the compliance officer for a medical device manufacturing firm. Your company maintains a cloud-based list of patients currently fitted with your devices for long-term care and quality assurance purposes. The list is maintained in a database that cross-references details about the hardware and some billing data. In this situation, who is likely to be considered the data custodian, under many privacy regulations and laws?

    A. You (the compliance officer)

    B. The cloud provider's network security team

    C. Your company

    D. The database administrator

69. You are conducting an audit of a cloud service provider and are unsure about the types of tests that you should plan. Which resource provides the most definitive guidance?

    A. Client organization management

    B. Applicable audit standard

    C. Client organization chief audit executive

    D. Auditor organization management

70. When a conflict of laws occurs, _____determines the jurisdiction in which the dispute will be heard.

    A. Tort law

    B. Doctrine of Proper Law

    C. Common law

    D. Criminal law

71. Chris is worried that the laptops that his organization has recently acquired were modified by a third party to include keyloggers before they were delivered. Where should he focus his efforts to prevent this?

    A. His supply chain

    B. His vendor contracts

    C. His post-purchase build process

    D. The original equipment manufacturer (OEM)

72. Greg is evaluating a new vendor that will be supplying networking gear to his organization. Due to the nature of his organization's work, Greg is concerned that an attacker might attempt a supply chain exploit. Assuming that both Greg's organization and the vendor operate under reasonable security procedures, which one of the following activities likely poses the greatest supply chain risk to the equipment?

    A. Tampering by an unauthorized third party at the vendor's site

    B. Interception of devices in transit

    C. Misconfiguration by an administrator after installation

    D. Tampering by an unauthorized third party at Greg's site

73. What is an accounting report on controls at a service organization that replaces older SAS 70 type reports?

    A. SOC 1

    B. SSAE 16

    C. GAAP

    D. SOC 2

74. In which of the following cases would it be most appropriate to engage an internal auditor?

    A. Confirming accuracy of financial statements

    B. Certifying against an international standard

    C. Investigating employee malfeasance

    D. Complying with PCI DSS requirements

75. Which one of the following frameworks is a U.S. federal law governing privacy?

    A. PCI DSS

    B. CCPA

    C. GDPR

    D. HIPAA

76. You operate a cloud service and would like to provide potential customers with a report that confirms the effectiveness of your security controls and is appropriate for use by the general public. What type of audit should you conduct?

    A. SOC 1

    B. SOC 2

    C. SOC 3

    D. SOC 4

77. Which one of the following individuals is normally responsible for fulfilling the operational data protection responsibilities delegated by senior management, such as validating data integrity, testing backups, and managing security policies?

    A. Data custodian

    B. Data owner

    C. Data user

    D. Auditor

78. A _____ typically employs a set of methods, principles, or rules for assessing risk based on absolute numerical values.

    A. Qualitative assessment

    B. One-sided assessment

    C. Vulnerability assessment

    D. Quantitative assessment

79. Nolan is a procurement officer for a U.S. federal government agency and is selecting a cloud service provider. What program offers a set of prescreened cloud providers authorized for use in the federal government?

    A. FIPS 140-2

    B. NIST 800-53

    C. ISO 27017

    D. FedRAMP

80. What procedures should an organization follow when collecting evidence from a security incident that may be used in court?

    A. Digital forensics

    B. ISO 27001

    C. Common law

    D. eDiscovery

81. Which one of the following principles requires that organizations put governance structures in place to ensure they are meeting their obligations?

    A. Due diligence

    B. Separation of duties

    C. Due care

    D. Least privilege

82. You would like to ensure that your organization's insurance policy covers the damage resulting from a security incident sufficiently to allow you to resume operations. What asset valuation technique should you use?

    A. Depreciated value

    B. Original cost

    C. Estimation

    D. Replacement cost

83. You are concerned that you may no longer have access to necessary source code if a cloud vendor ceases operations. What security control would best protect against this risk?

    A. Contractual terms

    B. Escrow

    C. SLA

    D. Litigation

84. What is a type of assessment that employs a set of methods, principles, or rules for assessing risk based on non-numerical categories or levels?

    A. Quantitative assessment

    B. Qualitative assessment

    C. Hybrid assessment

    D. SOC 2

85. Which one of the following terms is not commonly found in cloud service provider contracts?

    A. Right to access facilities

    B. Right to audit

    C. Termination provisions

    D. Right to access data

86. Ben is seeking a control objective framework that is widely accepted around the world and focuses specifically on information security controls. Which one of the following frameworks would best meet his needs?

    A. ITIL

    B. ISO 27002

    C. CMM

    D. PMBOK Guide

87. When an organization uses a cloud service provider to handle protected health information, who is responsible for securing that data?

   A. Customer

   B. Cloud provider

   C. Both the customer and the cloud provider

   D. Neither the customer nor the cloud provider

88. What term is used to describe an individual within an organization who has been delegated day-to-day responsibility for decision-making about a category of information?

   A. Data owner

   B. Data custodian

   C. Data processor

   D. Data steward

89. Ron is the CISO of a U.S. company that is entering into a business partnership with a European firm. The European firm will be sending his company customer records to run through Ron's firm's proprietary credit scoring algorithm. Under GDPR, what role will Ron's company have relative to the customer data?

   A. Data controller

   B. Data owner

   C. Data subject

   D. Data processor

90. Which of the following would normally be considered a supply chain risk? (Choose all that apply.)

   A. Adversary tampering with hardware prior to being shipped to the end customer

   B. Adversary hacking into a web server run by the organization in an IaaS environment

   C. Adversary using social engineering to compromise an employee of an SaaS vendor to gain access to customer accounts

   D. Adversary conducting a denial-of-service attack using a botnet

For questions 91–93, please refer to the following scenario:

Henry is the risk manager for Atwood Cloud Services, an SaaS provider in the midwestern United States. The firm's main datacenter is located in northern Indiana in an area that is prone to tornadoes. Henry recently undertook a replacement cost analysis and determined that rebuilding and reconfiguring the datacenter would cost $10 million.

Henry consulted with tornado experts, datacenter specialists, and structural engineers. Together, they determined that a typical tornado would cause approximately $5 million of damage to the facility. The meteorologists determined that Atwood's facility lies in an area where they are likely to experience a tornado once every 200 years.

91. Based on the information in this scenario, what is the exposure factor for the effect of a tornado on Atwood Landing's datacenter?

A. 10 percent

B. 25 percent

C. 50 percent

D. 75 percent

92. Based on the information in this scenario, what is the annualized rate of occurrence for a tornado at Atwood Landing's datacenter?

A. 0.0025

B. 0.005

C. 0.01

D. 0.015

93. Based on the information in this scenario, what is the annualized loss expectancy for a tornado at Atwood Landing's datacenter?

A. $25,000

B. $50,000

C. $250,000

D. $500,000

94. Tamara recently decided to purchase cyber-liability insurance to cover her company's costs in the event of a data breach at a cloud service provider. What risk management strategy is she pursuing?

A. Risk acceptance

B. Risk mitigation

C. Risk transference

D. Risk avoidance

95. The Domer Industries risk assessment team recently conducted a qualitative risk assessment and developed a matrix similar to the one shown here. Which quadrant contains the risks that require the most immediate attention?

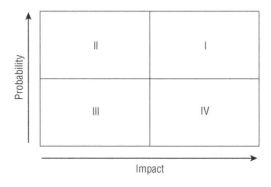

    A. I

    B. II

    C. III

    D. IV

96. Jim starts a new job as a system engineer, and he is reviewing a team document titled "Forensic Response Guidelines for Cloud Services." Which one of the following statements is not true?

    A. Jim must comply with the information in this document.

    B. The document contains information about forensic examinations.

    C. Jim should read the document thoroughly.

    D. The document is likely based on industry best practices.

97. Which one of the following laws does not contain breach notification requirements?

    A. GLBA

    B. HIPAA/HITECH

    C. FERPA

    D. GDPR

98. Which one of the following metrics would not commonly be found in an SLA?

    A. Network performance

    B. Compute capacity

    C. Help desk response time

    D. Number of security incidents

99. You are the CISO for a major hospital system and are preparing to sign a contract with a software as a service (SaaS) email vendor and want to perform a control assessment to ensure that its business continuity planning measures are reasonable. What type of audit might you request to meet this goal?

    A. SOC 1

    B. FISMA

    C. PCI DSS

    D. SOC 2

100. Which of the following is probably *least* suited for inclusion in the service-level agreement (SLA) between a cloud customer and cloud provider?

    A. Bandwidth

    B. Jurisdiction

    C. Storage space

    D. Availability

Chapter

7

Practice Test 1

1. You are selecting a datacenter environment to host a cloud application run by your organization. Your primary requirement is that the datacenter must require no shutdowns for equipment maintenance. What is the lowest level of datacenter that would be acceptable under the Uptime Institute tier system?

   A. Tier 1

   B. Tier 2

   C. Tier 3

   D. Tier 4

2. In an infrastructure as a service (IaaS) arrangement, who accepts responsibility for securing cloud-based applications?

   A. The cloud provider

   B. The cloud customer

   C. The regulator

   D. The end user/client

3. Brenda's company employs a number of application developers who create software to meet many different business needs. She is embarking on a project to validate the use of verified open source software and is concerned about the unknowing use of software libraries by those developers. Which of the following technologies will best assist with identifying these uses?

   A. Dynamic application security testing (DAST)

   B. Static application security testing (SAST)

   C. Software composition analysis (SCA)

   D. Interactive application security testing (IAST)

4. _____ are software or devices that monitor networks for malicious activities or policy violations and produce electronic alerts and/or reports to a management station.

   A. Host intrusion detection systems (HIDS)

   B. Hardware security modules (HSM)

   C. Network intrusion detection systems (NIDS)

   D. Virtual private networks (VPNs)

5. Carla works for an infrastructure as a service (IaaS) provider. She is analyzing the security settings for the hypervisors used in a multitenant environment. Who should have access to modify settings on those hypervisors?

   A. Only employees of Carla's company with the appropriate security training and access rights.

   B. Employees of Carla's company and customers with virtual machines running on that specific hypervisor.

   C. Employees of Carla's company and customers with appropriate security training.

   D. None of these groups should have hypervisor access.

6. In which cloud computing model does a customer share computing infrastructure with other customers of the cloud vendor where one customer may not know the other's identity?

    A. Public cloud

    B. Private cloud

    C. Community cloud

    D. Shared cloud

7. You work for a government research facility. Your organization often shares data with other government research organizations. You would like to create a single sign-on experience across the organizations, where users at each organization can sign in with the user ID/ authentication issued by that organization, then access research data in all the other organizations. Instead of replicating the data stores of each organization at every other organization (which is one way of accomplishing this goal), you instead want every user to have access to each organization's specific storage resources.

    What is the term for this kind of arrangement?

    A. Public-key infrastructure (PKI)

    B. Portability

    C. Federation

    D. Repudiation

8. Paul's organization maintains protected health information that is regulated under HIPAA. He would like to add a new security control capable of detecting when employees attempt to remove this sensitive information from his organization's systems and networks, either intentionally or unintentionally. What security control would best meet his needs?

    A. DLP

    B. CASB

    C. IPS

    D. NGFW

9. Which of the following is not an essential element defining cloud computing?

    A. Broad network access

    B. Metered service

    C. Off-site storage

    D. On-demand self-service

10. Justin recently participated in a disaster recovery plan test where the team sat together and discussed the response to a scenario but did not actually activate any disaster recovery controls. What type of test did he participate in?

    A. Checklist review

    B. Full interruption test

    C. Parallel test

    D. Tabletop exercise

11. Tonya is employed by a cloud service provider and is responsible for evaluating the provider's security program. What ISO standard can best help her ensure that her organization has a robust set of security controls in place?

   A. ISO 27001

   B. ISO 27002

   C. ISO 27017

   D. ISO 27701

12. Katie's organization recently suffered a data breach and exposed a database containing student records. The records contained no identifying information other than tokenized student ID numbers. Which of the following statements most accurately represents how Katie should feel about the exposure of these records?

   A. The data is safe only if data from the tokenization process was secure.

   B. The data is safe only if the cryptographic keys were not exposed.

   C. The data is safe only if a strong hash function was used in the tokenization process.

   D. The data is not safe and should be considered breached.

13. Bob is designing a datacenter to support his organization, a financial services firm. Which of the following actions would best enhance Bob's efforts to create resiliency in the datacenter?

   A. Ensure that all entrances are secured with biometric-based locks.

   B. Purchase uninterruptible power supplies (UPSs) from different vendors.

   C. Include financial background checks in all personnel reviews for administrators.

   D. Make sure all raised floors have at least 24 inches of clearance.

14. Under the Common Criteria, which one of the following EAL levels indicates that a system has been methodically designed, tested, and reviewed?

   A. EAL1

   B. EAL2

   C. EAL3

   D. EAL4

15. A(n) _____ consists of a computer, data, or a network site that appears to be part of a network but is actually isolated and monitored. It also appears to contain data or resources of value that are in fact fake.

   A. Honeypot

   B. HIDS

   C. Virtual application

   D. Sandbox

16. Rusty is evaluating the security of a web-based SaaS application and wants to verify that the site provides strong encryption between the web server and the client. What is the most common way to achieve this goal?

   A. Secure sockets layer (SSL)

   B. DNS Security Extensions (DNSSEC)

   C. Internet Protocol Secure (IPsec)

   D. Transport layer security (TLS)

17. You operate a cloud service and would like a report that confirms the effectiveness of your security controls and provides significant detail of control gaps that you can use for remediation. What type of audit should you conduct?

   A. SOC 1

   B. SOC 2

   C. SOC 3

   D. SOC 4

18. Adam's organization recently experienced a security breach that affected customer data. Which one of the following stakeholder groups might Adam be required to inform?

   A. Customers

   B. Regulators

   C. Partners

   D. All of the above

19. An application programming interface (API) gateway can typically offer all of the following capabilities *except* _____.

   A. Rate limiting

   B. Access control

   C. Content filtering

   D. Logging

20. When logging information about an internet user's location, what source provides the most accurate physical location data?

   A. GPS

   B. IP address correlation

   C. User attestation

   D. MAC address correlation

21. What type of device is designed to safely store and manage encryption keys?

   A. Hardware security module

   B. Secure BIOS

   C. Hardware token

   D. Host intrusion detection system

22. The Transport Layer Security (TLS) protocol creates a secure communications channel over public media (such as the internet). In a typical TLS session, who initiates the protocol?

A. The server

B. The client

C. The certifying authority

D. The internet service provider (ISP)

23. In what cloud computing service model is the customer responsible for installing and maintaining the operating system?

A. IaaS

B. PaaS

C. SaaS

D. FaaS

For questions 24–26, please refer to the following scenario:

Darcy is an information security risk analyst for Roscommon Cloud Solutions. She is currently trying to decide whether the company should purchase an upgraded fire suppression system for their primary datacenter. The datacenter facility has a replacement cost of $2 million.

After consulting with actuaries, datacenter managers, and fire subject matter experts, Darcy determined that a typical fire would likely require the replacement of all equipment inside the building but not cause significant structural damage. Together, they estimated that recovering from the fire would cost $750,000. They also determined that the company can expect a fire of this magnitude once every 50 years.

24. Based on the information in this scenario, what is the exposure factor for the effect of a fire on the Roscommon Cloud Solutions datacenter?

A. 7.5 percent

B. 15.0 percent

C. 27.5 percent

D. 37.5 percent

25. Based on the information in this scenario, what is the annualized rate of occurrence for a fire at the Roscommon Cloud Solutions datacenter?

A. 0.002

B. 0.005

C. 0.02

D. 0.05

26. Based on the information in this scenario, what is the annualized loss expectancy for a fire at the Roscommon Cloud Solutions datacenter?

A. $15,000

B. $25,000

    C. $75,000

    D. $750,000

27. What is the most significant barrier to eDiscovery efforts in organizations that make heavy use of many different cloud services?

    A. Identifying relevant records

    B. Coordinating multiple providers that might have relevant records

    C. Obtaining provider cooperation

    D. Determining when eDiscovery is necessary

28. David's organization is preparing to adopt an information rights management tool. What IRM capability focuses on securing data sent by the system while it is in transit over a network?

    A. Tagging

    B. Data labeling

    C. Encryption

    D. Provisioning

29. Which of the following best describes threat modeling?

    A. The idea of identifying specific points of vulnerability and then implementing counter-measures to protect or thwart those points from successful exploitation

    B. The idea of finding points and then implementing countermeasures to protect or thwart those points from successful exploitation

    C. The idea of identifying specific vulnerabilities and then patching them to protect or thwart them from successful exploitation

    D. The idea of identifying specific intrusion points and implementing countermeasures to protect or thwart those points from successful intrusion

30. Gary is concerned that the environmental controls in his organization's datacenter may not be effectively controlling humidity. Which of the following circumstances would not commonly result from humidity issues? (Choose all that apply.)

    A. Static electricity damaging equipment

    B. Fires in power supplies

    C. Corrosion of equipment

    D. Moisture buildup

31. Which of the following mechanisms *cannot* be used by a data loss prevention (DLP) solution to detect the presence of data?

    A. Pattern matching

    B. Metadata

    C. Content strings

    D. Tokenization

32. Gabriel's organization maintains a system of voting records. The system uses SHA3 to obscure the contents of sensitive records. What data obfuscation technique is this system using?

A. Hashing

B. Masking

C. Anonymization

D. Shuffling

33. Which Statement on Standards for Attestation Engagements (SSAE) 18 report is purposefully designed for public release (for instance, to be posted on a company's website)?

A. Service Organization Control (SOC) 1

B. SOC 2, Type 1

C. SOC 2, Type 2

D. SOC 3

34. Which of the following is a true statement about the virtualization management toolset?

A. It can be regarded as something public-facing.

B. It must be on a distinct, isolated management network (virtual local area network [VLAN]).

C. It connects physically to a dedicated storage area allocated to each customer.

D. The responsibility for securely installing and updating it falls on the customer.

35. You are the IT director for a small contracting firm. Your company is considering migrating to a cloud production environment. Which service model would *best* fit your needs if you wanted an option that reduced the chance of vendor lock-in but also did not require the highest degree of administration by your own personnel?

A. IaaS

B. PaaS

C. SaaS

D. SECaaS

36. You are the data manager for a retail company; you anticipate a much higher volume of sales activity in the final quarter of each calendar year than the other quarters. In order to handle these increased transactions, and to accommodate the temporary sales personnel you will hire for only that time period, you consider augmenting your internal, on-premises production environment with a cloud capability for a specific duration, and will return to operating fully on-premises after the period of increased activity. Which facet of cloud computing is *most* important for making this possible?

A. Broad network access

B. Rapid elasticity

C. Metered service

D. Resource pooling

37. Which one of the following individuals is typically responsible for making high-level data classification decisions for an organization?

   A. The data custodian

   B. The data owner

   C. The data processor

   D. The data user

38. Brad is assisting with the implementation of a cloud-based SaaS solution where users can post content that is viewed by other users. He is concerned that users might store executable content on the site that then might be executed automatically by the browsers of other site visitors. What type of vulnerability would permit this attack?

   A. SQL injection

   B. Cross-site scripting

   C. Cross-site request forgery

   D. Server-side request forgery

39. You are the security manager for an online marketing company. Your company has recently migrated to a cloud production environment and has deployed a number of new cloud-based protection mechanisms offered by both third parties and the cloud provider, including data loss prevention (DLP) and security information and event management (SIEM) solutions.

   After one week of operation, your security team reports an inordinate amount of time responding to potential incidents that have turned out to only be false-positive reports. Management is concerned that the cloud migration was a bad idea and that it is too costly in terms of misspent security efforts. What do you recommend?

   A. Change the control set so that you use only security products not offered by the cloud provider.

   B. Change the control set so that you use only security products offered by the cloud provider.

   C. Wait three weeks for additional data before making a final decision.

   D. Move back to an on-premises environment as soon as possible to avoid additional wasted funds and effort.

40. Which one of the following stakeholders is most likely to demand communication about service outages for a cloud service provider?

   A. Customers

   B. Vendors

   C. Partners

   D. Regulators

41. Which is the part of the SDLC in which all functional features of the system chosen for development in analysis are described independently of any computer platform?

   A. Physical design phase

   B. User story

   C. Agile phase

   D. Logical design phase

42. A group of clinics decides to create an identification federation for their users (medical providers and clinicians). In this federation, all of the participating organizations would need to be in compliance with what U.S. federal regulation?

    A. Family Educational Rights and Privacy Act (FERPA)

    B. Family and Medical Leave Act (FMLA)

    C. Payment Card Industry Data Security Standard (PCI DSS)

    D. Health Insurance Portability and Accountability Act (HIPAA)

43. You are the data manager for a retail company; you anticipate a much higher volume of sales activity in the final quarter of each calendar year than the other quarters. In order to handle these increased transactions, and to accommodate the temporary sales personnel you will hire for only that time period, you consider augmenting your internal, on-premises production environment with a cloud capability for a specific duration, and will return to operating fully on-premises after the period of increased activity. Which deployment model best describes this type of arrangement?

    A. Private cloud

    B. Community cloud

    C. Public cloud

    D. Hybrid cloud

44. How does representational state transfer (REST) make web service requests?

    A. XML

    B. SAML

    C. URIs

    D. TLS

45. Which of the following best describes a set of practices that focus on aligning IT services with business needs?

    A. ITIL

    B. ISO

    C. HIPAA

    D. GLBA

46. What type of cloud storage is typically used to provide disk volumes for use with virtual server instances that will store important long-term data?

    A. Object storage

    B. Block storage

    C. Ephemeral storage

    D. Archival storage

47. Lisa is working to develop a long-term relationship with a consulting firm that will assist in her organization's cloud migration. She has a contract in place that governs the terms of many different projects and would like to create a document that will describe one specific new project. What type of document should she create?

A. MSA

B. BPA

C. SOW

D. MOU

48. Full isolation of user activity, processes, and virtual network segments in a cloud environment is incredibly important because of risks due to _____.

A. Distributed denial of service (DDoS)

B. Unencrypted packets

C. Multitenancy

D. Insider threat

49. In a federated environment, who is the relying party, and what do they do?

A. The relying party is the service provider and they would consume the tokens generated by the identity provider.

B. The relying party is the service provider and they would consume the tokens generated by the customer.

C. The relying party is the customer and they would consume the tokens generated by the identity provider.

D. The relying party is the identity provider and they would consume the tokens generated by the service provider.

50. Christine is concerned about the risk that another customer will be able to access sensitive data elements stored in her organization's database in a multitenant public cloud environment. What control would best mitigate this risk?

A. TLS

B. IPsec

C. Volume encryption

D. VPN

51. Which one of the following fire suppression systems is least likely to damage sensitive electronic equipment in a datacenter?

A. Wet pipe

B. Dry pipe

C. Preaction

D. Inert gas

52. You are the security manager for a data analysis company. Your senior management is considering a cloud migration in order to use the greater capabilities of a cloud provider to perform calculations and computations. Your company wants to ensure that neither the contractual nor the technical setup of the cloud service will affect your data sets in any way so that you are not locked into a single provider.

Which of the following criteria will probably be *most* crucial for your choice of cloud providers?

    A. Portability

    B. Interoperability

    C. Resiliency

    D. Governance

53. Which one of the following standards is most likely to contain detailed technical requirements for a hardware security module (HSM) used in a cloud environment?

    A. FIPS 140-2

    B. PCI DSS

    C. ISO 27017

    D. Common Criteria

54. Which of the following is *not* a reason for conducting audits?

    A. Regulatory compliance

    B. Enhanced user experience

    C. Determination of service quality

    D. Security assurance

55. Migrating to a cloud environment will reduce an organization's dependence on

    _____.

    A. Capital expenditures for IT

    B. Operational expenditures for IT

    C. Data-driven workflows

    D. Customer satisfaction

Questions 56–58 refer to the following scenario:

Arlene ran a vulnerability scan of a VPN server used by contractors and employees to gain access to her organization's network. An external scan of the server found the vulnerability shown below:

56. Which one of the following hash algorithms would *not* trigger this vulnerability?
    A. MD4
    B. MD5
    C. SHA-1
    D. SHA-256

57. What is the most likely result of failing to correct this vulnerability?
    A. All users will be able to access the site, but some may see an error message.
    B. All users will be able to access the site.
    C. Some users will be unable to access the site.
    D. All users will be unable to access the site.

58. How can Arlene correct this vulnerability?
    A. Reconfigure the VPN server to only use secure hash functions.
    B. Request a new certificate.
    C. Change the domain name of the server.
    D. Implement an intrusion prevention system.

59. You are also concerned about the availability of data stored on servers that support your organization's cloud services. You would like to add technology that would enable continued access to files located on the server even if a hard drive in a server fails. What integrity control allows you to add robustness without adding additional servers?
    A. Server clustering
    B. Load balancing
    C. RAID
    D. Scheduled backups

60. MTTR is best described as which of the following?
    A. The average cost to repair a device that has failed or is in need of repair
    B. The average time it takes to return a defective device to the manufacturer
    C. The average time it takes to repair a device that has failed or is in need of repair
    D. The time it takes to repair a device that has failed or is in need of repair

61. What is a set of technologies designed to analyze application source code and binaries for coding and design conditions that are indicative of security and vulnerabilities?

A. Dynamic application security testing (DAST)

B. Static application security testing (SAST)

C. Secure coding

D. OWASP

62. You are participating in a data discovery effort and begin to explore a relational database server. What type of data should you most likely expect to encounter?

A. Unstructured data

B. Semi-structured data

C. Structured data

D. Unorganized data

63. Domain Name System Security Extensions (DNSSEC) provides all of the following *except* _____.

A. Payload encryption

B. Origin authority

C. Data integrity

D. Authenticated denial of existence

64. Alice received an encrypted message from Bob. Bob encrypted the message for confidentiality using an asymmetric encryption algorithm. What key should Alice use to decrypt the message?

A. Bob's public key

B. Bob's private key

C. Alice's private key

D. Alice's public key

65. Bobbi is investigating a security incident and discovers that an attacker began with a normal user account but managed to exploit a system vulnerability to provide that account with administrative rights. What type of attack took place under the STRIDE threat model?

A. Spoofing

B. Repudiation

C. Tampering

D. Elevation of privilege

66. Which type of hypervisor has an operating system installed on the hardware and then the virtual manager software installed on top of it?

A. Type 1

B. Type 3

C. Type 2

D. Type 4

67. The government-wide program that provides for a standardized approach to security assessments, authorization, and continuous monitoring of cloud products and services is called_____.

   A. FISMA

   B. HIPAA

   C. FedRAMP

   D. GLBA

68. In a cloud context, who determines the risk appetite of your organization?

   A. The cloud provider

   B. Your internet service provider (ISP)

   C. Federal regulators

   D. Senior management

69. Yolanda is analyzing a business process that uses a cloud service to send invoices to clients. What phase of the cloud data lifecycle is most directly occurring?

   A. Create

   B. Archive

   C. Store

   D. Share

70. Carla is completing an IT audit that involves very sensitive log records that may later be disputed. She would like to collect a copy of the log records now and then protect them with a technology that will provide nonrepudiation. Which one of the following technologies would best meet her needs?

   A. Multifactor authentication

   B. Strong encryption

   C. Cryptographic hash

   D. Digital signature

71. You are the security manager for a small application development company. Your company is considering the migration of your testing environment to the cloud. As part of your testing methodology, you use several third-party cloud testing vendors.

   Which of the following traits of cloud functionality is probably the *most* crucial in terms of deciding which cloud provider you will choose?

   A. Portability

   B. Interoperability

   C. Resiliency

   D. Governance

72. Luis is concerned about the proliferation of sensitive data in his organization and is searching for systems containing Social Security numbers. He uses a tool that detects any data matching the pattern "XXX-XX-XXXX" where each X is a digit. What type of data discovery is Luis performing?

   A. Metadata-based discovery

   B. Content-based discovery

   C. Classification-based discovery

   D. Label-based discovery

73. You work for a government research facility. Your organization often shares data with other government research organizations. You would like to create a single sign-on experience across the organizations, where users at each organization can sign in with the user ID/authentication issued by that organization, then access research data in all the other organizations. Instead of replicating the data stores of each organization at every other organization (which is one way of accomplishing this goal), you instead want every user to have access to each organization's specific storage resources.

   In order to pass the user IDs and authenticating credentials of each user among the organizations, what protocol, language, or technique will you *most* likely utilize?

   A. Representational State Transfer (REST)

   B. Security Assertion Markup Language (SAML)

   C. Simple Object Access Protocol (SOAP)

   D. Hypertext Markup Language (HTML)

74. Warren is helping his organization build a new datacenter that will support a cloud service they provide to their customers. Which one of the following is a reasonable minimum amount of time to expect the uninterruptible power supply (UPS) to provide power to the systems in the datacenter?

   A. 10 minutes

   B. 60 minutes

   C. 3 hours

   D. 12 hours

75. The practice of using strong magnets to erase and scramble data on magnetic media is called _____.

   A. Degaussing

   B. Scrubbing

   C. Crypto-shredding

   D. Bit splitting

Questions 76 and 77 refer to the following scenario:

Gary is responsible for managing a large data set from a university research project that is stored with a cloud service provider in their object storage mechanism.

He is concerned about managing costs of the service but also wants to make sure that they do not violate any legal obligations.

The policies governing this data set specify a retention period of five years but note that litigation holds may override this requirement. Researchers rarely access data after 90 days but occasionally have a need to review older data.

76. Which one of the following actions should Gary take to minimize costs?

- **A.** Set a lifecycle policy that moves data to archival storage after 90 days and destroys it after five years.
- **B.** Set a lifecycle policy that moves data to archival storage after 90 days.
- **C.** Set a lifecycle policy that destroys data after five years.
- **D.** None of these actions are appropriate.

77. Gary receives a litigation hold notice for data related to tests performed in March 2022. What should he do?

- **A.** Suspend all data deletion.
- **B.** Suspend deletion of data from March 2022 only.
- **C.** Suspend all data archival.
- **D.** None of these actions are necessary.

78. In regard to most privacy guidance, the data subject is _____.

- **A.** The individual described by the personally identifiable information (PII)
- **B.** The entity that collects or creates the PII
- **C.** The entity that uses the PII on behalf of the controller
- **D.** The entity that regulates the PII

79. Which term refers to a system's ability to cordon off or protect certain aspects of the compute environment such as processing, memory, and other resources needed in the compute transaction?

- **A.** Virtualization
- **B.** Emulation
- **C.** ASLR
- **D.** Sandboxing

80. You are the security policy lead for your organization, which is considering migrating from your on-premises, traditional IT environment into the cloud. You are reviewing the Cloud Security Alliance Cloud Controls Matrix (CSA CCM) as a tool for your organization.

Which of the following benefits will the CSA CCM offer your organization?

- **A.** Simplifying regulatory compliance
- **B.** Collecting multiple data streams from your log files
- **C.** Ensuring that the baseline configuration is applied to all systems
- **D.** Enforcing contract terms between your organization and the cloud provider

81. ISO 31000 is most similar to which of the following regulations, standards, guidelines, and frameworks?

    A. NIST 800-37

    B. COBIT

    C. ITIL

    D. GDPR

82. Which one of the following technologies is typically contained within a computer and manages the encryption keys used for full-disk encryption?

    A. HSM

    B. PKI

    C. TPM

    D. IPS

83. You are the IT security manager for a video game software development company. In order to test your products for security defects, your firm decides to use a small team of game testers recruited from a public pool of interested gamers who apply for a chance to take part. This is an example of _____.

    A. Static testing

    B. Dynamic testing

    C. Code review

    D. Open source review

84. Which one of the following principles imposes a standard of care upon an individual that is broad and equivalent to what one would expect from a reasonable person under the circumstances?

    A. Due diligence

    B. Separation of duties

    C. Due care

    D. Least privilege

85. Which one of the following is the *most* important security consideration when selecting a new computer facility?

    A. Local law enforcement response times

    B. Location adjacent to competitor's facilities

    C. Aircraft flight paths

    D. Utility infrastructure

86. Which one of the following storage types is typically the most inexpensive class of storage?

    A. Block storage

    B. Object storage

    C. Archival storage

    D. Raw storage

87. Andy is concerned that his organization is not meeting uptime requirements to their cloud service customers. Which one of the following ITIL control categories is least directly impacted?

   A. Incident management

   B. Change management

   C. Availability management

   D. Service level management

88. Firewalls, DLP (data loss prevention or data leak protection) and digital rights management (DRM) solutions, and security information and event management (SIEM) products are all examples of _____ controls.

   A. Technical

   B. Administrative

   C. Physical

   D. Competing

89. Brenda's organization recently completed the acquisition of a competitor firm. Which one of the following tasks would be *least* likely to be part of the organizational processes addressed during the acquisition?

   A. Consolidation of security functions

   B. Integration of security tools

   C. Protection of intellectual property

   D. Documentation of security policies

90. What is the term used to describe loss of access to data because the cloud provider has ceased operation?

   A. Tokenization

   B. Vendor lockout

   C. Vendor lock-in

   D. Masking

91. Which one of the following is not commonly used as a criterion for data classification decisions?

   A. Sensitivity

   B. Criticality

   C. Age

   D. Jurisdiction

92. All of the following are activities that should be performed when capturing and maintaining an accurate, secure system baseline *except* _____.

   A. Updating the OS baseline image according to a scheduled interval to include any necessary security patches and configuration modifications

   B. Starting with a clean installation (hardware or virtual) of the desired OS

   C. Including only the default account credentials and nothing customized

   D. Halting or removing all unnecessary services

93. Richard is a data custodian who recently received a litigation hold notice for a set of records he administers. How long should he set the retention period for the affected data?

    A. 1 year

    B. 5 years

    C. 7 years

    D. Indefinite

94. What technology can serve as a connection between the virtual guest operating system and the hypervisor, improving the services provided to the guest?

    A. Virtualization sandbox.

    B. Virtualization bridge.

    C. Virtualization tools.

    D. It is not advised to create a connection between the virtual guests and the hypervisor in order to preserve tenant isolation.

95. Matt needs to revoke a digital certificate that is used as part of his organization's information rights management (IRM) program. Which one of the following options would best meet this need?

    A. Update the certificate's OCSP record.

    B. Add the certificate to the CRL.

    C. Change the public key.

    D. Change the private key.

96. You are the IT security subject matter expert for a hobbyist collective that researches and archives old music. Your collective is set up in such a way that the members own various pieces of the network themselves, pool resources and data, and communicate and share files via the internet. This is an example of what cloud model?

    A. Hybrid

    B. Private

    C. Public

    D. Community

97. What ITIL process ensures that IT resources are sufficient to meet current and future business demand?

    A. Availability management

    B. Service level management

    C. Configuration management

    D. Capacity management

98. What is the correct order of the phases of the data lifecycle?

    A. Create, Store, Use, Archive, Share, Destroy

    B. Create, Store, Use, Share, Archive, Destroy

    C. Create, Use, Store, Share, Archive, Destroy

    D. Create, Archive, Store, Share, Use, Destroy

99. Carolyn is using ephemeral storage to process data in a machine learning application using a virtual server instance. Which one of the following best describes this storage?

    A. It will remain until Carolyn explicitly deletes it.

    B. It will be deleted if the server is rebooted.

    C. It will be deleted only if the server is stopped.

    D. It will be deleted only if the server is terminated.

100. You are the security manager for a small retailer engaged in e-commerce. A large part of your sales is transacted through the use of credit and debit cards and you need to store these numbers for use in future transactions.

    You have determined that the costs of maintaining an encrypted storage capability in order to meet compliance requirements are prohibitive. What other technology can you use instead to meet those regulatory needs?

    A. Obfuscation

    B. Masking

    C. Tokenization

    D. Hashing

101. Which one of the following actions might be taken as part of a business continuity plan?

    A. Restoring from backup tapes

    B. Implementing RAID

    C. Relocating to a cold site

    D. Restarting business operations

102. Bob is designing a datacenter to support his organization, a financial services firm. Bob's datacenter will have to be approved by regulators using a framework under which law?

    A. Health Industry Portability and Accountability Act (HIPAA)

    B. Payment Card Industry Data Security Standard (PCI DSS)

    C. Gramm–Leach–Bliley Act (GLBA)

    D. Sarbanes–Oxley Act (SOX)

103. Which one of the following is most likely to be stored as unstructured data?

    A. Interview videos

    B. Sales transactions

    C. Customer contact information

    D. Website visitor logs

104. _____ is a symmetric block type of cipher used to encrypt information and is currently the standard for the U.S. government in protecting sensitive and secret documents.

    A. MD5

    B. SSL

    C. Blowfish

    D. AES

105. Tom is conducting a business continuity planning effort for Orange Blossoms, a fruit orchard located in Central Florida. During the assessment process, the committee determined that there is a small risk of snow in the region but that the cost of implementing controls to reduce the impact of that risk is not warranted. They elect to not take any specific action in response to the risk. What risk management strategy is Orange Blossoms pursuing?

A. Risk mitigation

B. Risk transference

C. Risk avoidance

D. Risk acceptance

106. Linda is selecting a disaster recovery facility for her organization, and she wants to retain independence from other organizations as much as possible. She would like to choose a facility that balances cost and recovery time, allowing activation in about one week after a disaster is declared. What type of facility should she choose?

A. Cold site

B. Warm site

C. Mutual assistance agreement

D. Hot site

107. Helen's organization handles large quantities of highly sensitive information. To help address this risk, she purchased a cyber-liability insurance policy. What type of risk response action is Helen taking?

A. Transfer

B. Avoid

C. Mitigate

D. Accept

108. Which type of attack occurs when an application receives untrusted data and then sends it to a web browser without proper validation?

A. SQL injection

B. Brute-force

C. Cross-site scripting (XSS)

D. Man-in-the-middle/on-path

109. Which federal standard is for the accreditation and distinguishing of secure and well-architected cryptographic modules produced by private sector vendors who see to or are in the process of having their solutions and services certified by the U.S. government departments and regulated industries that collect, store, transfer, or share data that is deemed to be sensitive but not classified?

A. ISO 27036

B. ISO 27050

C. COBIT

D. FIPS 140-2

110. Which one of the following technologies is least commonly associated with semi-structured data?

   A. JSON

   B. XML

   C. SQL

   D. MongoDB

111. Which of the following describes a SYN flood attack?

   A. Rapid transmission of internet Relay Chat (IRC) messages

   B. Creating a high number of partially open TCP connections

   C. Disabling the Domain Name Service (DNS) server

   D. Excessive list linking of users and files

112. What concept from the field of digital forensics requires that you document who handles evidence from the time of collection until the time of use in court?

   A. eDiscovery

   B. Probable cause

   C. Chain of custody

   D. The Doctrine of the Proper Law

113. Chris is investigating a security incident where he believes that an attacker placed fraudulent orders using his organization's website. He believes that critical evidence may be stored in the website's logs and is concerned that those logs may be modified because the web server is still in production. The web server is hosted in a virtualized environment. What action should Chris take?

   A. Keep the website offline until the investigation is complete.

   B. Take the virtualization platform offline as evidence.

   C. Take a snapshot of the web server instance and use that for the investigation.

   D. No action is necessary.

114. The Transport Layer Security (TLS) protocol creates a secure communications channel over public media (such as the internet). In a typical TLS session, what form of cryptography is used for the session key?

   A. Symmetric key

   B. Asymmetric key pairs

   C. Hashing

   D. One asymmetric key pair

115. Which of the following is *not* typically a phase in the software development life cycle (SDLC)?

   A. Define

   B. Test

   C. Develop

   D. Sanitize

116. What component of a virtualized environment is responsible for enforcing tenant isolation?

   A. Guest operating system

   B. Hypervisor

   C. Kernel

   D. Protection manager

117. In a public cloud services arrangement, who creates governance that will determine which controls are selected for the datacenter and how they are deployed?

   A. The cloud provider

   B. The cloud customer

   C. The regulator(s)

   D. The end user

118. Which one of the following entities is dedicated to helping application developers improve software security?

   A. ATASM

   B. PASTA

   C. DREAD

   D. SAFEcode

119. Gavin is creating a report to management on the results of his most recent risk assessment. In his report, he would like to identify the remaining level of risk to the organization after adopting security controls. What term best describes this current level of risk?

   A. Inherent risk

   B. Residual risk

   C. Control risk

   D. Mitigated risk

120. Tina is gathering evidence as part of a cybersecurity investigation. Which one of the following evidence types is most volatile?

   A. Firmware contents

   B. File stored in archival storage

   C. File stored on a server hard drive

   D. RAM contents

121. The Agile Manifesto for software development focuses largely on _____.

   A. Secure build

   B. Thorough documentation

   C. Working prototypes

   D. Proper planning

122. You are the IT security manager for a video game software development company. In order to test the functionality of online multiplayer game content, your testing team wants to use a cloud service independent from the internal production environment. You suggest that a(n) _____ service model will best meet this requirement.

   A.   IaaS

   B.   PaaS

   C.   SaaS

   D.   FaaS

123. Why is Simple Object Access Protocol (SOAP) used for accessing web services instead of the Distributed Component Object Model (DCOM) and the Common Object Request Broker Architecture (CORBA)?

   A.   SOAP provides a much more lightweight solution.

   B.   SOAP provides for stronger interoperability.

   C.   SOAP is much more secure.

   D.   SOAP is newer.

124. _____ is an exercise designed to determine the impact of losing the support of or availability of any particular resource to an organization.

   A.   BIA

   B.   PCP

   C.   BCD

   D.   DR

125. Which of the following best describes the characteristics of a private cloud?

   A.   An infrastructure provisioned for exclusive use by a single organization consisting of multiple customers (e.g., business units)

   B.   An infrastructure provisioned for exclusive use by a single organization consisting of multiple customers hosted exclusively off-premises

   C.   An infrastructure provisioned for exclusive use by a single organization consisting of multiple customers (e.g., business units) hosted exclusively on-premises

   D.   An infrastructure provisioned for exclusive use by a single organization consisting of multiple customers (e.g., business units) that is owned and managed by the organization

Chapter

8

Practice Test 2

1. Juanita has configured her virtualization cluster for high availability mode. The virtualization management plane detects that one of her servers has failed and is no longer sending heartbeat information. What will the cluster do if the node cannot be restarted?

    A. Attempt to reboot the failed system.

    B. Shut down the failed system and send an alert.

    C. Restart the VMs hosted on that system on other cluster nodes.

    D. Migrate the hosts from the failed system to its backup mirror.

2. Will wants to use containerized applications in his cloud-hosted environment. Which of the following is a best practice he should use as he builds them?

    A. Package a single application per container.

    B. Use default installs wherever possible.

    C. Retain all normal tools and utilities.

    D. Avoid tagging to reduce complexity.

3. Jason wants to adopt a cloud service security standard. Which of the following is specifically designed to cover cloud service providers?

    A. ISO/IEC 20000:1

    B. ISO/IEC 27017

    C. PCI DSS

    D. GDPR

4. Helen's organization operates an e-commerce website housed by a cloud service provider. Which of the following compliance standards is she likely to have to comply with?

    A. PCI DSS

    B. FedRAMP

    C. COBIT

    D. ITIL

5. Ilya wants to ensure that systems in his cloud environment are properly patched. Which of the following options will give him the most flexibility and control over patching, including when patches are installed and what patches are installed if his organization has a strong emphasis on using prebuilt tools?

    A. Automatically install patches using built-in OS tools.

    B. Use a patching script developed by the organization.

    C. Set up automatic updates for all applications and the OS.

    D. Use the cloud provider's patching tools and patch baselines.

6. Yasmine is validating her software's performance under load, including testing for higher numbers of users than her organization expects to ever use the application. What type of testing is she conducting?

   A. Functional testing

   B. Black-box testing

   C. Nonfunctional testing

   D. White-box testing

7. Adam's organization uses Google cloud services and he wants to ensure that his organization's logs are secure. What best practice should he recommend to his organization to ensure that the logs are secure at rest?

   A. Ensure the cloud provider regularly rotates keys for the logs.

   B. Use customer-managed encryption keys for logs.

   C. Use provider-managed encryption keys for logs.

   D. Avoid encrypting logs to ensure they remain accessible.

8. Charleen wants to implement multifactor authentication for her organization. Which of the following MFA options is considered the least secure?

   A. Application-based code generation

   B. Hardware token–based code generation

   C. SMS-based code delivery

   D. USB hardware tokens

9. Email and web pages are both examples of what type of data?

   A. Unstructured data

   B. Structured data

   C. Semi-structured data

   D. Partially structured data

10. Felix wants to ensure that members of his organization only access management consoles while they are in approved locations. Which of the following network security capabilities will best allow him to accomplish that task?

   A. Zero trust

   B. Geofencing

   C. Traffic inspection

   D. Network security groups

11. Valerie, an Amazon AWS user, is concerned about potential outages that might impact her current US-East region. What risk mitigation strategy should she take to ensure her organization can handle a region-wide outage?

   A. Configure DR in another region.

   B. Configure DR in another availability zone.

   C. Deploy redundant systems in her current availability zone.

   D. Deploy redundant systems in her current region.

12. Casey is transitioning from an on-premises datacenter to a cloud datacenter. What hardware monitoring will she still be able to access in her new environment?

  A. CPU utilization

  B. Fan speeds

  C. System temperature

  D. System voltages

13. Kirk is adopting a platform as a service tool for his organization. Who is responsible for application and data security in PaaS environments?

  A. The customer

  B. The provider

  C. The regulator

  D. Both the customer and provider

14. Alaina wants to protect her on-premises datacenter from power issues. Which of the following options is best suited to handling brownouts?

  A. A generator

  B. Purchasing power from two different providers

  C. UPS

  D. PDUs

15. What term is used to describe a cloud service provider that allows customers to create virtual machines, define their own networking using virtual networks, and use storage and other services to create and manage their own infrastructure?

  A. IaaS

  B. PaaS

  C. SaaS

  D. CaaS

16. When Susan logs into her organization's service portal, she sees customer data that has names and addresses removed. What data obfuscation technique is her organization using?

  A. Randomization

  B. Data masking

  C. Hashing

  D. Anonymization

17. Hui wants to conduct a point in time SOC audit that covers her organization's security practices. What type of SOC audit should she select?

  A. A SOC 1 Type 1

  B. A SOC 2 Type 1

  C. A SOC 1 Type 2

  D. A SOC 2 Type 2

18. The Cloud Security Alliance notes that specific log types may only be available to cloud service providers when conducting forensic investigations. Which of the following log types will not typically be under service provider control in an IaaS environment?

    A. Logs from DNS servers

    B. Billing records

    C. API logs

    D. Web server logs

19. ITIL v4 defines one primary responsibility for availability. What role is key to availability efforts in ITIL?

    A. System architect

    B. Availability tester

    C. Risk manager

    D. Availability manager

20. Wayne's organization employs cloud architects who have broad responsibility for the implementation and oversight of their cloud environment. He wants to provide the architects with appropriate rights in his environment. What should he do to provide them with the proper rights?

    A. Use the vendor's best practices definitions for cloud architect rights.

    B. Use only built-in roles.

    C. Define a custom role.

    D. Use multifactor authentication to map roles as needed.

21. Jack is considering a cloud service policy as part of his organization's move to the cloud. Which of the following is not a common principle to follow when building a cloud service policy?

    A. Obtain input from all relevant stakeholders.

    B. Change organizational culture for the cloud.

    C. Follow the chain of command.

    D. Meet external requirements.

22. Lucca wants to define technical risks to his cloud environment. Which of the following is not a technical risk for his cloud services?

    A. Privacy issues

    B. Data breaches

    C. System outages

    D. Denial-of-service attacks

23. What defines a Type 2 hypervisor?

    A. It runs in the cloud.

    B. It runs on top of an existing operating system.

    C. It is installed on a bare-metal system.

    D. It cannot run inside of a virtualization system.

24. Amazon's S3 relies on collections of objects in buckets and is accessible via REST APIs. What common type of cloud storage is Amazon's S3?

    A. Object

    B. Block

    C. Native

    D. Network file

25. Which of the following is not a typical goal of a privacy impact assessment (PIA)?

    A. Identifying the cost of privacy efforts

    B. Ensuring that the organization meets legal and policy-based privacy requirements

    C. Identifying the risks of privacy breaches

    D. Identifying privacy controls

26. Mike wants to ensure that his data labeling travels with the data as it is used in his organization. What is the most effective and feasible option to ensure this?

    A. Include the data labels in file metadata.

    B. Include the data labels in the filename.

    C. Include the data labels as s second file sent with the first.

    D. Include the data labels as part of a cryptographic wrapper.

27. After a breach has been discovered, what group is most likely to have a legally required time frame to be notified about the breach?

    A. Customers

    B. Partners

    C. Regulators

    D. Law enforcement

28. Google's Cloud Architecture Framework suggests a number of common security design practices. Which of the following is not a common cloud IaaS design security practice?

    A. Meet compliance requirements for your regions.

    B. Use a layered security approach.

    C. Emphasize manual monitoring.

    D. Automate deployment of sensitive tasks.

29. Olivia is using a waterfall SLDC. Which of the following is not a phase in typical waterfall-based SDLCs?

    A. Requirements gathering

    B. Reverse engineering

    C. Implementation

    D. Maintenance

30. Michelle wants to store and manage cryptographic keys for her cloud environment. What solution should she require her cloud IaaS provider to have if she is selecting a new provider?

    A. TPM

    B. Cloud HSM

    C. PKI

    D. SAS 70

31. What is the most common method for allocation of compute power in cloud IaaS environments?

    A. Each customer uses a dedicated CPU per instance.

    B. Each customer uses a dedicated core per instance.

    C. Computation time is virtualized and allocated based on performance.

    D. Computation time is virtualized and allocated based on time.

32. Gurvinder want to ensure that his cloud environment is available and reliable. What type of agreement should he ensure his organization receives from the cloud vendor?

    A. QSA

    B. NDA

    C. MSA

    D. SLA

33. Ben is exploring new security options for his organization and wants to learn about confidential computing. Which of the following best describes what confidential computing does?

    A. It ensures only authenticated users can access data.

    B. It protects data both in transit and at rest.

    C. It allows you to secure data in use, even while being processed.

    D. It destroys data before it can be accessed by unauthorized parties.

34. Susan wants to detect and alert on potential malicious traffic, but she does not want to risk causing service outages due to false positives. What technology should she deploy?

    A. IDS

    B. Network security group

    C. IPS

    D. Firewall

35. Which of the following elements is not a typical service catalog component as defined by ISO/IEC 20000-1?

    A. Contact points

    B. A description of the service

    C. Dependencies on other services

    D. Risk ratings

36. What does the acronym STRIDE stand for?

    A. Spoofing, Tampering, Repudiation, Information Disclosure, Denial of Service, Elevation of Privilege

    B. Security, Testing, Reconnaissance, Investigation, Data Security, Escalation

    C. Security, Testing, Repudiation, Information Disclosure, Data Security, Escalation

    D. Spoofing, Tampering, Reconnaissance, Incident Response, Deletion, Evidence

37. Brian's organization uses Google Workspace. What type of cloud service are they using?

    A. IaaS

    B. PaaS

    C. SaaS

    D. DaaS

38. What security testing model is used to verify the components that make up open source software packages?

    A. Static testing

    B. Software composition analysis

    C. Interactive security testing

    D. Fuzzing

39. Chris has been notified by a partner about a recent breach of their cloud-hosted environment. What should Chris ask for from the partner organization?

    A. A full list of compromised systems and services

    B. A list of impacted customers

    C. Disclosure of any relevant information based on their partnership agreement

    D. Disclosure of other impacted partners

40. Gary is assessing risks and wants to describe how vendors are handling their risks. What term should he use to describe the risk remaining after the vendor has implemented their controls?

    A. Inherent risk

    B. Opportunity risk

    C. Residual risk

    D. Controlled risk

41. Jaime wants to explain the technology that allows cloud vendors to sell access to portions of their underlying hardware in the form of compute. What building block technology provides the foundation for this?

    A. APIs

    B. Virtualization

    C. Segmentation

    D. SLAs

42. Yuri wants to avoid the OWASP Top 10 application security risks. What should he do to help prevent cryptographic failures for data in transit?

A. Use TLS for all communications.

B. Use AES-256 encryption for all stored data.

C. Require all connections be done via UDP.

D. Require a three-way handshake for all data connections.

43. Rick wants to ensure that his organization will not be held accountable if something goes wrong that his PaaS provider is responsible for. What should he require in his cloud contract?

A. OLA

B. Service-level management

C. SLA

D. Indemnification

44. Hillary wants to publish an SSAE-18 SOC report to her website for public use. What type of SOC report should she provide if she wants to provide information about her organization's controls over time?

A. An SOC 1 Type 2

B. An SOC 2 Type 2

C. An SOC 3 Type 2

D. An SOC 4 Type 2

45. Christina wants to ensure that her vendor is using appropriate, strong encryption technology. What standard could she ask her vendor to meet to ensure this?

A. EBCDIC

B. FIPS 140-2

C. SecureCERT

D. AESCert

46. Jerome wants to implement DevOps for his organization and is considering how security should be designed in. Which practice is best suited to a DevOps CI/CD environment?

A. Automation of security processes

B. Creation of major releases on a yearly cycle

C. Testing for security in production

D. Static code review

47. Michelle wants to consider the legal risks relevant to her cloud environment. What risk should she highlight if she is concerned about how her organization will handle responses to lawsuits?

A. Cybersecurity risks

B. eDiscovery

C. Data security

D. Copyright infringement

48. Amanda wants to ensure that she can identify systems that performed actions in her cloud environment. What information is most critical to log to ensure she can properly identify ephemeral systems?

 A. Their public IP address

 B. Their private IP address

 C. Tags

 D. Usernames

49. Justin's IRM system deployment uses tagging to document data sensitivity. How can he use tagging later to most effectively decrease the chance of a data breach?

 A. Implement a DLP system.

 B. Use tags to manage data lifecycles.

 C. Use tags to help IDS detection.

 D. Implement a honeypot to capture tags.

50. Ramon wants to use a cloud identity provider for his organization. Which of the following options is most likely to be supported by cloud identity providers?

 A. SAML

 B. RDP

 C. LDAP

 D. FedID

51. Hyun wants to assess whether the cloud providers his organization is considering adopting have appropriate security-focused risk management methods in place. What type of audit artifact should he request to obtain the most information about controls and practices?

 A. An SOC 2 Type 2

 B. An SOC 2 Type 1

 C. An SOC 1 Type 2

 D. An SOC 1 Type 1

52. Kayla deploys multiple small instances with a load balancer in front of them as part of her cloud environment. What benefit is she most likely to receive from this?

 A. Greater confidentiality

 B. Fewer vulnerabilities

 C. High availability

 D. Shorter patching windows

53. Rene is designing her cloud environment to ensure business continuity. Which of the following design elements is best suited to ensuring business continuity?

 A. Setting up a backup VPC in another region

 B. Configuring backups to another cloud provider

 C. Deploying instances to multiple availability zones

 D. Ensuring staff are not all working the same location

54. Henry wants to reduce the risk of secrets being exposed in the event of a breach. What practice should he adopt to help prevent an attacker with access to application source code or the running application from using the secrets they can recover for future access?

   A. Use multifactor authentication.

   B. Use dynamic secrets.

   C. Use strong passwords.

   D. Use certificates and passphrases.

55. Jim has mounted a local C: drive for his Windows instance in his cloud service provider's IaaS environment. What type of storage is he most likely using?

   A. Ephemeral block storage

   B. Long-term

   C. Object

   D. Container

56. Lisa wants to audit actions taken in her cloud environment. Which of the following mechanisms is typically not permitted when dealing with cloud service management backplanes?

   A. User access logs

   B. Packet capture

   C. Specialized cloud service logs

   D. Configuration review

57. Emily needs to identify the data elements in an existing customer database that match customers in a newly acquired customer database. What process will Emily need to engage in to accomplish this?

   A. Data migration

   B. Data mining

   C. Data consolidation

   D. Data mapping

58. Wayne's organization considers their data to be highly sensitive and wants to ensure that the cloud provider itself cannot access the data while it is stored on the provider's large-scale bulk storage. What type of encryption should he select to accomplish this in a secure manner?

   A. AES-256

   B. MD5

   C. SHA-1

   D. CRC

59. What is operating system–level sandboxing most frequently used for?

   A. Building redundant infrastructure

   B. Rapid application development

   C. Testing malicious software

   D. Performing FIPS 140-2 testing

60. The North American Electric Reliability Corporation Critical Infrastructure Protection (NERC/CIP) points to what it calls "mutually managed encryption" as a useful model for cloud environments where the cloud service provider and registered entity (covered by NERC/CIP's requirements) share access and management of encryption keys. What advantage does this type of shared responsibility provide?

    A. Flexibility and easier operational support

    B. Lowered risk of unauthorized disclosure

    C. Simpler control structure

    D. Guaranteed confidentiality

61. Jason wants to detect common vulnerabilities during his software development life cycle. What type of assessment is most likely to identify business logic issues?

    A. Static code analysis

    B. Vulnerability scanning

    C. Dynamic testing

    D. Software composition analysis

62. Stacey wants to preserve forensics artifacts from a running instance in her cloud environment. What two key steps should she take to ensure she can perform forensic analysis?

    A. Create a snapshot of the running instance and make bit-for-bit copies of any mounted volumes.

    B. Shut down the instance and tag it for forensic investigation.

    C. Shut down the instance and then create a snapshot for forensic investigation.

    D. Use the cloud provider's forensic response team and validate their process.

63. Damian knows that misconfiguration is one of the common cloud threats and wants to decrease the chances of a misconfiguration causing significant issues for his organization. What practice is most likely to help his entire organization avoid misconfiguration issues?

    A. Using multifactor authentication

    B. Conducting regular vulnerability scanning

    C. Create and use configuration baselines

    D. Using default settings to ensure proper configuration

64. What document is typically created after a master service agreement (MSA) to determine what tasks a business will actually perform?

    A. SLA

    B. SOW

    C. NDA

    D. SOP

65. Christina wants to use Google as an identity provider, allowing her organization to simply determine what rights account holders would have while allowing Google to perform authentication and identity management for her. What is this type of relationship called?

   A. A client/server infrastructure

   B. Collaboration

   C. A service provider

   D. Federation

66. Naomi wants to understand what open source components are part of the containerization tool she is considering adopting. What testing process should she use to understand potential risks of the software based on its components?

   A. Interactive application security testing

   B. Software composition analysis

   C. Manual static testing

   D. Automated static testing

67. Selah has deployed open source software in her cloud environment and wants to validate the licensing for the software. What concern is most frequently involved in open source software licensing?

   A. The cost of licensing

   B. The license type

   C. The length of the license period

   D. Changes to the license for the deployed software

68. The company that Eric works for uses an authentication process that allows Eric to log in once and then use a variety of systems and services the organization provides. What technology is the company using?

   A. Federation

   B. MFA

   C. IAM

   D. SSO

69. ITIL v4 includes three major tasks for configuration management. Which of the following lists correctly identifies those tasks?

   A. Configuration design, configuration control, configuration deletion

   B. Configuration identification, configuration control, configuration verification and audit

   C. Configuration identification, configuration management, configuration modification

   D. Configuration design, configuration modification, configuration documentation

70. Chuck wants to conduct a gap analysis for the security controls in his cloud environment. What artifact will he need first?

    A. OLA

    B. Configuration baseline

    C. DR/BC plan

    D. ITIL-based configuration item (CI)

71. Annie wants to test software as part of her quality assurance efforts. What type of quality assurance testing will provide the greatest insight into the quality of the software being produced?

    A. Automated QA testing tools

    B. Fuzzing

    C. Manual QA testing

    D. Software composition analysis

72. Dave logs into a service using a federated identity. What does the identity provider send to his browser to present to the service provider?

    A. A token

    B. A password

    C. A password and a URL

    D. A sessionID

73. Theresa's organization has determined that a maximum of 30 minutes of data is acceptable as a data loss in the event of a major disaster. What term is used to describe this type of definition?

    A. A recovery time objective

    B. A snapshot window

    C. A recovery point objective

    D. A snapshot duration

74. Alaina wants to establish metrics for her risk management program. Which of the following isn't a metric that will help her manage her program effectively?

    A. Cost of the risk management program

    B. The number of risks identified

    C. The number of risks that have occurred

    D. The rate of risk occurrence per day

75. What is the primary driver in cloud IaaS environments for storage capacity monitoring?

    A. Performance management

    B. Cost management

    C. Continuity management

    D. Security management

76. Lisa is auditing her customer's cloud-hosted services. She has been asked to perform an external audit of all the cloud services in use. What is the largest challenge she is likely to face?

A. Accessing audit trails in customer-managed environments

B. Determining appropriate audit targets

C. Understanding the scope of the cloud environment

D. Gathering information about controls from provider audit artifacts

77. Which of the following is not typically stored in cloud secrets management tools?

A. MFA tokens

B. API keys

C. Passwords

D. Certificates

78. Gary's organization uses a combination of cloud infrastructure and organizationally issued laptops to allow their remote workforce to access organizational data anywhere. What DLP deployment option will help Gary protect data in use by staff?

A. On central file servers

B. On endpoint devices as a client

C. At the network border

D. At the network core

79. Lucca wants to apply data classification to his organization's data. What phase of the data lifecycle should he ensure tags are applied at?

A. Create

B. Use

C. Share

D. Destroy

80. Susan knows that serverless technology provides a number of security benefits for her organization. Which of the following isn't a common benefit of serverless computing?

A. Not needing to handle patching

B. Broad privileges available via IAM

C. Ephemeral infrastructure

D. High levels of instrumentation

81. Nick operates a service that hosts e-commerce websites. His infrastructure runs in AWS, and each customer is allocated their own S3 storage bucket. What type of logical design is Nick using?

A. Storage aggregation

B. Virtualization

C. Containerization

D. Tenant partitioning

82. Katie's organization creates their software in an environment hosted in the Azure cloud. They use a continuous integration/continuous delivery (CI/CD) process that focuses on automated testing and deployment. What risk is most likely to make it through an automated security testing process?

    A. Business logic risk

    B. SQL injection flaws

    C. Cross-site scripting flaws

    D. Vulnerable components

83. Thulani keeps documentation for her forensic activities and writes down how data was acquired, as well as where the data is stored, who has access to it, and any transfers of the data or media. What is Thulani documenting?

    A. Chain of custody

    B. Forensic proof

    C. Data logging

    D. Investigation notes

84. Derek operates cloud-hosted environments in both the U.S. and the European Union (EU). His organization captures customer data in both locations, and he wants to use that data as a central, shared resource for his company. What concern should he raise about this potential use of the data?

    A. There are different privacy laws in the U.S. and the EU, creating compliance concerns.

    B. The EU does not allow U.S. data to be imported to EU servers.

    C. The U.S. does not allow EU data to be imported to U.S. servers.

    D. U.S. and EU privacy laws have the same penalties, but they are significant and can be costly.

85. Ibrahim wants to securely configure SSH. Which of the following is not a common best practice for modern SSH environments?

    A. Using SSH keys

    B. Enabling password complexity requirements

    C. Changing the default SSH port number

    D. Limiting which users can log in via SSH

86. What ISO/IEC standard defines business continuity plans, systems, and processes?

    A. ISO/IEC 270001

    B. ISO/IEC 853-1

    C. ISC/IEC 28000:2022

    D. ISO/IEC 22301:2019

87. What ports and protocol does DHCP operate on?

    A. UDP ports 21 and 22

    B. TCP ports 80 and 443

    C. TCP ports 3389 and 4780

    D. UDP ports 67 and 68

88. Sara wants to operate some of her infrastructure in a datacenter that she controls and some in third-party cloud-hosted environments. What type of cloud deployment model best describes this?

    A. Private cloud

    B. Hybrid cloud

    C. Multicloud

    D. Community cloud

89. Isabelle wants to retrieve forensic data from her cloud provider's native logging facility. What technique is most likely to be supported for this type of data access?

    A. Transfer to removable media

    B. Manual copying

    C. API-based

    D. Printed copies

90. Wesley wants to ensure that sensitive data used by his organization cannot be accessed or recovered by third parties. Once his organization stops using data stored in the cloud, what deletion process should he recommend they use?

    A. Cryptographic shredding

    B. Zero wiping

    C. Deletion

    D. Random data-based wiping

91. Mark uses Terraform to design and deploy his infrastructure by creating code and configuration files that define what will be deployed and how it will be set up. What is this type of strategy called?

    A. Infrastructure as code

    B. Dynamic scaling architecture

    C. Containerization-based

    D. Software as a cloud

92. Diana wants to have the highest level of security possible for her secret keys stored in her cloud environment. What solution should she choose if her cloud service provider has it available?

    A. Dedicated TPM

    B. Cloud HSM

    C. Cloud TPM

    D. Dedicated HSM

93. Ashley's testing process involves approaching software testing like an attacker would. She will attempt to compromise or misuse the software, and report on its responses and any issues she identifies. What type of testing is Ashely conducting?

A. Abuse case testing

B. Interactive application security testing

C. User acceptance testing

D. Static testing

94. Lisa wants to advise her organization on a standard that they can adopt that defines information security controls. What standard should she recommend that will be broadly accepted by auditors?

A. ISO 27001

B. SOC 1

C. GDPR

D. HIPAA

95. What step is typically first in an ITIL-based change management process?

A. CAB review.

B. Create the RFC.

C. Change authorization.

D. Deployment.

96. Specific customer data in Gina's database has been replaced with alternate values that allow Gina to look up the original information from another database without exposing the actual data in the database she is using. Each unique data element is given a replacement value that is consistent any time that data element is used. What type of technique is in use in Gina's database?

A. Masking

B. Hashing

C. Anonymization

D. Tokenization

97. Amanda's company is being sued, and has received a letter from opposing counsel requiring them to retain information related to the lawsuit. What is this called?

A. Statute-based retention

B. Legal hold

C. DR/BC requirements

D. Legislative hold

98. Freya wants to revoke a certificate used by her organization. What will happen when she revokes the certificate via her certificate authority?

    A. The certificate will no longer work to encrypt data.

    B. The certificate will be placed on a certificate revocation list.

    C. A message about the revocation will be sent to all users of the certificate.

    D. The CA will set the certificate's expiration date to the revocation date.

99. Bart wants to perform data discovery on information stored in a SQL database that his company uses for customer information. What type of data is this?

    A. Structured data

    B. Semi-structured data

    C. Unstructured data

    D. Consolidated data

100. Patricia wants to analyze the data from her IPS for unexpected behavior. If she wants to use a known baseline, then analyze IPS data for potential malicious activity in an automated way that includes the ability to adapt to changes in attack behavior using information it gathers, what technology should she select?

    A. A WAF

    B. A SIEM

    C. IDS

    D. AI

101. Kathleen is concerned about country-specific privacy regulations because her organization is opening a location in a new country. What should she advise her organization's leadership to do?

    A. Follow OWASP-defined best practices.

    B. Engage external counsel with appropriate expertise.

    C. Identify an appropriate NIST standard to follow.

    D. Carefully review the laws and design the new policy based on them.

102. Which of the following is not a typical driver for data retention policies?

    A. Business requirements

    B. Legal requirements

    C. Regulatory requirements

    D. Data integrity requirements

103. Parker is concerned about customers abusing his organization's APIs and wants to control the volume of requests they are allowed to send. Which of the following solutions is best suited to meet his needs?

    A. An API gateway

    B. An API firewall

    C. An API load balancer

    D. An API engine

104. Ron has implemented his IaaS design using an infrastructure as code model. His team has leveraged native APIs and functions within the IaaS environment and uses many of the vendor's specialized capabilities. What issue may arise for Ron if the vendor begins to significantly increase prices?

    A. Interoperability

    B. Vendor lock-in

    C. API contention

    D. Code escrow

105. Rick's company spreads its data across multiple cloud vendors to help ensure that a data loss event or disaster at a single provider doesn't cause the organization to lose the data. What technique is Rick's company using?

    A. Data mapping

    B. Data cloning

    C. Data dispersion

    D. Data modeling

106. Jonah wants to address the OWASP Top 10 vulnerable and outdated components issue for his organization. What can he do to most effectively help identify them for his open source tools?

    A. Use software composition analysis tools.

    B. Engage a penetration tester.

    C. Perform static code review.

    D. Set up automatic updates.

107. Megan is accountable for the financial data in her organization, and she delegates responsibility for data-related actions to others in her organization. What role does she play?

    A. Data owner

    B. Data custodian

    C. Data processor

    D. Data steward

108. What makes vendor risk assessment difficult for open source software?

    A. There is no vendor for many open source packages.

    B. Open source software cannot undergo static code review.

    C. Open source software vendors do not offer software support contracts.

    D. Risk information about historical issues is not available.

109. The law enforcement officer that Henry is working with on a digital forensics effort has asked Henry for a forensic copy of the hard drive for a cloud-hosted desktop as a service system. What should Henry explain to the officer about the differences between cloud-hosted and physical systems?

    A. The forensic copy process will take far longer than normal.

    B. There is not a physical disk that Henry can access, and a snapshot is the closest equivalent to a forensic copy that he can provide.

    C. The forensic copy cannot be verified because the disk will change during the process.

    D. Cloud providers do not allow forensic copies of systems in their environments, and only logs will be available.

110. ITIL v4 identifies four information management subprocesses related to information security management. What ITIL v4 subprocess includes audits?

    A. Design of security controls

    B. Security testing

    C. Management of security incidents

    D. Security review

111. Diana wants to increase the bandwidth available to her cloud infrastructure as a service-hosted system. What would she need to do to increase the speed at which her instance is connecting to the provider's network?

    A. Replace the network interface card.

    B. Request that the cloud provider upgrade the network card.

    C. Increase the instance's network bandwidth.

    D. Change the network interface speed setting inside the instance's operating system.

112. What step occurs at point X in the following diagram as part of the cloud secure data lifecycle?

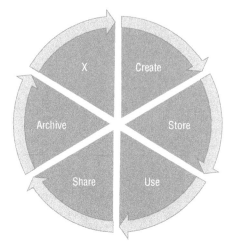

- **A.** Reclassify
- **B.** Back up
- **C.** Manage
- **D.** Destroy

113. What requirement for data breach reporting does the Sarbanes–Oxley Act place on organizations that must comply with it?

- **A.** All impacted customers must be notified.
- **B.** Data breaches must be reported in annual and quarterly reports.
- **C.** Law enforcement must be informed as soon as the breach is discovered.
- **D.** Breach disclosure is required in local news media.

114. Renee wants to gather requirements as part of her Agile SDLC. Which of the following is not a common requirements-gathering process for Agile teams?

- **A.** Interviews
- **B.** Questionnaires
- **C.** Workshops
- **D.** Reverse engineering

115. Christina wants to train developers in her organization on common issues in web application development for the cloud. What tool can she use to base her training on?

- **A.** MITRE's ATT&CK
- **B.** The OWASP Top 10
- **C.** The SANS Blue Book
- **D.** NIST's CMDB

116. Emily's company aggregates cloud service contracts for multiple customers to allow for a better discount rate. They also provide integration services for their customers. What role is Emily's company playing?

    A. Cloud service provider

    B. Regulator

    C. Cloud service broker

    D. Cloud steward

117. Mike wants to use a standards-based rating system to identify, define, and catalog vulnerabilities. Which of the following options should he choose?

    A. CVE

    B. VulnRank

    C. CPE

    D. MITRE

118. What privacy regulation will impact Susan's organization as they begin to operate in France?

    A. ISO/IEC 27018

    B. Generally Accepted Privacy Principles (GAPP)

    C. FERPA

    D. GDPR

119. Fiona wants to back up virtual machines hosted in her on-premises datacenter. What technique is typically used to back up guest operating systems?

    A. Backup clients on the guest OS

    B. Copies of the underlying guest OS disks

    C. Snapshots through the VM host

    D. Snapshots through the guest OS

120. Olivia's industry requires yearly audits of their business, and she knows that she needs to provide audit artifacts to the auditors about her cloud-hosted services. What should Olivia do to meet her audit requirements?

    A. Engage external auditors to audit the cloud provider.

    B. Contact the cloud service provider to obtain the required audit artifacts.

    C. Engage internal auditors to audit the cloud provider.

    D. Contact the cloud service provider and provide the required audit artifacts to them.

121. What happens at the end of the release management process flow according to ITIL?

    A. Release closure

    B. Release deployment

    C. Release build

    D. Release documentation

122. What type of hypervisor is most commonly used to host cloud IaaS services?

    A. Type 1

    B. Type 2

    C. Type 3

    D. Type 4

123. Sean's company has grown its IT infrastructure and no longer considers the converted closet that its servers have been hosted in sufficient to the organization's needs. If Sean wants to meet an Uptime Institute Level 3 rating, what option will most efficiently and effectively meet his needs?

    A. Buy a datacenter.

    B. Build a datacenter.

    C. Rent space in a datacenter facility.

    D. Build a datacenter in an existing building.

124. Which of the following is true of most cloud service providers datacenters?

    A. Access to inexpensive power is not a major driver in datacenter placement.

    B. Datacenters are placed without regard to weather-based threats.

    C. Customers are not allowed physical access to machines.

    D. Redundant design is not critical due to the number of datacenters.

125. Maria logs into her company's service portal and looks at a customer's information. In the credit card field she sees the credit card listed in a format that reads:

XXXX-XXXX-XXXX-1980

What type of data security technique is in use?

    A. Hashing

    B. Masking

    C. Randomization

    D. De-identification

Appendix

Answers to Review Questions

Chapter 1: Domain 1: Cloud Concepts, Architecture, and Design

1. B. The key to answering this question is recognizing that the multitenancy model involves many different customers accessing cloud resources hosted on shared hardware. That makes this a public cloud deployment, regardless of the fact that access to a particular server instance is limited to Matthew's company. In a private cloud deployment, only Matthew's company would have access to any resources hosted on the same physical hardware. This is not multitenancy. There is no indication that Matthew's organization is combining resources of public and private cloud computing, which would be a hybrid cloud, or that the resource use is limited to members of a particular group, which would be a community cloud.

2. A. Cryptographic erasure is a strong sanitization technique that involves encrypting the data with a strong encryption engine and then taking the keys generated in that process, encrypting them with a different encryption engine, and destroying the resulting keys of the second round of encryption. This technique is effective on both magnetic and solid-state drives. Degaussing and overwriting are not effective on SSDs. Physical destruction would effectively sanitize the media but would prevent Zeke from reusing the drives.

3. A. Containers do not provide easy portability because they are dependent upon the host operating system. Hypervisors are used to host virtual machines on a device, so that is another incorrect answer. Serverless computing is a platform as a service model that allows cloud customers to run their own code on the provider's platform without provisioning servers, so that is also incorrect. Virtual machines are self-contained and have their own internal operating system, so it is possible to move them between different host operating systems.

4. B. Under the cloud reference architecture, the activities of customers are to use cloud services, perform service trials, monitor services, administer service security, provide billing and usage reports, handle problem reports, administer tenancies, perform business administration, select and purchase service, and request audit reports. Preparing systems is one of the responsibilities of cloud service providers.

5. C. The reality is that Seth will likely achieve all of these goals, but the most relevant one is elasticity. Elasticity refers to the ability of a system to dynamically grow and shrink based on the current level of demand. Scalability refers to the ability of a system to grow as demand increases but does not require the ability to shrink.

6. B. The defining characteristic of zero-trust network architecture is that trust decisions are not based on network location, such as IP address. It is appropriate to use other characteristics, such as a user's identity, the nature of the requested access, and the user's geographic (not network!) location.

7. A. If a cloud provider is able to choose between types of hypervisors, the bare-metal (Type 1) hypervisor is preferable to the hypervisor that runs off the OS (Type 2) because it will offer less attack surface. Type 3 and 4 hypervisors do not exist.

8. D. Network security groups provide functionality equivalent to network firewalls for cloud-hosted server instances. They allow the restriction of traffic that may reach a server instance. Joe would not be able to modify the network firewall rules because those are only available to the cloud provider. Geofencing would restrict the geographic locations from which users may access the servers, which is not Joe's requirement. Traffic inspection may be used to examine the traffic reaching the instance but is not normally used to create port-based restrictions.

9. D. Object storage services are susceptible to disk failures and user error that may unintentionally destroy or modify data. They are also vulnerable to ransomware attacks that infect systems with access to the object store and then encrypt data stored on the service. They are unlikely to be affected by traditional viruses because they do not have a runtime environment.

10. B. Geofencing may be used to trigger actions, such as an alert, when a user or device leaves a defined geographic area. Firewalls and intrusion prevention systems may incorporate geographic information into their decision-making processes but would not provide the immediate notification that Vince desires. Geotagging simply annotates log records or other data with the geographic location of the user performing an action but does not directly provide alerting based on geographic location.

11. C. Cloud computing is a model for enabling ubiquitous, convenient, on-demand network access to a shared pool of configurable computing resources (e.g., networks, servers, storage, applications, and services) that can be rapidly provisioned and released with minimal management effort or service provider interaction. This definition does not include multitenancy, which is a characteristic of public cloud computing but not all cloud computing models.

12. A. The Cloud Security Alliance (CSA) provides an enterprise architecture reference guide that offers vendor-neutral design patterns for cloud security. Amazon Web Services (AWS) and Microsoft do provide cloud design patterns but they are specific to the service offerings of those vendors. (ISC)² does not provide cloud design patterns.

13. B. The use of an API is an example of accessing data programmatically during the Use phase of the lifecycle. If Lori were simply placing data into a cloud service or maintaining data there, that would be an example of the Store phase. Lori is not creating or destroying data; she is simply using the data that is already stored in the cloud service.

14. D. This is an example of block storage, storage that is available as disk volumes. Object storage maintains files in buckets. Virtualized servers are compute capabilities, not storage capabilities. Network capacity is used to connect servers to each other and the internet and is not used for the storage of data.

15. D. The sudo command allows a normal user account to execute administrative commands and is an example of privileged access, not standard user access. There is no indication in the scenario that Ben lacks proper authorization for this access. Service access is the access to resources by system services, rather than individual people.

16. D. The greatest risk when a device is lost or stolen is that sensitive data contained on the device will fall into the wrong hands. Confidentiality protects against this risk. Nonrepudiation is when the recipient of a message can prove the originator's identity to a third party. Authentication is a means of proving one's identity. Integrity demonstrates that information has not been modified since transmission.

17. B. Qualitative tools are often used in business impact assessment to capture the impact on intangible factors such as customer confidence, employee morale, and reputation. Quantitative tools, such as the computation of annualized loss expectancies and single loss expectancies, are only appropriate for easily quantifiable risks.

18. B. EAL2 assurance applies when the system has been structurally tested. It is the second-to-lowest level of assurance under the Common Criteria.

19. D. Orchestration tools are designed to manage workloads and seamlessly shift them between cloud service providers. Virtualization platforms allow a cloud provider to host virtual server instances, but they do not provide the ability to migrate workloads between different providers. Databases are a cloud service offering that allows for the organized storage of relational data. Cloud access service brokers (CASBs) allow for the consistent enforcement of security policies across cloud providers.

20. B. The Payment Card Industry Data Security Standard (PCI DSS) governs the storage, processing, and transmission of credit card information. The Health Insurance Portability and Accountability Act (HIPAA) governs protected health information. The Sarbanes–Oxley (SOX) Act regulates the financial reporting of publicly traded corporations. The Gramm–Leach–Bliley Act (GLBA) protects personal financial information.

21. C. Cloud governance programs try to bring all of an organization's cloud activities under more centralized control. They serve as a screening body helping to ensure that cloud services used by the organization meet technical, functional, and security requirements. They also provide a centralized point of monitoring for duplicative services, preventing different business units from spending money on similar services when consolidation would reduce both costs and the complexity of the operating environment. Cloud orchestration tools are designed to manage workloads and seamlessly shift them between cloud service providers. Cloud access service brokers (CASBs) allow for the consistent enforcement of security policies across cloud providers. Cloud migration is the transition from an on-premises environment to a cloud environment or between two cloud environments.

22. C. Asymmetric cryptosystems use a pair of keys for each user. In this case, with 1,000 users, the system will require 2,000 keys.

23. B. The use of multiple public cloud providers to achieve diversity is known as a multicloud strategy. That is the scenario that Erin is creating. Community clouds are shared cloud resources open to members of an affinity group. Private cloud resources are limited to the use of a single organization. Hybrid cloud strategies combine public and private cloud resources, not resources from multiple public cloud providers.

24. B. Email is an application-level service that is offered by cloud providers as a software as a service (SaaS) capability. Block storage and network capacity are infrastructure as a service

(IaaS) offerings and are infrastructure capabilities. Serverless computing is a platform as a service (PaaS) offering and is a platform capability.

25. A. Oversubscription means that cloud providers can sell customers a total capacity that exceeds the actual physical capacity of their infrastructure because, in the big picture, customers will never use all of that capacity simultaneously. Undersubscription would be when a cloud provider does not sell all of their available capacity and this would not require that users not access services simultaneously. Overprovisioning occurs when a customer (not a service provider) purchases more capacity than they need. Similarly, underprovisioning occurs when a customer does not purchase enough capacity to meet their needs.

26. D. The scenario describes a mix of public cloud and private cloud services. This is an example of a hybrid cloud environment.

27. D. In an infrastructure as a service environment, security duties follow a shared responsibility model. Since the vendor is responsible for managing the storage hardware, the vendor would retain responsibility for destroying or wiping drives as they are taken out of service. However, it is still the customer's responsibility to validate that the vendor's sanitization procedures meet their requirements prior to utilizing the vendor's storage services.

28. A. When Lucca reviews the recovery time objective (RTO) data, he needs to ensure that the organization can recover from an outage in less than two hours based on the maximum tolerable downtime (MTD) of two hours.

29. D. The recipient of a message that was encrypted using asymmetric cryptography always decrypts that message using their own private key. The sender of the message would have previously encrypted it using the recipient's public key. The sender's public and private keys are not used in this process.

30. B. Jen's organization is a cloud service partner—an organization that helps cloud service customers use the services offered by cloud service providers. In this case, Jen's clients are cloud service customers and they are moving to services offered by cloud service providers. Cloud service brokers are cloud service providers who offer a managed identity and access management service to cloud customers that integrates security requirements across cloud services.

31. D. This is a tricky question because all of these publications may have some relevance to Carla's work. NIST 800-53 provides general cybersecurity standards for federal agencies, whereas NIST 800-171 applies specifically to the use of controlled unclassified information (CUI). The Common Criteria (CC) provide a certification process for hardware and software products. However, the most relevant standards are FIPS 140-2, the Security Requirements for Cryptographic Modules. This guidance is specific to the cryptographic requirements of systems such as HSMs and would have the most directly relevant guidance.

32. A. The greatest risk in this situation is that the service offering will depend on features provided only by a single vendor, preventing Ryan's organization from moving to a different vendor and locking them into their current provider. Interoperability is the concern that services should be able to integrate and work well together. There is no indication that interoperability is at risk in this scenario. There is also no indication that the use of this vendor creates any special auditability or confidentiality concerns.

33. D. EAL7 is the highest level of assurance under the Common Criteria. It applies when a system has been formally verified, designed, and tested.

34. B. The blockchain is technology that uses cryptography to create a distributed immutable ledger. It is the technical foundation behind cryptocurrency and many other applications. Quantum computing is an emerging technology that uses principles of particle physics to perform computing. Edge computing moves compute power to Internet of Things (IoT) devices located at the "edge" of the network. Confidential computing is an area of research into methods for protecting data in use through the protection provided by a trusted execution environment (TEE).

35. C. The verification process is similar to the certification process in that it validates security controls. Verification may go a step further by involving a third-party testing service and compiling results that may be trusted by many different organizations. Accreditation is the act of management formally accepting an evaluating system, not evaluating the system itself.

36. C. One of the core capabilities of infrastructure as a service is providing servers on a vendor-managed virtualization platform. Web-based payroll and email systems are examples of software as a service. An application platform managed by a vendor that runs customer code is an example of platform as a service.

37. D. The brand associated with the cloud provider should not influence the cost–benefit analysis; the cloud provider's brand (and even which cloud provider an organization uses) will most likely not even be known to the consumers who have a business relationship with the organization.

    The provider does not absorb the cost when the customer requests a modification of the SLA. Though an even split of the cost between customer and provider may seem fair, the customer pays for all costs associated with modifications to the SLA by the customer. Finally, customer modifications to their SLA are chargeable expenses that will almost certainly be paid for by the customer.

38. C. Ephemeral computing means that you can create computing resources, such as servers and storage spaces, to solve a particular problem and then get rid of them as soon as you no longer need them. There is no indication in the scenario that Barry will be using confidential computing, quantum computing, or parallel processing.

39. A. This type of provision is best described as an availability commitment because the service provider is guaranteeing that the service will be available 99.9% of the time. It could also be described as a security provision because availability is a subset of security, but availability is a more specific term and, therefore, a better answer. Resiliency is the ability of a system to withstand failures and, while related to availability, is not what is guaranteed in this agreement. There is no discussion of privacy-related concerns.

40. C. Users have the most control over environments hosted on an IaaS platform because they are able to manually adjust the resources assigned to the application. Users do not have this configurability in the SaaS, FaaS, or PaaS environment.

41. C. ISO 27017 provides guidance on the security controls that should be implemented by cloud service providers and would be useful to Gavin in evaluating such a provider. ISO 27001 is a general description of controls appropriate for a cybersecurity program, whereas ISO 27701 provides control guidance for privacy programs. ISO 17789 provides a cloud reference architecture and does not offer specific security guidance.

42. D. The Payment Card Industry Data Security Standard (PCI DSS) is overseen by the Payment Card Industry Security Standards Council (PCI SSC). This is not the responsibility of the Securities and Exchange Commission (SEC), the Food and Drug Administration (FDA), or the Federal Trade Commission (FTC).

43. B. Cloud computing systems where the customer only provides application code for execution on a vendor-supplied computing platform are examples of platform as a service (PaaS) computing. Software as a service (SaaS) offerings provide a fully functional application to customers as a cloud service. Infrastructure as a service (IaaS) offerings provide basic infrastructure building blocks to customers. CaaS is a subcategory of IaaS for computing resources provided as a service.

44. C. In a risk acceptance strategy, the organization chooses to take no action other than documenting the risk. Purchasing insurance would be an example of risk transference. Relocating the datacenter would be risk avoidance. Reengineering the facility is an example of a risk mitigation strategy.

45. D. Predictive analytics seek to use our existing data to predict future events. In this case, Matthew is seeking to predict the likelihood that a customer will place an order, so he is performing predictive analytics. Descriptive analytics simply seeks to describe our data. Prescriptive analytics seek to optimize our behavior by simulating many scenarios. Neither prescriptive nor descriptive analytics are being used in this scenario. Optimal analytics is not a class of analytics techniques.

46. B. Resource pooling is the characteristic that allows the cloud provider to meet various demands from customers while remaining financially viable. The cloud provider can make capital investments that greatly exceed what any single customer could provide on their own and can apportion these resources as needed so that the resources are not underutilized (which would mean a wasteful investment) or overtaxed (which would mean a decrease in level of service). Elasticity and scalability allows the customer to grow or shrink the IT footprint (number of users, number of machines, size of storage, and so on) as necessary to meet operational needs without excess capacity. On-demand self-service refers to the model that allows customers to scale their compute and/or storage needs with little or no intervention from or prior communication with the provider.

47. A. The risk assessment team should pay the most immediate attention to those risks that appear in quadrant I. These are the risks with a high probability of occurring and a high impact on the organization if they do occur.

48. A. The service-level agreement (SLA) is between a service provider and a customer and documents in a formal manner expectations for availability, performance, and other parameters. An MOU may cover the same items but is not as formal a document. An OLA is between internal service organizations and does not involve customers. An SOW is an addendum to a contract describing work to be performed.

49. A. Bianca's concern in this situation is reversibility—the ability to back out the change if it does not go well. Portability is the capability to move workloads easily between environments but would only apply after the services are up and running. Similarly, resiliency is the ability of an environment to withstand disruptions and is not a primary concern in the middle of a migration. There are no regulatory concerns raised in this scenario.

50. B. The FBI does not produce cloud security guidance documents. The SANS Institute, Cloud Security Alliance, and vendors such as Microsoft all produce cloud security guidance documents.

51. D. Measured service means that almost everything you do in the cloud is metered. Cloud providers measure the number of seconds you use a virtual server, the amount of disk space you consume, the number of function calls you make, and many other measures. This allows them to charge you for precisely the services you use—no more and no less. Elasticity and scalability allows the customer to grow or shrink the IT footprint (number of users, number of machines, size of storage, and so on) as necessary to meet operational needs without excess capacity. On-demand self-service refers to the model that allows customers to scale their compute and/or storage needs with little or no intervention from or prior communication with the provider.

52. D. Operating systems do exist in PaaS environments where they are maintained by the service provider. The customer has no access to or ability to maintain the operating system in a PaaS environment.

53. A. Organizations moving from an on-premises datacenter to the cloud should expect to see a reduction in utility expenses due to the reduction in on-site equipment. Software licensing fees are unlikely to change. Security expenses may increase or decrease depending on the nature of the transition. There is no reason to believe that executive compensation will change.

54. B. Block storage is used to provide disk volumes and is the appropriate choice in this situation. Object storage is used to store individual files but cannot be mounted as a disk. There is no indication that Devon needs to use a database in this scenario. Archival storage should only be used in cases where data does not need to be frequently accessed and is not appropriate for a disk attached to a server instance.

55. C. The first thing Casey should do is notify her management, but after that, replacing the certificate and using proper key management practices with the new certificate's key should be at the top of her list.

56. D. The checklist review is the least disruptive type of disaster recovery test. During a checklist review, team members each review the contents of their disaster recovery checklists on their own and suggest any necessary changes. During a tabletop exercise, team members come together and walk through a scenario without making any changes to information systems. During a parallel test, the team actually activates the disaster recovery site for testing but the primary site remains operational. During a full interruption test, the team takes down the primary site and confirms that the disaster recovery site is capable of handling regular operations. The full interruption test is the most thorough test but also the most disruptive.

57. D. In a software as a service solution, the vendor manages both the physical infrastructure and the complete application stack, providing the customer with access to a fully managed application. Infrastructure as a service (IaaS) offerings provide customers with basic technology building blocks. Platform as a service (PaaS) offerings provide customers with an environment where they can execute their own code. CaaS is a subcategory of IaaS for computing resources provided as a service.

58. C. Security baselines provide a starting point to scope and tailor security controls to your organization's needs. They aren't always appropriate to specific organizational needs, they cannot ensure that systems are always in a secure state, and they do not prevent liability.

59. C. The DevOps approach to technology management seeks to integrate software development, operations, and quality assurance in a seamless approach that builds collaboration between the three disciplines. Agile is a development methodology often used in DevOps environments. Lean is a process improvement strategy. The IT Infrastructure Library (ITIL) is a collection of best practices for managing IT organizations.

60. B. In all likelihood, the vendor will immediately deny this request because customers should not have access to underlying infrastructure in a PaaS environment. If Stacey truly needs this access, she should consider an IaaS offering instead of a PaaS offering.

61. D. Installing a device that will block attacks is an attempt to lower risk by reducing the likelihood of a successful application attack. Controls that lower the impact of a risk attempt to reduce the amount of damage caused when a risk materializes. The recovery point objective (RPO) addresses the amount of data loss that is acceptable due to an incident. The maximum tolerable outage (MTO) is the amount of downtime that the business can safely withstand.

62. A. OpenID Connect is an authentication layer that works with OAuth 2.0 as its underlying authorization framework. It has been widely adopted by cloud service providers and is widely supported. SAML, RADIUS, and Kerberos are alternative authentication technologies but do not have the same level of seamless integration with OAuth.

63. B. The most appropriate standard to use as a baseline when evaluating vendors is to determine whether the vendor's security controls meet the organization's own standards. Compliance with laws and regulations should be included in that requirement and are a necessary, but not sufficient, condition for working with the vendor. Vendor compliance with their own policies also fits into the category of necessary, but not sufficient, controls, as the vendor's policy may be weaker than the organization's own requirements. The elimination of all identified security risks is an impossible requirement for a potential vendor to meet.

64. A. This is an example of a vendor offering a fully functional application as a web-based service. Therefore, it fits under the definition of software as a service (SaaS). In infrastructure as a service (IaaS), compute as a service (CaaS), and platform as a service (PaaS) approaches, the customer provides their own software. In this example, the vendor is providing the email software, so none of those choices is appropriate.

65. B. In this case, most cloud service models (including IaaS, SaaS, and serverless/FaaS) would require transmitting most information back to the cloud. The edge computing service model would be far more appropriate, as it places computing power at the sensor, minimizing the data that must be sent back to the cloud over limited connectivity network links.

66. C. Security Assertion Markup Language (SAML) is the best choice for providing authentication and authorization information, particularly for browser-based SSO. HTML is primarily used for web pages, SPML is used to exchange user information for SSO, and XACML is used for access control policy markup.

67. A. In an IaaS server environment, the customer retains responsibility for most server security operations under the shared responsibility model. This includes managing OS security settings, maintaining host firewalls, and configuring server access control. The vendor would be responsible for all security mechanisms at the hypervisor layer and below.

68. C. This is an example of providing a fully developed and hosted application to a customer, so it is an example of software as a service (SaaS) computing. In a platform as a service (PaaS) offering, the customer provides application code for execution on a vendor-supplied computing platform. Infrastructure as a service (IaaS) offerings provide basic infrastructure building blocks to customers. Function as a service (FaaS) offerings are a subcategory of PaaS for serverless computing applications.

69. C. The DevOps and DevSecOps philosophies are closely linked to the Agile method of software development. The waterfall, modified waterfall, and spiral models are more traditional approaches that are not commonly used with DevOps and DevSecOps.

70. C. Cloud access security brokers (CASBs) are designed to enforce security policies consistently across cloud services and would best meet Bailey's needs. Data loss prevention (DLP) and digital rights management (DRM) solutions may be able to detect, block, and control some use of information in the cloud, but they would not provide a way to consistently enforce security policies across cloud platforms. Intrusion prevention systems (IPSs) are designed to detect and block malicious activity and would not be relevant in this scenario.

71. C. In an infrastructure as a service environment, the vendor is responsible for hardware- and network-related responsibilities. These include configuring network firewalls, maintaining the hypervisor, and managing physical equipment. The customer retains responsibility for patching operating systems on its virtual machine instances.

72. A. In the public cloud computing model, the vendor builds a single platform that is shared among many different customers. This is also known as the multitenancy model.

73. C. A cloud IaaS vendor will allow Kristen to set up infrastructure as quickly as she can deploy and pay for it. A PaaS vendor provides a platform that would require her to migrate her custom application to it, likely taking longer than a hosted datacenter provider. A datacenter vendor that provides rack, power, and remote hands assistance fails the test based on Kristen's desire to not have to acquire or ship hardware.

74. B. IaaS networking is generally configurable by the end customer through the use of network security groups, bandwidth provisioning, and similar mechanisms. Security groups are the equivalent of firewall rules for IaaS networking. PaaS and SaaS networking are managed by the cloud service provider. Customers may connect to cloud service provider networks using a VPN.

75. D. In a serverless computing model, the vendor does not expose details of the operating system to its customers. Therefore, the vendor retains full responsibility for configuring it securely under the shared responsibility model of cloud computing.

76. C. ISO 27001 is an international standard for the creation of an information security management system (ISMS). NIST SP 800-37 is the Risk Management Framework created by the U.S. government for assessing the security of systems. NIST SP 800-53 is the list of security controls approved for use by U.S. government agencies and a means to map them to the Risk Management Framework. The Payment Card Industry Data Security Standard (PCI DSS) is the payment card industry's framework of compliance for all entities accepting or processing credit card payments.

77. A. This is the definition of cloud migration interoperability challenges. Portability is the measure of how difficult it might be to move the organization's systems/data from a given cloud host to another cloud host. Stability has no specific meaning here and is just a distractor. Security might be an element of this challenge but is not the optimum answer; the question posed a concern about functionality, not disclosure or tainting the information.

78. D. Mike's concern in this situation is portability—the capability to move workloads easily between environments. Reversibility is the ability to back out the change if it does not go well. Resiliency is the ability of an environment to withstand disruptions and is not a primary concern in the middle of a migration. There are no regulatory concerns raised in this scenario.

79. C. Elasticity refers to the ability of a system to dynamically grow and shrink based on the current level of demand. Scalability refers to the ability of a system to grow as demand increases but does not require the ability to shrink. Services that are elastic must also be scalable, but services that are scalable are not necessarily elastic.

80. D. In an IaaS configuration, the customer still has to maintain the OS, so option D is the only answer that is not a direct benefit for the cloud customer.

81. B. Encryption consumes processing power and time; as with all security controls, additional security means measurably less operational capability—there is always a trade-off between security and productivity. Option A is gibberish and only a distractor. Option C is incorrect because vendor lockout does not result from encryption; it is what might happen if the cloud provider goes out of business while holding your data. Data subjects are the individuals whose personally identifiable information (PII) an organization holds; usually, they will not know or care if something is encrypted (unless there is a breach of that PII, and then investigators will want to determine how that PII was protected) and would probably welcome total encryption, even though that might mean a decrease in operational capability.

82. A. Due care is the minimal level of effort necessary to perform your duty to others; in cloud security, that is often the care that the cloud customer is required to demonstrate in order to protect the data it owns. Due diligence is any activity taken in support or furtherance of due care. This answer, then, is optimum: the due care is set out by the policy, and activities that support the policy (here, auditing the controls the policy requires) are a demonstration of due diligence.

The General Data Protection Regulation (GDPR) and GLBA are both legislative mandates; these might dictate a standard of due care, but they are not the due care or due diligence, specifically.

Door locks and turnstiles are physical security controls; they both might be examples of due care efforts, but neither demonstrates due diligence.

Due care and diligence can be demonstrated by either internal or external controls/processes; there is no distinction to be made based on where the control is situated.

83. A. Confidential computing protects data in use by using a trusted execution environment (TEE). Confidential computing environments may also make use of other security technologies, including trusted platform modules (TPMs), hardware security modules (HSMs), and public key infrastructure (PKI), but those technologies do not protect data in use and are not, therefore, required for a confidential computing environment.

84. C. The Common Criteria provide a general certification process for computing hardware that might be used in government applications. FIPS 140-2 provides similar guidance but is specific to cryptographic modules and is not used for generalized hardware. NIST 800-53 provides security control guidance but is not a certification process. FedRAMP provides a certification process for cloud computing services but not for hardware.

85. B. The distinguished name (DN) is the nomenclature for all entries in an LDAP environment.

A domain name is used to identify one or more IP addresses. For instance, Microsoft.com and google.com are domain names. Option A is incorrect.

A directory name is typically associated with a filesystem structure and not something related to LDAP. Option C is incorrect.

"Default Name" is not a common term and is made up. Option D is not the correct answer.

86. C. Databases are used to store information that is collected into related tables. Storage could also be used for this purpose, but it does not provide the table structure of a database, so it would not be the best solution. Networking and virtualization technologies are not used to store data.

87. B. Confidential computing is an emerging technology designed to support the protection of data that is actively stored in memory.

88. D. The cloud customer is ultimately responsible for all legal repercussions involving data security and privacy; the cloud provider might be liable for financial costs related to these responsibilities, but those damages can only be recovered long after the notifications have been made by the cloud customer.

All the other options are incorrect because they do not correctly identify who is required to make data breach notifications in accordance with all applicable laws. That responsibility rests with the cloud customer.

89. D. An IaaS service model allows an organization to retain the most control of their IT assets in the cloud; the cloud customer is responsible for the operating system, the applications, and the data in the cloud. The private cloud model allows the organization to retain the greatest degree of governance control in the cloud; all the other deployment models would necessitate giving up governance control in an environment with pooled resources.

90. D. Henry's biggest concern should be the long-term security and supportability of the IoT devices. As these devices are increasingly embedded in buildings and infrastructure, it is important to understand the support model and the security model. Both the lack of separate administrative access and the lack of strong encryption can be addressed by placing the IoT devices on a dedicated subnet or network that prevents other users from accessing the devices directly. This will help limit the risk without undue expense or complexity and is a common practice. Finally, lack of storage space can be a concern, but it is not the most important when looking at the risks IoT devices can create.

91. B. In the private cloud computing model, the cloud computing environment is dedicated to a single organization and does not follow the shared tenancy model. The environment may be built by the company in its own datacenter or built by a vendor at a colocation site. Public cloud computing makes use of vendor datacenters. Hybrid cloud computing combines the use of public and private cloud resources. Shared cloud computing is not a cloud service model.

92. A. Hypervisors enforce isolation between virtual machines and are, therefore, most susceptible to escape attacks. Hardware security modules and trusted platform modules store and manage cryptographic keys and are not vulnerable to escape attacks. Databases may be hosted on a virtual platform that is vulnerable to an escape attack, but the database itself is not vulnerable to that attack.

93. A. Traffic inspection technology would allow Steve to examine the contents of encrypted HTTPS traffic and detect sensitive information. Port blocking may be used to stop HTTPS traffic entirely, but that would not detect a security violation. Patching and geofencing technologies would play no role in this scenario.

94. B. Hot sites, cold sites, and warm sites all require a significant investment in physical facilities. Hot sites and warm sites also require investments in hardware and/or software. Using the cloud provides a way to minimize costs by configuring but not activating resources until they are actually needed.

95. A. Authentication is verifying that the user is who they claim to be and assigning them an identity assertion (usually a user ID) based on that identity.

Authorization is granting access based on permissions allocated to a particular user/valid identity assertion.

Nonrepudiation is the security concept of not allowing a participant in a transaction to deny that they participated.

Regression is a statistical concept not relevant to the question in any way.

96. A. Software as a service (SaaS) models place the primary burden of security (and other administration) on the service provider. Platform as a service (PaaS) and infrastructure as a service (IaaS) shift some responsibility from the provider to the customer under the shared responsibility model. Function as a service (FaaS) is a subcategory of PaaS.

97. A. In a symmetric encryption algorithm, all data is encrypted and decrypted with the same shared secret key. This key is the only key required for the communication.

98. C. When an individual receives a copy of a digital certificate, the person verifies the authenticity of that certificate by using the CA's public key to validate the digital signature contained on the certificate.

99. C. Quantum computing uses advanced particle physics to perform computing tasks in a revolutionary manner that might render modern encryption algorithms insecure. Ephemeral computing refers to the use of computing assets on a temporary basis. Confidential computing uses trusted execution environments (TEE) to protect data in use. Parallel computing uses multiple processors to perform different parts of a calculation simultaneously.

100. C. Technically, BC efforts are meant to ensure that critical business functions can continue during a disruptive event, and DR efforts are supposed to support the return to normal operations. However, in practice, the efforts often coincide, use the same plans/personnel, and have many of the same procedures.

Option A is incorrect; both BC and DR use the RTO and RPO as metrics to determine success.

Option B is incorrect; BC and DR efforts are not specific to the cause of a disruptive event.

Option D is incorrect; health and human safety should be paramount in all security efforts, with very few exceptions.

Chapter 2: Domain 2: Architecture and Design

1. D. Emails and other freeform text are examples of unstructured data. Structured data like the data found in databases is carefully defined, whereas semi-structured data like XML and JSON applies structure without being tightly controlled. While email itself is defined by an RFC, the term RFC-defined data is not used in this context.

2. A. Data labeling typically occurs during the Creation phase of the data lifecycle. Data labels may also be changed or added during use as data is modified.

3. B. Jacinda is likely to face challenges using her DLP system due to the broad and consistent use of encryption for data in transit or data in motion in cloud environments. She will need to take particular care to design and architect her environment to allow the DLP system to have access to the traffic it needs. Data labeling can be a challenge, if it is lacking or if it isn't done properly, but DLP systems can use pattern matching and other techniques to identify data. Data at rest is typically not as much of a concern for a DLP system since preventing loss requires understanding when data is going somewhere, not when it is remaining in a location.

4. C. Passwords are intentionally not captured or logged since creating an audit log that contains passwords would be a significant security issue. The source and destination IP address as well as the account used for privileged access are all common log data that can help when events need to be audited.

5. A. Cryptographic erasure, or crypto-shredding, is the only way to ensure that drives and volumes hosted by third parties are securely cleared. Zero-wiping may result in remnant data, particularly where drives are dynamically allocated space in a hosted environment. Degaussing or other physical destruction is typically not possible with third-party-hosted systems without a special contract and dedicated hardware.

6. D. Legal holds require organizations to identify and preserve data that meets the hold's scope. Jason should identify the files and preserve them until they are required. Restoring files might erase important data, deleting files is completely contrary to the concept of the hold, and holds do not require immediate production—they are just what they sound like, a requirement to hold the data.

7. B. Masking data involves replacing data with alternate characters like X or *. This is typically done via controls in the software or database itself, as the underlying data remains intact in the database. Anonymization or deidentification removes data that might allow individuals to be identified. Hashing is used to allow data to be referenced by a hash without displaying the actual data, but it causes properties of the data that may be needed for testing to be lost. Randomization or shuffling data moves it around, disassociating the data but leaving real data in place to be tested.

8. C. XML and JSON are both examples of semi-structured data. Other examples include CSV files, XML, NoSQL databases, and HTML files.

9. B. The provider's own logging function is the best option. Information about systems being created and destroyed won't exist on the local systems, and thus syslog, syslog-ng, and local logs won't work. In addition, Linux typically doesn't have an application log—both event and application logs are common for Windows systems.

10. A. Original source IP addresses may not be visible in the local web server log. Fortunately, load-balancer logs can be used if they are available. The destination IP address will typically remain, as well as the destination port and the actual query.

11. A. Hashing converts variable length data to fixed-length outputs, meaning that the length, formatting, and the ability to perform operations on the data using strings or numbers will be lost. Its ability to be uniquely identified won't be lost—Isaac just needs to know the hash of a given address to continue to reference that data element.

12. B. Data dispersion is the practice of ensuring that important data is stored in more than one location or service. It does not necessarily require specific distances or geographic limits, doesn't require deletion of data not in secure storage, and doesn't require you to use multiple data sets to access data.

13. B. Storage that is associated with an instance that will be destroyed when the instance is shut down is ephemeral storage. Raw storage is storage that you have direct access to like a hard drive, or an SSD that has access to the underlying device. Long-term storage is storage that is intended to continue to exist, and is often used for logs or data storage. Volume-based storage is storage allocated as a virtual drive or device within the cloud.

14. A. The size of the data or files is not typically a data classification type or field. Sensitivity, jurisdiction, and criticality are all commonly used to classify data.

15. A. Data labels can help DLP systems identify and manage data, so Chris should ensure that data is labeled as part of its creation process to help his DLP identify and protect it. Classification is important, but without tags it won't be useful to the DLP. Hashing can be used to help a DLP identify specific files, but tends to be done by the DLP system itself if needed, and geolocation tagging is not a typical DLP protection.

16. D. Chain of custody documentation, often including actions like hashing files to ensure they are not changed from their original form, is commonly done to support nonrepudiation. Digitally signing files and data dispersion won't prevent copying and does not encrypt them.

17. C. Ephemeral storage will have the performance of its overall storage type, so low performance isn't an expected issue. Inadvertent exposure, malicious access, and loss of forensic artifacts are all concerns for ephemeral storage.

18. B. Raw storage provides direct access to a disk, and without crypto-shredding is likely to have remnant data on the disk after it is used. Since long-term and ephemeral storage is typically abstracted, it is less likely to have remnant data in unallocated or reallocated sectors that would not be purged through typical wipe operations.

19. A. Unstructured data is the most difficult to perform discovery against because the data is unlabeled and requires discovery to be done using searches or other techniques that can handle arbitrary data. Rigidly structured data is not a common description of a type of data for the purposes of the CCSP exam.

20. C. While it isn't always perfectly accurate, geolocation (sometimes called geoIP) data attempts to identify the location of a given IP address. Isaac can use that data to attempt to match authentication events to logins, although VPNs and other tools may obscure the actual login location for users.

21. B. While there may be some concerns about real data being used, Charleen's goal is to have actual data for testing, making shuffling her best option. Hashing, randomization, and masking all remove or modify data in meaningful ways, resulting in testing not being as accurate as it might be against real-world data.

22. D. Michelle should be aware that logging deletion events, like any other high-volume event, may incur additional costs for her organization. Since the question specifically mentions ephemeral files and heavy usage, this may be a more significant concern for her organization. Logs will show the relevant information, and there is nothing to indicate they would not be accurate, logging is enabled or disabled by the account holder or owner, and creation and deletion event logging is supported by object-based filesystems.

23. B. Data's confidentiality level is often contained in a label, but the monetary value is not a common data label. Creation and scheduled destruction date are also common data labels.

24. B. Retention policies often include language that addresses legal holds because holds can impact retention practices and requirements. Data classification, acceptable use, and data breach response policies typically do not include legal hold language.

25. A. Keys should never be stored in plaintext format and should instead be stored in a secure manner—typically encrypted in a hardware security module or other key vault.

26. C. While IRMs are useful through many of the phases of the cloud data lifecycle, Marco knows that sharing data is when an IRM is most heavily used to ensure that data is not inadvertently exposed or misused.

27. B. JSON is an example of semi-structured data. Other examples include CSV files, XML, NoSQL databases, and HTML files.

28. A. Cloud archival storage is typically designed primarily as a storage location with infrequent and smaller scale access, not for large-scale interactive access like a discovery process will use. It is likely to be a slow and potentially costly effort if the data is scanned while in the archival location. Charleen should validate if scanning the archived data makes sense, or if moving it to a different storage tier may fit the organization's needs better. The data should exist as archival storage is used to preserve data; archival storage is online but may be slow; and no mention of encryption was made, so we cannot assume that it was encrypted.

29. B. Data mapping is the process of matching fields in databases to allow them to be integrated or for purposes such as data migration.

30. C. Adding labels as part of the file's metadata is a common practice and is less likely to be changed than including them in the filename. Modifying the files themselves with data at the beginning or end of the file can cause issues with processing that may not be prepared to handle labeled data.

31. D. Key escrow and backup is incredibly important, and once a key is lost, it cannot be recovered and the data should be considered lost. Generating new keys will not decrypt the data, the passphrase isn't sufficient to recover keys, and hashing is not a form of encryption and cannot be reversed.

32. D. Madani knows that structured data is well-defined and organized, and will be the easiest to perform discovery actions on. It isn't possible to perform discovery against encrypted data unless it is decrypted for the discovery process. Unstructured data is harder than semi-structured data discovery in most cases.

33. A. Ashley is documenting the chain of custody for the image to ensure it can be used in court. Repudiation might occur if the chain of custody was not properly documented. A legal hold does not necessarily require chain of custody documentation, although organizations may choose to or be required to ensure it. Forensic accounting is a term used to describe financial investigations.

34. D. Data mapping is a term used to describe matching fields in databases to allow data migration or integration. Data classification policies do identify classification levels, assign responsibilities, and define roles.

35. B. Labeling data at creation ensures that it can be properly handled through the rest of its lifecycle. Automated labeling is preferable where possible to avoid human error and to accommodate the volume of data that most organizations create.

36. A. Anonymizing access using a key removes the ability to provide accountability and works against organizational best practices. Identifying the key, the user, and when and how it is used supports accountability for usage.

37. B. Crypto-shredding is the only viable option in environments controlled or managed by a third-party organization in most circumstances. Physical destruction is not permitted or supported by third-party providers, nor is degaussing, which will also not work on many modern drives. Overwriting may be appealing, but remnant data is an issue with SSDs and volumes that are dynamically allocated.

38. B. Tokenization relies on two distinct databases, one with actual data and one with tokenized data. Token servers then pull the data the token represents from the real data database when needed. This process does not require encryption, specify FIPS 140 requirements, or involve deidentification practices.

39. A. With the source database ready and a tokenization database prepared to be populated, the next step is to identify which data should be tokenized. Not all data is sensitive, and thus not all data needs to be tokenized. Once you know what data will be tokenized, you can tokenize it—sometimes by hashing the data. Randomization is not part of this process.

40. C. Dataflow diagrams are a critical part of organizational understanding of how data is created, moves, and is used throughout an organization. They often include details like ports, protocols, data elements and classification, and other details that can help you understand not only where data is, but how it gets there and what data is in use.

41. A. Annie should map the data between the database fields and then use the mappings to help her sort and manage data as needed. Data labeling is used to tag data with important information like classification, creation date or time, or other elements. Column consolidation and columnar aggregation were made up for this question.

42. D. Data lifespan is not a typical entry in a dataflow diagram since they focus on flows, not policies. Data types, fields or names, services, systems, ports, protocols, and security details are all commonly included in dataflow diagrams.

43. C. Encrypting the drive or volume at creation ensures that any data written to the drive or volume through its lifespan will be encrypted and that destruction of the encryption key will result in secure destruction of the data.

44. C. Unstructured data does not have the structure required to be easily stored in a database. Semi-structured and structured data is easier to store in a relational database since it has descriptors and elements that make it easier to map into fields.

45. A. Retention policies often include retention periods, regulatory and compliance requirements, data classification impacts on retention, how and when data should be deleted, and archiving and retrieval processes. In addition, Olivia may want to include monitoring, maintenance, and enforcement.

46. C. An IRM needs to maintain a certificate revocation list that allows users and applications to validate certificates, just like any other service that uses certificates. That means that Hui should be able to check to see if the revoked certificate is in the list to validate her actions. Issuing a new certificate using the same information, accessing the data using her own certificate, or deleting the private keys will not invalidate the existing certificate.

47. D. The provisioning capability of IRM systems focuses on providing rights to individuals based on roles and job functions. Tagging and data labeling are used to ensure that data is handled appropriately based on rules. Encryption secures data at rest and in transit.

48. A. Business impact analysis helps to determine what data is needed to continue the operations of the business. This is an assessment of the criticality of the data, and Randy knows that the data he flags may be necessary in the event of a disaster or other business continuity issue.

49. C. Susan should prepare a dataflow diagram to share with her application developers and cloud architects to make sure that the application and service environment is correctly documented. Data mapping matches fields in databases, business impact analysis work assesses the importance of data to an organization's work, and data classification describes data based on things like sensitivity, jurisdiction, or criticality.

50. C. The most common risk, and thus the most impactful risk in this list, is the potential for a provider outage to result in the inability to access dispersed data.

51. B. Installation of a local agent is typically required by IRM systems to ensure data is properly handled on endpoint systems. The question doesn't specify the use of a server either in the cloud or locally, and the endpoints mentioned are not cloud-based.

52. A. Unstructured data includes data like images, audio, video, word processing files, and other data that does not have a formally defined structure like structured data does. There's no information that indicates that this is sensitive information, and there isn't any mention of labeling in the question.

53. B. Ingress and egress fees are often some of the highest expenses involved in this effort. Since the data is already contained in a storage tier, no new expenses should arise. Logs are text-based and can be stored efficiently, so it is unlikely that log files will be a major cost driver.

54. C. Amanda knows that the original drive should be preserved, and actions should only be taken on a forensic copy. Working with the original, regardless of the process, is not a forensic best practice.

55. A. While IRM systems can control actions on the system, taking a photo (or even a screenshot) of displayed text is typically outside of their capabilities. Preventing copying, printing, and making copies are all common IRM features.

56. B. Regulatory compliance is important for organizations, and Felix needs to point out that discovery across multiple countries and regions may involve a complex set of regulations to comply with. Costs may vary in different regions, but that is not the primary concern Felix needs to raise. There isn't any mention in the question of whether data is structured or not, and while encryption import and export may be covered by law, discovery can be conducted using local tools in each region if necessary.

57. B. Archiving data to a lower-cost, and typically lower-performance storage tier, is a common strategy for cloud data retention. Examples like Amazon's Glacier allow for long-term storage with infrequent or slow access and may come with additional costs for retrieval, but optimize costs when data is unlikely to be accessed. Deleting the data does not allow it to be used, moving to a third-party service provider is more complex, and moving to a higher-performance storage tier does not meet his cost needs.

58. B. The Use phase of the data lifecycle often includes modification of data, and thus will require labels to change or be added.

59. D. TLS, or Transport Layer Security, is the encryption protocol of choice for web application traffic. It replaced SSL. Both MD5 and SHA-1 are hashing algorithms, not encryption.

60. A. Data dispersion best fits this description, and bit splitting is a form of data dispersion, although it is one that is more frequently associated with malicious use to avoid forensic analysis and investigations.

61. C. Legal holds normally take precedence over other deletion requirements. While Gurleen should check with her organization's legal counsel, in general she should continue to preserve the data.

62. D. Ephemeral storage that is associated with instances in most cloud provider's infrastructure is wiped and reclaimed for reallocation when instances are terminated. If the instance were merely shut down, the storage would be retained for when the system was reactivated.

63. A. Ephemeral data is often kept for shorter time periods like 45 days, a time period sufficient to allow investigations without building up large volumes of data that will not be used and which can be expensive to store. Longer-term storage may be required by law or contracts or due to specific contractual requirements.

64. A. While it may seem quite simple, securely erasing all copies of the encryption key is all that it takes to complete the destruction process for crypto-shredding.

65. A. Service outages are the only direct threat to availability on this list. Lincoln should review the service provider's history of service outages and issues as he makes decisions about adopting the service.

66. D. Information rights management systems typically rely on certificates to identify systems. They can be issued centrally and managed, as well as used for digital signatures and encryption.

67. C. Derek's organization is using hashing, which uses a one-way cryptographic function to replace data with values that can be referenced without exposing the actual data. Anonymization focuses on removing data that can be associated with specific users or individuals, masking uses alternate characters to conceal data, and shuffling switches data around while retaining actual data for testing.

68. A. Long-term storage is storage that is intended to continue to exist and is often used for logs or data storage. Storage that is associated with an instance that will be destroyed when the instance is shut down is ephemeral storage. Raw storage is storage that you have direct access to like a hard drive or an SSD that has access to the underlying device. Volume-based storage is storage allocated as a virtual drive or device within the cloud.

69. C. OWASPs Secrets Management Cheatsheet describes three main requirements for "break-glass" secrets backup environments: ensuring automated backups are in place and executed regularly based on the number of secrets and their lifecycle, frequently testing the restore procedures, and encrypting backups and placing them on secure, monitored storage.

70. B. Using standard test secrets makes them easier to detect if they are in an exposed location. Since Alaina specifically has an internal test environment, this is the right location to use standard secrets. Secrets managers should be used in all locations, but they won't help with identifying issues with secrets exposure. Multiple utilities may be tempting, but they add overhead and additional work where a properly configured and tested utility will provide sufficient detection in most cases. High entropy secrets are useful, but secrets with a known and consistent format can more easily be detected and thus problems with exposure can be detected.

71. D. Retrieval time, the amount of time before data can be accessed, is a primary driver for the cost of archival storage in cloud environments. The size of the data in the question is fixed, so Angie needs to figure out what other options she can control. The type and sensitivity of the data do not impact costs but may impact practices that Angie will put in place to secure and manage it.

72. D. The figure shows a data mapping process between two database tables matching names, phone numbers, and email addresses. String comparison compares two strings to determine if they are the same. Field hashing and table matching were made up for this question.

73. B. Provisioning for IRM systems gives users the rights and permissions that they need to access files they have rights to. Tagging and labeling help to mark files based on data classification guidelines, allowing the IRM to apply rules appropriately, and data mapping maps fields in databases to each other.

74. B. Data access patterns are one of the most important things to understand before selecting archival storage. Archival storage classes and services often focus on inexpensive, low frequency, slow access, but other options can include more dynamic access capabilities—often at a higher cost since the storage needs to be capable of higher performance. The cost of the storage is just that—cost, not performance. The volume of the data, and the amount of time that the data will be stored for, also influence cost, not performance.

75. B. Data owners are defined by data classification policies and hold overall responsibility for data that they own. Data custodians are responsible for the data, ensuring access control, proper storage, and other operational controls. Data processors are often third parties who process the data as part of a business process, and data users are end users who use the data for their job.

76. C. Tokenized data is only a concern if the database with original data that it references is also exposed. Tokens are not encrypted, and while hashing is used in many tokenization processes, hashes are a one-way function and should have additional transformations performed to ensure that simply hashing data to get matches will not succeed.

77. A. Versioning tools like those found in Amazon's S3 environment allow you to revert to a previous version if an inadvertent change occurs, if data is corrupted, or if the file is deleted. This can take up significant amounts of additional space in some circumstances, so Asha should carefully consider where and when she enables versioning in her cloud environment. Daily backups, recurring snapshots, or archiving processes will take longer to restore from in most cases and may allow for multiple changes before backup, snapshot, or archiving occurs.

78. C. The concept of least privilege is used for secrets too, and maximizing the number of rights a secret provides instead of minimizing it is a bad idea. Brian should instead seek to limit the rights a given secret provides to constrain the impact of a potential breach or misuse.

79. B. Access logging will allow Chris to monitor for access to specific buckets by individuals, including privileged accounts. Authentication logging won't show access, nor will bandwidth logging. Timestamps should be on by default for any log event.

80. C. Jaime is performing content-based discovery by searching for specific terms in unstructured data. Label-based discovery would rely on data labels, metadata-based discovery uses metadata information, and structure-based discovery was made up for this question.

81. B. Mike should immediately revoke the certificate so that any malicious use will be limited. He may then want to determine why the certificate was exposed and issue a new certificate to ensure that the user or owner can continue to perform their job.

82. A. Tagging data will help the DLP manage it appropriately without having to rely on pattern matching. Reducing the overall amount of data may help, but Dan's first priority should be using more effective methods. Classifying data helps, but only if you tag it or otherwise help the DLP to easily manage it. Regular expressions are part of pattern matching. Refining them may help, but the underlying issue of relying on the most challenging matching mode will remain.

83. C. Tags are an important tool when working with ephemeral systems. While IP addresses may be reused and administrative accounts are likely to be the same across systems, tags can be unique, allowing events to be tracked to an instance. The system's deletion time should be logged, as should the time it is instantiated, but this obviously wouldn't be in every log event created by the machine.

84. B. Legal holds typically override other agreements and lifecycles. Valerie should preserve only the data requested or covered by the legal hold, and she should continue with normal practices for the remaining data.

85. A. Heikki's next step will be to set up policies that apply appropriate controls to the data that he has categorized and labeled. Once those policies are set, he can train users and run the DLP.

86. A. Kara is performing metadata-based discovery using the metadata that already exists in most digital photos. Content-based discovery might compare the photos looking for specific subjects, and label- or tag-based discovery would leverage data labels.

87. D. Rick knows that the tokenized data can be looked up against a database that contains the original customer data, allowing it to be accessed as needed. The actual customer data is stored in a separate database, meaning that a breach of the token database would not result in a customer data breach. The customer data is more secure but could still be breached if attackers leveraged the tokens and their lookup capability.

88. B. Hashes can be used to validate whether an image has been modified, but it is important to note that a running machine will have a different hash than the original. Jack may need to check specific file hashes instead. Cloud provider logs may not show changes to an instance, timestamps are time-consuming to check and may be modified when files are copied, and rebuilding the machine will typically result in differences.

89. B. Dispersion is the concept of ensuring that data is in multiple locations so that a single failure, event, or loss cannot result in the destruction or loss of the data. Deduplication involves removing duplicates from a data set; protected supply chain and lifecycle management are how data is managed throughout its life and doesn't specifically describe where data is stored for redundancy.

90. A. When data is created and used in other countries, it may be subject to regulations specific to those countries. Christina should point out that regulatory compliance is critical and could prove complex in this scenario. Exposure issues should be accounted for through best practices like using encryption for all transfers. Transfer speeds for archival data are typically not as critical as for operational data, and permissions should be set to be appropriate for the data regardless of location.

91. D. The Use stage occurs after Classification and before Transfer or Archiving.

92. D. Ben knows that hashes are one-way functions and cannot be reversed. They generate fixed-length output from variable-length input, and identical files will generate identical output. Two different files should never generate the same output—this is known as a collision and is not acceptable in a hashing algorithm.

93. C. IRM can be particularly useful during the sharing stage of the cloud data lifecycle since information rights management tools can ensure privileges and access to data are appropriately managed as data moves around the organization and potentially leaves it.

94. A. Storage occurs after creation in the cloud data lifecycle. Labeling is typically done as part of the creation process. Provisioning may be done at any time but is often associated with use. Encryption is not a stage in the cycle.

95. A. Naomi has attempted to anonymize the data by removing personally identifiable data. Hashes use a one-way cryptographic function to reference data without having the data itself exposed or in use. Shuffling moves data around so it is not associated with its original entries, but allows actual data to be used for testing. Tokenization uses two databases with data mapped to reference items known as tokens, allowing tokens to be referenced and then data that those tokens refer to be accessed.

96. B. Data value is typically not included in a data retention policy. Instead, retention periods, compliance requirements, and data classification are included as well as lifecycle requirements and archiving and retrieval procedures.

97. C. Raw storage is storage that you have direct access to like a hard drive or an SSD that has access to the underlying device. Long-term storage is storage that is intended to continue to exist and is often used for logs or data storage. Storage that is associated with an instance that will be destroyed when the instance is shut down is ephemeral storage. Volume-based storage is storage allocated as a virtual drive or device within the cloud.

98. C. IRM tools require that client devices and applications support IRM or that they access files via web applications that can provide IRM controls. Fortunately, SharePoint users tend to use Microsoft Office heavily, meaning that many, if not most, of the files will be opened using tools that natively support IRM.

99. B. Using existing metadata will help Angelo with his data discovery process, so he should start with that. Once he has the metadata processed, he can use it to speed up other cataloging efforts like scanning for sensitive data, classifying data, and mapping the data to compliance requirements.

100. B. This is an example of raw storage, which directly presents underlying hardware to users.

Chapter 3: Domain 3: Cloud Platform and Infrastructure Security

1. D. Barry should recruit an independent moderator to facilitate the session. Having a moderator who was not directly involved in the effort encourages honest and open feedback. While it is not necessary to use an external consultant, they may easily fill this role. It's also possible to find a qualified internal employee to fill this position, but it should not be someone who was involved in the incident response effort or who has a major stake in the plan, such as Barry, the CISO, or the DR team leader.

2. D. Without ISP connectivity, nobody will be able to use the internet and, thus, the cloud. Of course, realistically, without internet connectivity not much business will get done anyway, for most organizations, regardless of whether they were operating in the cloud or on-premises.

Option A is incorrect because the loss of any single cloud administrator is unlikely to gravely affect your organization's RTO.

The loss of a specific VM will probably not gravely affect your organization's RTO. VMs can be reinstantiated with ease. Option B is incorrect.

The loss of your policy and contract documentation cannot gravely affect your organization's RTO. Option C is untrue.

3. C. Generators are capable of providing backup power for a sustained period of time in the event of a power loss, but they take time to activate. Uninterruptible power supplies (UPS) provide immediate, battery-driven power for a short period of time to cover momentary losses of power, which would not cover a sustained period of power loss. Redundant arrays of inexpensive disks (RAID) and redundant servers are high-availability controls but do not cover power loss scenarios.

4. C. Data loss prevention (DLP) systems may identify sensitive information stored on endpoint systems or in transit over a network. This is their primary purpose. DLP systems are commonly available as a third-party managed service offering. Intrusion detection and prevention systems (IDSs/IPSs) may be used to identify some sensitive information using signatures built for that purpose, but this is not the primary role of those tools and they would not be as effective as DLP systems at this task. TLS is a network encryption protocol that may be used to protect sensitive information, but it does not have any ability to identify sensitive information.

5. A. The management plane of a cloud service provider's datacenter should be reserved for use by that provider's own engineers. Traffic on the management plane controls the operation of the infrastructure itself, and granting customers (even highly trained engineers) access to that network could jeopardize the security of other customers.

6. C. Radio frequency identification (RFID) technology is a cost-effective way to track items in a facility. While Wi-Fi could be used for the same purpose, it would be much more expensive to implement.

7. A. A cold site includes the basic capabilities required for datacenter operations—space, power, HVAC, and communications—but it does not include any of the hardware required to restore operations.

8. C. It's best to have your backup at another cloud provider in case whatever causes an interruption in service occurs throughout your primary provider's environment; this will be more complicated and expensive, but it provides the best redundancy and resiliency. Using the same provider for production and backup is not a bad option, but it entails the risk of the same contingency affecting both copies of your data. Having either the backup or the production environment localized does not provide the best protection, so neither option B nor option D is desirable.

9. D. All of these terms accurately describe this use of technology. However, the use of Docker is best described as a containerization technology, so this is the best possible answer choice.

10. C. Health and human safety is always paramount in all security activity. All of these assets require some type of protection; however, human safety must always be the highest priority.

11. D. All of these technologies play some role in tenant partitioning. However, this question asked specifically about the partitioning of virtual machines belonging to different tenants. This is the responsibility of the hypervisor on a virtualization platform.

12. C. Datacenters should be located in the core of a building. Locating it in the basement makes it susceptible to flooding. The first floor is the normal point of entry to a building, making it more susceptible to physical break-ins. Locating it on the top floor makes it vulnerable to wind and roof damage.

13. A. The due care principle states that an individual should react in a situation using the same level of care that would be expected from any reasonable person. It is a very broad standard. The due diligence principle is a more specific component of due care that states that an individual assigned a responsibility should exercise due care to complete it accurately and in a timely manner.

14. C. In an infrastructure as a service environment, the vendor is responsible for hardware-related and network-related responsibilities. These include configuring network firewalls, maintaining the hypervisor, and managing physical equipment. The customer retains responsibility for patching operating systems on its virtual machine instances. The customer is responsible for managing network ingress and egress but does so by manipulating network security groups, rather than directly configuring the network firewall.

15. A. Incremental backups provide the option that includes the smallest amount of data. In this case, that would be only the data modified since the most recent incremental backup. A differential backup would back up all data modified since the last full backup, which would be a substantial amount. The full backup would include all information on the server. Transaction log backups are specifically designed to support database servers and would not be effective on a file server.

16. D. Security information and event management (SIEM) systems do correlate information from multiple sources and perform analysis, but they stop short of providing automated playbook responses. That is the realm of security orchestration, automation, and response (SOAR) platforms. Intrusion prevention platforms have a more limited scope, allowing the blocking of traffic based on analysis performed by the IPS itself. Log repositories simply collect log information and do not perform analysis.

17. C. This is a classic example of the "buy vs. build" decision. Any time an organization chooses to build out capital resources, such as an on-premises datacenter, it involves very high upfront investments. The other offerings here involve leveraging the capital investments made by others and will involve lower (or no) up-front costs but will have higher recurring costs.

18. A. Security information and event management (SIEM) solutions aggregate log entries from many different sources and correlate them to create an interpretable audit trail. Intrusion prevention systems (IPSs) analyze and block suspicious network traffic. Endpoint detection and response (EDR) platforms monitor endpoints for malware and respond to malware infections. Cloud access security brokers (CASBs) enforce an organization's security policies across cloud providers. IPS, EDR, and CASB solutions are important components of an organization's security program but they do not aggregate and correlate log entries.

19. D. Because supply chain dependencies can affect service, the cloud customer will need assurance that any third-party reliance is secure.

Regulators and end users do not provide security to the enterprise, so options A and B are incorrect.

The vendors used for on-premises security will no longer affect the data, so option C is incorrect.

20. A. When Brittney reviews the recovery time objective (RTO) data, she needs to ensure that the organization can recover from an outage in less than 30 minutes based on the maximum tolerable downtime (MTD) of 30 minutes.

21. A. A content delivery network (CDN) run by a major provider can handle large-scale DDoS attacks more easily than any of the other solutions. Using DDoS mitigation techniques via an ISP is the next most useful capability, followed by both increases in bandwidth and increases in the number of servers in the web application cluster.

22. A. A denial-of-service (DoS) attack is designed to overwhelm a system until it is unable to process legitimate requests. The purpose of this attack is to deny legitimate users access to the system, which is a violation of the principle of availability.

23. C. Risk mitigation strategies attempt to lower the probability and/or impact of a risk occurring. Intrusion prevention systems attempt to reduce the probability of a successful attack and are, therefore, examples of risk mitigation.

24. C. The business impact analysis (BIA) is designed for this purpose: to determine the critical path of assets/resources/data within the organization. It is a perfect tool to use in shaping the BC/DR plan.

The risk analyses options and the risk appetite option may provide input for the BIA, but they are not what is used to determine the critical assets necessary to protect in the BC/DR activity. So, options A, B, and D are incorrect.

25. B. A well-designed datacenter should have redundant systems and capabilities for each critical part of its infrastructure. That means that power, cooling, and network connectivity should all be redundant. Kim should determine how to ensure that a single system failure cannot take her datacenter offline.

26. D. The principle of least privilege should guide Joe in this case. He should apply no access permissions by default and then give each user the necessary permissions to perform their job responsibilities. Read only, editor, and administrator permissions may be necessary for one or more of these users, but those permissions should be assigned based on business need and not by default.

27. B. Application programming interfaces (APIs) allow for the programmatic interaction with services and platforms. Jason can use APIs to tie together different technologies and interact with them programmatically. Python scripts may play a role in that automation but they do not, on their own, allow the automation to occur because the script must use the API to interact with services. Cloud access security brokers (CASBs) enforce customer security policies across a variety of services and are not a backend security solution. The hypervisor is a component of the management plane and would be a target of the automation, rather than a facilitator of it.

28. B. The question describes an HSM. KMB is a nonsense term used as a distractor, so it is incorrect. TGT is a term associated with Kerberos single sign-on systems and is incorrect. The TCB includes the elements of hardware and software (usually in the operating system) that ensure that a system can only be controlled by those with the proper permissions (i.e., admins with root control), so it is also incorrect.

29. D. The key to successfully answering this question is noticing that it asks who bears "ultimate responsibility." The chief executive officer (CEO) bears ultimate responsibility for the success of the organization and, therefore, will be the one held accountable if the business fails. Of course, everyone in the organization has some accountability for their own roles in the program's success.

30. C. Michael should conduct his investigation, but there is a pressing business need to bring the website back online. The most reasonable course of action would be to take a snapshot of the compromised system and use the snapshot for the investigation, restoring the website to operation as quickly as possible while using the results of the investigation to improve the security of the site.

31. B. The hypervisor is responsible for coordinating access to physical hardware and enforcing isolation between different virtual machines running on the same physical platform.

32. B. To avoid a situation where severing a given physical connection results in severing its backup as well (such as construction/landscaping, etc.), have redundant lines enter on different sides of the building.

    For health and human safety, multiple egress points from each facility is preferred (and often required by law); option A is incorrect.

    Emergency lighting should receive power regardless of their proximity to the power source, and parking vehicles near generators is a bad idea from a safety perspective; option C is incorrect.

    Not all facilities need to withstand earthquakes; this may be true of datacenters in California, but not in Sydney, so it is not an industry-wide best practice. Option D is incorrect.

33. C. Virtual local area networks (VLANs) are used to create logical separation between systems in a datacenter and are the most cost-effective way to provide network segmentation. Creating separate LANs would require redundant equipment and unnecessary expense. Virtual private networks (VPNs) are used to connect remote users and sites over an insecure network and are not relevant within a secure datacenter. Border Gateway Protocol (BGP) is used to route traffic between network sites and is not relevant to this scenario.

34. D. The only reason organizations accept any level of risk is because of the potential benefit also afforded by a risky activity.

    Profit is not the hallmark of every opportunity (or every organization—many organizations are nonprofit or government-based), so option A is incorrect.

    Likewise, not all risky activities offer a chance to enhance performance, so option B is incorrect.

    Cost is not a benefit, so that doesn't even make sense in the context of the question; option C is not correct and a distractor.

35. C. Tier 2 datacenters are expected to achieve 99.741% availability. Tier 1 datacenters are expected to achieve 99.671% availability. Tier 3 datacenters are expected to achieve 99.982% availability. Tier 4 datacenters are expected to achieve 99.995% availability.

36. B. Running unnecessary services on a server increases the attack surface and exposes an organization to unnecessary risk. Therefore, Ursula should work through the organization's normal change management processes to remove the service.

37. C. The compute nodes of a cloud datacenter can be measured in terms of how many central processing units (CPUs) and how much random access memory (RAM) is available within the center.

Option A is incorrect because routers would be considered a part of the networking of a datacenter (and because option C is a better answer).

Option B involves applications and how traffic flows between them and storage controllers; it has nothing to do with the compute nodes and is therefore wrong.

Option D might obliquely be considered correct because it's technically true (compute nodes will include both virtual and hardware machines), but option C is a much better and more accurate choice.

38. B. Block storage, also known as volume storage, provides disk volumes for use by servers. Cloud environments generally do not provide dedicated disks because that approach would be highly inefficient. Object storage is used to store files as individual objects and cannot be used as a disk volume. Any type of storage may be encrypted or unencrypted, but the fact that storage is encrypted does not make it useful for disk volumes.

39. D. VMs are snapshotted and simply stored as files when they are not being used; an attacker who gains access to those file stores could ostensibly steal entire machines in highly portable, easily copied formats. Therefore, these cloud storage spaces must include a significant amount of controls.

It is possible to sanitize cloud file spaces by using crypto-shredding. Virtualization does not prevent the use of application-based security controls. Administrators are free to encrypt cloud-based file stores.

40. A. SQL injection vulnerabilities allow an attacker to send commands through a web application to the database supporting that application. Cross-site scripting attacks execute code on a remote user's system. Cross-site request forgery and server-side request forgery attacks seek to exploit trust relationships by tricking systems into authorizing unauthorized activity.

41. B. The recovery point objective (RPO) is a measure of data that can be lost in an outage without irreparably damaging the organization. Data replication strategies will most affect this metric, as the choice of strategy will determine how much recent data is available for recovery purposes.

Recovery time objective (RTO) is a measure of how long an organization can endure an outage without irreparable harm. This may be affected by the replication strategy, but not as much as the RPO. Option A is incorrect.

The maximum allowable downtime (MAD) is how long an organization can suffer an outage before ceasing to be an organization. This is not dependent on the RPO, and the data replication strategy won't have much effect on it at all. Option C is incorrect.

The mean time to failure (MTTF) is a measure of how long an asset is expected to last (usually hardware), as determined by the manufacturer/vendor. The data replication strategy will have no bearing on this whatsoever. Option D is incorrect.

42. B. Transport Layer Security (TLS) is the primary protocol used to implement the HTTPS standard for secure communication between servers and users. Virtual private networks (VPNs) will also encrypt web traffic, but they are a separate service normally provided by a user's employer and not the remote website. Virtual local area networks (VLANs) are used for network segmentation and not for encryption. IPsec is a protocol used to implement VPNs.

43. B. Theoretically, all the options are possibly true. However, option B is the most likely to occur; the cost and risk of moving operations from one environment/provider to another is sizable, so staying with the secondary provider (making them the new primary) is a good way to reduce some of the risk involved in returning to normal.

44. B. Gary should follow the least privilege principle and assign users only the permissions they need to perform their job responsibilities. Aggregation is a term used to describe the unintentional accumulation of privileges over time, also known as privilege creep. Separation of duties and separation of privileges are principles used to secure sensitive processes.

45. A. The matrix shown in the figure is known as a separation of duties matrix. It is used to ensure that one person does not obtain two privileges that would create a potential conflict. Aggregation is a term used to describe the unintentional accumulation of privileges over time, also known as privilege creep. Two-person control is used when two people must work together to perform a sensitive action. Defense in depth is a general security principle used to describe a philosophy of overlapping security controls.

46. B. Before granting access, Gary should verify that the user has a valid security clearance and a business need to know the information. Gary is performing an authorization task, so he does not have to verify the user's credentials, such as a password or biometric scan.

47. D. Gary should follow the principle of two-person control by requiring simultaneous action by two separate authorized individuals to gain access to the encryption keys. He should also apply the principles of least privilege and defense in depth, but these principles apply to all operations and are not specific to sensitive operations. Gary should avoid the security through obscurity principle, the reliance upon the secrecy of security mechanisms to provide security for a system or process.

48. A, B, C. Privileged access reviews are one of the most critical components of an organization's security program because they ensure that only authorized users have access to perform the most sensitive operations. They should take place whenever a user with privileged access leaves the organization or changes roles as well as on a regular, recurring basis. However, it is not reasonable to expect that these time-consuming reviews would take place on a daily basis.

49. A. Type 1, or "bare-metal" hypervisors, run directly on top of hardware and provide a greater degree of security than Type 2 hypervisors. This is because Type 2 hypervisors must run on top of another operating system, increasing the total attack surface. Types 3 and 4 hypervisors do not exist.

50. A. The major factor driving organizations to lease space in a colocation facility is a reduction in cost achieved through economies of scale. Leased facilities are not necessarily more or less secure or complex than custom-built facilities, and they do not necessarily have greater capability.

51. B. Tier 1 datacenters require dedicated space for IT systems, an uninterruptible power supply (UPS) system for line conditioning and backup purposes, sufficient cooling systems to serve all critical equipment, and a power generator for extended electrical outages, with at least 12 hours of fuel to run the generator at sufficient load to power the IT systems. Dual-power supplies are a requirement of a Tier 3 datacenter and are not required in Tier 1 datacenters.

52. B. The most important detail in this question is that the access must be automated. This means that systems will connect to each other without any human intervention. Because of this requirement, biometric controls are not useful because they require that a person be involved in the authentication process. Using passwords would require storing that password on the remote server. This is possible, but not ideal from a security perspective. Since we don't want to use passwords or biometrics, multifactor authentication is also not feasible. That leaves digital certificates as the most viable option for securing these connections.

53. B. The NBI usually handles traffic between the SDN controllers and SDN applications.

Options A and C are incorrect because neither of those options lists any of the SDN infrastructure, be that the controllers or the applications. Option D may be arguably correct, as there might be an NBI handling that traffic between those nodes, but option B is more specific and always true for this definition, so it is the better choice.

54. C. This is a very popular function of federated identity.

Single sign-on (SSO) is similar to federation, but it is limited to a single organization; federation is basically SSO across multiple organizations. Option A is incorrect.

Options B and D are threats listed in the Open Web Application Security Project (OWASP) Top 10; they are incorrect.

55. B. Hardware security modules (HSMs) are security solutions designed to manage the processes surrounding cryptographic keys. Key management boxes (KMBs) provide for the management of physical keys. Ticket-granting tickets (TGTs) are a component of the Kerberos authentication process. The trusted computing base (TCB) provides a secure operating environment inside a computer system.

56. C. Sprawl needs to be addressed from a managerial perspective because it is caused by allowed user actions (usually in a completely authorized capacity).

Technical and logical mean the same thing and could be considered as contributing to sprawl because the technological capabilities of virtualization create the ease of use that can cause sprawl. However, management is a better answer because this is primarily a human problem.

External is incorrect; sprawl occurs within the organization.

57. B.. A trained and experienced moderator can guide the participants through the activity, enhancing their training and noting pitfalls and areas for improvement. Option A is not preferable because having the participants gathered together ensures their full attention and provides interaction that remote participation might not yield. Option C is a baseline; all participants should have copies of the policy as a matter of course. Option D is not useful in a tabletop exercise; only critical participants in the organization should take part in the tabletop.

58. C. The baseline will contain the suite of security controls applied uniformly throughout the environment.

A VM image audit is unlikely to involve any form of physical security; A is incorrect.

Baselines won't predictively show malicious activity; B is incorrect.

Baselines also do not have anything to do with user training and awareness; option D is incorrect.

59. B. This is a difficult question that requires a great deal of thought. Option B is correct because appropriate cloud data security practices will require encrypting a great deal of the data, and having the keys will be necessary during contingency operations in order to access the backup; without the keys, you won't be able to access your data. Option A is not correct because using the cloud for BC/DR will allow personnel to access the backup from anywhere they can get broadband connectivity, not specifically a recovery site. Option C is not correct because the customer will rarely have physical access to servers in the cloud environment. Option D is not correct because forensic analysis is not a significant consideration in BC/DR; it is much more important for incident response.

60. A. Ping is a term used to describe the ability of customers to access their systems remotely. Power is shorthand for electrical power to the systems. Pipe refers to the network connectivity that supports servers' connections to the internet.

61. B. Sharing resources with other, unknown customers (some of whom may be competitors of or even hostile to the organization) is a risk not faced by organizations that maintain their own, on-premises datacenters.

All the other answers are threats that exist in both environments and are therefore incorrect.

62. D. Software-defined networks allow administrators to perform a variety of automated functions. These include rerouting traffic based on current customer demand, creating logical subnets without having to change any physical connections, and filtering access to resources based upon specific rules or settings. Delivering streaming media content in an efficient manner by placing it closer to the end user is a function of content delivery networks (CDNs), not SDNs.

63. A. The illustration shows an example of a failover cluster, where DB1 and DB2 are both configured as database servers. At any given time, only one will function as the active database server, while the other remains ready to assume responsibility if the first one fails. Although the environment may use UPS, tape backup, and cold sites as disaster recovery and business continuity controls, they are not shown in the diagram.

64. B. Having an additional backup with a different provider means that if your primary provider becomes unusable for any reason (including bankruptcy or unfavorable contract terms), your data is not held hostage or lost.

    Custom VMs may or may not work in a new environment; this is actually a risk when porting data out of the production environment; option A is incorrect.

    Performance probably will not increase if data is replicated to another cloud provider; in fact, you will probably lose some load-balancing capability you might have had if you kept the data and backups together. Option C is incorrect.

    Having two providers will always be more costly than a single provider; option D is incorrect.

65. B. The "sensitive information," in this case, is whatever knowledge of the datacenter's security controls and processes might be gathered by physically visiting the datacenter. Even though a cloud customer cannot get access to the facility, this also means that other cloud customers (some of whom may be hostile to another customer's interests) also will not have access, so none would have advantage over the other(s).

    Option A is incorrect because qualified personnel are still required whether or not a cloud environment has limited access to their datacenter. In fact, security may be degraded by having unqualified personnel rather than qualified personnel working in the cloud datacenter.

    Option C is incorrect because reducing jurisdictional exposure does not enhance security.

    There may be a correlation between ensuring statutory compliance and enhancing security as it applies to limiting access to the cloud datacenter. However, option B is a better answer because it is certainly true. Therefore, option D is not the best answer to the question.

66. C. Virtual server instances and containers provide direct computing resources to cloud service users. Function as a service provides a platform upon which computing may be performed. Object storage does not provide any compute capability, as it is solely a storage service.

67. C. While options A and B are both also true, C is the most significant reason cloud datacenters use VMs. If the cloud provider had to purchase a new box for every user, the cost of cloud services would be as much as running a traditional environment (or likely cost even more), and there would be no reason for any organization to migrate to the cloud, especially

considering the risks associated with disclosing data to a third party. Option D is simply untrue. VMs are not easier to operate than actual devices.

68. A. Full tests, also known as full interruption tests, shut down the primary operating facility and shift operations to the backup facility. These tests are very likely to have a serious impact on production operations. The parallel test activates the backup facility but does not move production responsibility to it. Walkthroughs and simulations do not activate the backup facility or impact production operations in any way.

69. A. This is an example of an escape attack because the attacker was able to leave the confines of their own virtual machine and access resources belonging to another customer. There is no indication in the scenario that the attack used any specific overflow, injection, or scripting vulnerability.

70. B. Escape attacks always occur as the result of a vulnerability or malfunction in the hypervisor because the hypervisor is responsible for performing the separation that prevents one customer from accessing resources belonging to another customer.

71. D. Disk volumes used to support virtual machines are typically stored on block storage. However, when snapshotting is used to create backups of those disks, the backups are commonly stored in less expensive object storage. Dedicated disks are not generally used in cloud environments. The backups may be encrypted while in object storage, but this is not a technical requirement.

72. D. Having your data backed up and accessible in the cloud eliminates any need for having a distinct hot site/warm site separate from your primary operating environment; instead, your personnel can recover operations from anywhere with a good broadband connection.

Cloud BC/DR capability does not remove the necessity of security personnel and appropriate policies; both options A and B are incorrect.

Option C makes no sense as an answer to the question. It is unclear how you can cut costs by eliminating your old access credentials. In fact, it is difficult to imagine how that is a true statement. Therefore, option C is a poor choice and option D is the best choice.

73. B. A specified configuration built to defined standards and with a controlled process can be used to demonstrate that all VMs within an environment include certain controls; this can greatly enhance the efficiency of an audit process.

The VM's image has very little to do with physical security or training; options A and C are incorrect.

Baseline images are the opposite of customization; option D is incorrect.

74. D. Log entries do provide some insight into user activity but they generally do not provide the full context of user communication. Netflow records only provide the "telephone bill" level detail of communications and not the content. While those sources would be useful, full packet capture provides the most accurate reconstruction of user activity, but it is costly to implement due to data storage requirements.

75. C. It's best to have your backup at another cloud provider in case whatever causes an interruption in service occurs throughout your primary provider's environment; this will be more complicated and expensive, but it provides the best redundancy and resiliency. Using the same provider for production and backup is not a bad option, but it entails the risk of the same contingency affecting both copies of your data. Having either the backup or the production environment localized does not provide the best protection because you no longer operate secure cloud datacenters.

76. C. This is not an easy question, because every plan/policy should include mention of the governance documents that drive the formation of the plan/policy; however, these can be included by reference only—you don't need to include full copies of these governance documents. All the other options should be included in the BC/DR plan/policy.

77. A. Security Assertion Markup Language (SAML) is based on XML. HTTP is used for port 80 web traffic; HTML is used to present web pages. ASCII is the universal alphanumeric character set.

78. A. Depending on your industry and the nature of your data, moving information into another jurisdiction may affect or invalidate your regulatory compliance.

Cloud providers, wherever they are located, should compensate for environmental and physical security factors, so this should have no impact on your potential risk; options B and C are incorrect.

Option D is incorrect because it is a blanket statement that is not always true. In fact, for some organizations, the physical location where their data is stored can have serious regulatory consequences.

79. C. Under current legal frameworks, some risks (such as legal liability for privacy data breaches) cannot be transferred to a contracted party, so the data owners (that is, cloud customers) will still retain those risks. It is important to note that customers are always responsible for managing risk in some way, even if risk is transferred to a cloud provider.

Option A is not correct; risks can and should be mitigated, even in the cloud.

Option B is not correct; cloud migration will require some risk acceptance, but that is true for everything except avoided risk.

Option D is incorrect; cloud providers can choose not to offer services or not to accept certain clients.

80. C. The administrative offices of a cloud datacenter rarely are part of the critical functions of the operation; a datacenter could likely endure the loss of the administrative offices for a considerable length of time, so redundancy here is probably not cost effective.

81. B. The recovery point objective (RPO) is a measure of data that can be lost in an outage without irreparably damaging the organization. Data replication strategies will most affect this metric, as the choice of strategy will determine how much recent data is available for recovery purposes.

Recovery time objective (RTO) is a measure of how long an organization can endure an outage without irreparable harm. This may be affected by the replication strategy, but not as much as the RPO. Option A is incorrect.

The maximum allowable downtime (MAD) is how long an organization can suffer an outage before ceasing to be an organization. This is not dependent on the RPO, and the data replication strategy won't have much effect on it at all. Option C is incorrect.

The mean time to failure (MTTF) is a measure of how long an asset is expected to last (usually hardware), as determined by the manufacturer/vendor. The data replication strategy will have no bearing on this whatsoever. Option D is incorrect.

82. C. Authorization is the process of granting users and other security principles access to resources in an environment.

Identification and authentication are part of the overall identity and access management (IAM) process, as is authorization, but they do not specifically describe granting access to resources.

Federation is a means of conducting IAM across organizations; authorization is a more specific answer, so federation is incorrect.

83. B. When using two different cloud providers, a cloud customer runs the risk that data/software formats used in the operational environment can't be readily adapted to the other provider's service, thus causing delays during an actual failover.

Risks of physical intrusion are neither obviated nor enhanced by choosing to use two cloud providers; option A is incorrect.

Using a different cloud provider for backup/archiving actually reduces the risks of outages due to vendor lock-in/lockout and natural disasters, so options C and D are not correct.

84. C. As the models increase in level of abstraction and service, the customer's control over the environment decreases. Therefore, the customer has the most control over the configuration of IaaS services, a moderate degree of control over PaaS/FaaS services, and the least control over SaaS services.

85. C. Without a full test, Warren can't be sure the BC/DR plan/process will work the way it is intended.

Audits are good, but they will not demonstrate actual performance the way a test will, so options A and B are incorrect.

It is important that the BC/DR capacity and performance be included in the contract, but that will not truly ensure that the functionality exists; a test is required, so option D is incorrect.

86. C. A premature return to normal operations can jeopardize not only production, but personnel; if the contingency that caused the BC/DR action is not fully complete/addressed, there may still be danger remaining.

The BC/DR plan/process should take into account both the absence of essential personnel and telecommunications capabilities, so options A and D are incorrect.

Option B does present a serious problem for the organization, but option C is still a greater risk, so B is incorrect.

87. C. Systems that use water always pose a greater failure risk to electronic equipment than those that use gas because water can destroy equipment. Of the systems listed, wet pipe systems pose the greatest risk because water is always present in the pipes.

88. B. Guest escape (a malicious user leaving the confines of a VM and able to access other VMs on the same machine) is less likely to occur and to have a significant impact in an environment provisioned for and used by a single customer.

In a public cloud, this is more likely and would be more significant, so option A is incorrect.

The service model doesn't specifically dictate the likelihood of occurrence or impact (both PaaS and IaaS could be in a private or public cloud, which is the more important factor), so both options C and D are incorrect.

89. A. Many cloud providers restrict activities that are common for administrative and security purposes but can also be construed/used for hacking; this includes port scanning and penetration testing. These restrictions can reduce the customer's ability to perform basic security functions. Customers should review these practices with service providers and confirm that they are allowed to conduct routine security activities.

While geographical dispersion of cloud assets might make securing those assets more difficult in the notional sense (customer administrators can't physically visit the devices that host their data), remoteness does not necessarily inhibit good security practices, which can be performed at a remove. This is not as detrimental as rules against port scanning/pen testing, so option B is incorrect.

There are no rules against user training or laws against securing your own assets, in the cloud or otherwise; options C and D are incorrect.

90. B. The question describes a software-defined network (SDN).

A VPN is used for creating an encrypted communications tunnel over an untrusted medium, so option A is incorrect.

ACLs are used as centralized repositories for identification, authentication, and authorization purposes, so option C is incorrect.

RBAC is an access control model used to assign permissions based on job functions within an organization, so option D is incorrect.

91. C. Cloud providers may be reluctant to grant physical access, even to their customers, on the assumption that allowing access would disclose information about security controls. In some cases, cloud customers won't even know the location(s) of the datacenter(s) where their data is stored.

The other options are all untrue. Data in the cloud and controls in the cloud can most certainly be audited. So, options A and B are incorrect. D is untrue; there are regulators for all industries, including those that operate in the cloud.

92. A. The business requirements will determine the crucial aspects of BC/DR.

All the other options may constitute some input that will influence the BC/DR, but they are not the prevailing factors and so are incorrect.

93. C. Because cloud access is remote access, pen tests will be remote tests; it doesn't really matter what the physical origin of the simulated attack is.

Cloud providers will want notice before the customer launches the test and that notice should include a description of the scope of the test, knowledge of the timeframe for the test, and the logical (not physical!) addresses of the testing systems.

94. D. The checklist review is the least disruptive type of disaster recovery test. During a checklist review, team members each review the contents of their disaster recovery checklists on their own and suggest any necessary changes. During a tabletop exercise, team members come together and walk through a scenario without making any changes to information systems. During a parallel test, the team actually activates the disaster recovery site for testing, but the primary site remains operational. During a full interruption test, the team takes down the primary site and confirms that the disaster recovery site is capable of handling regular operations. The full interruption test is the most thorough test but also the most disruptive.

95. D. DDoS prevents all these things except for data integrity. DDoS only prevents communication; it does not usually result in modified data.

96. C. Health and human safety is a paramount goal of security; all facilities must have multiple emergency egress points. All the other options are distractors as they are included in option C.

97. B. Because VMs don't take updates when they are not in use (snapshotted and saved as image files) and updates may be pushed while the VMs are saved, it's important to ensure that they receive updates when they are next instantiated. Systems may be configured to perform automatic updates.

A physical tracking mechanism won't be of much aid for virtual devices because they aren't physically stolen like hardware boxes, so option A is incorrect.

Having an ACL in the image baseline would create a situation where every user from every cloud customer could access every VM in the datacenter; option C is incorrect.

Write protection is used in forensic analysis of machines (virtual or otherwise); it would not be useful in an operational baseline. Option D is incorrect.

98. D. Performing live deception and trickery against employees of the cloud provider (or its suppliers/vendors) could be construed as unethical and possibly illegal, especially without their knowledge and/or consent. Social engineering probably won't be involved in penetration tests run by customers.

All the other options are legitimate activities a customer might perform during a penetration test (with provider permission).

99. D. Having the backup within the same environment can allow easy rollback to a last known good state or to reinstantiate clean VM images after minor incidents (e.g., a malware infection in certain VMs).

Ease of compliance will not be determined by the location of the backup, so option A is incorrect.

Traveling should not be a major cost for cloud usage; option B is incorrect.

The location of the backups won't have any effect on user training; option C is incorrect.

100. C. Event logging is essential for incident management and resolution; this can be set as an automated function of the CM tools.

Not all systems need or can utilize biometrics; option A is incorrect.

Usually, tampering refers to physical intrusion of a device; since the question is about VMs, it is probably not applicable. Option B is incorrect.

Hackback is illegal in many jurisdictions; option D is incorrect.

Chapter 4: Domain 4: Cloud Application Security

1. D. Mikayla can't validate third-party software's lack of vulnerabilities or other security issues simply by validating that it is signed, that its hash matches an officially posted hash, or that the checksum matches ensuring the file is intact. She'll need to test the software herself or identify a third party that she can rely on that does appropriate software testing. Even then, the software could still contain flaws.

2. C. Lin will need to provide authorization to use her organization's services. The third-party identity provider will supply user IDs and will authenticate them, then provide Lin with a token or validation that the user is who they claim to be. Identity proofing is not necessarily provided by either party in this scenario, which can make accepting third-party credentials challenging if verifying that someone is who they claim to be is important instead of just allowing access to the service.

3. D. Joanna knows she can't access the source code meaning that static analysis isn't an option, and that identifying secrets may be difficult.

4. A. The Agile development model is most frequently associated with cloud services and development. Rapid application development, spiral, and waterfall methods are more frequently associated with traditional development environments but can be used for cloud services and systems.

5. D. Susan knows that cloud services will allow her to build her applications on reliable, scalable infrastructure that can leverage redundancy in multiple ways. She also knows that securing code remains a concern regardless of the environment that it is built or run in.

6. C. Susan knows that encryption in transit, typically via TLS, is the right solution to prevent third parties from intercepting and accessing data that is sent to her customers via API calls. Tokenization and masking are used to protect data in applications, but they do not meet the need to prevent interception, and the data will be in transit rather than at rest in the scenario described.

7. B. Brainstorming, surveys, workshops, user observation, and many other techniques are commonly used to gather business requirements. Documentation, however, doesn't involve user requirements or feedback.

8. B. Since multiple tenants share the same underlying infrastructure, encryption at rest provides protection against inadvertent data exposure or remnant data on reused infrastructure. Elasticity, measured services, and scalability do not require encryption at rest and may in fact result in slightly higher costs due to encryption overhead.

9. C. Having multiple deployment paths means that elements or processes in a CI/CD system can be avoided. A single path with an emergency process backing it up helps to avoid this problem. Automation, use of metrics, and using version control are all recommended best practices for CI/CD pipelines.

10. C. Maria knows that IdPs typically integrate with either OpenID Connect or SAML. OpenLDAP is an open source implementation of LDAP, but it isn't used for this type of integration since it is a directory service. ConnectID and IDPL were made up for this question.

11. A. Jack knows that languages that best fit cloud applications make the most sense and that assembly language isn't likely to fit his CI/CD environment. Use of automated release pipelines, containers, and microservices are all common elements in cloud application development and design.

12. A. While some development models allow for user involvement in the entirety of the process, user input is most necessary in the Define phase, where developers can understand the business/user requirements—what the system/software is actually supposed to produce, in terms of function and performance. Involvement throughout the process is helpful, but without user input in Define, the entire process won't have the right starting point.

13. A. Brian needs to bring up regulatory compliance during the Requirements Gathering phase of the SDLC. If it isn't a requirement, it won't make it into the design and implementation. Testing for regulatory compliance can be challenging as not all compliance can be tested for by technical means.

14. A. Angie is using a white box, or full knowledge, testing methodology. Gray box, or partial knowledge, testing provides some but not all access to an environment or system. Black box, or zero knowledge, testing requires testers to act like attackers without insider knowledge of the systems. Red box was made up for this question.

15. C. KMSs, or key management services, are used to securely store and access secrets, allowing them to be used when needed without hard-coding them. TPMs are used to store secrets for hardware devices, MFA tokens are used for multifactor authentication, and API keys are used to securely authenticate to and access APIs, but none of them provide the functionality needed to avoid hard-coded credentials in cloud applications.

16. A. A software bill of materials (SBOM) is used to identify each component in a software package. Dana knows that having a SBOM will help her to track the versions and updates available for each component of her software stack.

17. A. API gateways are designed to aggregate API access, provide authentication for API use, rate-limit, and gather statistics and data about API usage. API proxies are used to decouple software components, API firewalls are purpose-built firewalls for APIs that protect specific APIs, and next-generation API managers were made up for this question.

18. B. Interactive application security testing (IAST) uses software instrumentation to monitor applications as they run and to gather information about what occurs and how the software performs. It is normally implemented during the QA or Testing phase of the SDLC.

19. B. Unsecured APIs are a common issue, and lack of authentication is a major problem. How data is provided—structured, unstructured, or semi-structured—is not a security issue. Encryption is typically not provided by the API and is instead provided by the web server or underlying service.

20. B. AES-256 is a commonly accepted and used standard for encryption of data at rest. TLS is used for encryption in transit. SSL is outmoded, and Blowfish has known vulnerabilities including birthday attacks.

21. C. Checking whether included software is internally or externally developed is a best practice, and only checking your own components will often leave a lot of unchecked software in a package. You can find the full list at `www.nist .gov/itl/executive-order-improving-nations-cybersecurity/ recommended-minimum-standard-vendor-or-developer`.

22. B. Lori's best option is to conduct a software composition analysis (SCA) process using an SCA tool that can identify open source libraries and other components. Vulnerability scans won't identify all of the components associated with software, and a version number validation process was made up for this question.

23. A. Christine is preparing for abuse case testing, which documents abuse of software functionality. Static testing reviews source code, QA testing validates the quality of software, and SCA is software composition analysis, which looks at underlying components of software.

24. B. ASVS is intended to be used as a metric to assess the degree of trust that can be placed in web applications, to provide guidance to developers on how to build in security controls, and as part of procurement processes to specify application security validation requirements in contracts. It isn't designed as an audit standard.

25. A. The OWASP Top 10 is a cloud-specific list, whereas the SANS Top 25 describes software errors in general. The NIST Dirty Dozen and the MITRE ATT&CK-RS were made up for this question.

26. D. Major.minor.patch is a common format for versioning. While there's no industry standard, having the versioning numbers in an order of scale is a common practice.

27. B. A software bill of materials (SBOM) is a listing of all of the components of a software package or program, and it is considered increasingly important as part of a software security program.

28. B. Web application firewalls (WAFs) typically have built-in protection against common attacks like SQL injection. Valerie should choose a WAF to protect against both the SQL injection she's aware of and other common attacks against web applications.

29. B. Containers allow applications to be moved easily because they contain the dependencies and components the application needs without requiring a complete operating system to be packaged with them. Packages are software components, and virtual machines run on hypervisors.

30. B. Charles is using a single sign-on (SSO) technology to allow him to log in once and use many services and systems. SAML and OpenID Connect are used for federation, while OTP is a one-time password.

31. A. Henry's organization should use API keys to ensure that only authorized users are able to use the APIs that they expose for customer use.

32. A. Nancy knows that she should keep track of the license term, or how long the license is valid for, so that the software does not disable itself when the license or contract expires. The cost, whether the terms can be disclosed, and if there is third-party software involved are less likely to be the cause of service interruptions.

33. B. FIPS 140-2, a Federal Information Processing Standard, defines the requirements for cryptographic modules and is a commonly used standard to assess cryptographic systems, and it's the only currently valid cryptographic standard listed here. SSL is outdated and has been replaced by TLS, SHA-2 is a hashing algorithm, and GDPR is a European Union data protection regulation.

34. C. Using dynamic secrets—secrets that are generated and used as they are needed—allows for granular auditing of uses because each secret is created as needed and thus their specific usage can be reviewed as needed. Shared accounts don't allow auditing because actions cannot be provably linked to individual users. Multifactor authentication helps prevent stolen credential and brute-force attacks but won't increase the auditability of usage, and API keys allow API authentication, but like multifactor authentication, don't increase the individual auditability of usage as much as dynamic secrets do.

35. D. Testing the performance and security of software is expected in the Testing phase of the SDLC. The version, complexity, and size of the code are not commonly tested elements.

36. A. Chris should look for a key management service (KMS). KMSs allow creation, storage, management, and auditing of keys. A PKI is a public key infrastructure, a CA is a certificate authority, and a KCS was made up for this question—none of them will provide the services that Chris is looking for.

37. A. Identity providers (IdPs) provide authentication as well as create, manage, and maintain identities and identity information. Relying parties and service providers both trust IdPs to handle authentication, and SSO is single sign-on.

38. C. Docker is a containerization tool.

39. D. Yasmine knows that in an SaaS environment the vendor is responsible for the applications, data storage, runtime and middleware, operating systems and servers, storage, and networking. Yasmine's company will be responsible for how they operate the software, who they provide access to, and what rights they provide to their users, as well as ensuring that her data is safe and secure.

40. B. Multifactor authentication relies on using two different types of factors: something you know, like a password or PIN; something you have, like a hardware token or application-generated PIN; or something you are, such as a biometric identifier. Jason knows that a password and an app-generated PIN counts as using multiple factors.

41. C. Git provides version management as part of its capabilities. Jenkins is a CI/CD tool used for continuous integration tooling. Puppet and Chef are both infrastructure automation tools.

42. A. Ramon's organization is using Azure's federation capability to leverage their existing on-site credentials in the cloud. Structured, shared, and constrained identity were made up for this question.

43. D. Having a complete software inventory allows organizations like Gretchen's to ensure that they are aware of their software license compliances, terms, and conditions as well as their license expiration dates. While only using open source software might seem like an easy solution, there are multiple open source software licenses that have different requirements, making a software inventory necessary. Using only commercial software doesn't simplify the requirement, and software versioning is important but would be part of a complete inventory.

44. A. DREAD has been replaced with STRIDE by Microsoft. PASTA and ATASM are in active use.

45. A. CASBs are often used to control usage based on roles and rights, but they aren't used to monitor based on costs in the cloud service itself—instead, cost limiting rules are often used in the cloud services themselves. They are also used to limit the potential for sensitive data loss and to detect anomalous usage patterns.

46. C. Kathleen knows that sandboxing, or creating a secure and isolated environment, is commonly used for malicious software testing. An IPS or antivirus can be used to detect malicious activities and might be deployed in the sandbox as part of the instrumentation. A SIEM solution is used to centralize and correlate security events and information.

47. A. Using the CASB to enforce encryption between an on-premises location and cloud providers will provide the most effective protection against third parties seeing the data in transit. Tokenization and masking help protect data while it is being accessed but don't prevent it from being exposed in transit. Upload prevention doesn't prevent downloads from being accessed.

48. A. Containers contain elements of the operating system but share the host's kernel. They also contain libraries, configuration files, and the application files or binaries themselves.

49. A. API keys should be unique, random, and non-guessable to ensure that attackers cannot guess or otherwise identify them.

50. C. Ian can filter based on user identity and the service the users are attempting to use to most effectively filter service usage by role. Activity and data don't identify the user, and activities don't necessarily uniquely identify a service.

51. A. ATASM considers architecture, threats, attack surfaces (*not* attacks) and mitigations.

52. A. Testing done against running code is called dynamic testing. Static testing reviews source code. Automatic and structured testing are not commonly used testing terms.

53. D. WAFs focus on web traffic and thus typically scan HTTP traffic rather than BGP, ICMP, or SMTP traffic.

54. B. The Design phase allows Henry to include security design elements that will help ensure that his application is secure. The Requirements phase should include the need for security but won't specify how it will be accomplished, and deployment and maintenance are too late as the architecture has already been designed and implemented.

55. C. A sandbox can be used to run malware for analysis purposes as it won't affect (or infect) the production environment; it's worth noting, though, that some malware is sandbox-aware, so additional antimalware measures are advisable. Optimizing production by moving tasks isn't a typical use for a sandbox, remote secure access systems are called jumpboxes, and subnets are created using network configurations.

56. B. Containerization best meets the platform-agnostic approach that matches Valerie's requirements. While serverless is powerful, moving between native serverless platforms typically requires building to each provider's requirements. Virtual machines have more overhead than Valerie needs, and not configuring them for the application only makes them less suited to the task.

57. D. A Database Activity Monitor (DAM) solution provides database activity monitoring that includes privileged account usage logging and monitoring in addition to other security and monitoring features. A WAF would help with web application security issues but doesn't meet the need described here. DB-IPS and database SIEMs were made up for this question.

58. D. Requiring authentication and setting throttling limits and quotas help to prevent denial-of-service attacks on APIs. Scalable architecture can help handle the load but won't stop the attacks from occurring, and using an IPS might help stop attacks but an API gateway would be more likely to understand API traffic.

59. C. Software that has either been purchased from a vendor or developed internally can be tested in a sandboxed environment that mimics the production environment in order to determine whether there will be any interoperability problems when it is installed into actual production. It isn't used for user awareness or regulatory requirement evaluation or API security testing in most cases.

60. C. FIPS 140-2 is a U.S. government standard that specifies the security requirements for cryptographic modules. If the module Jen is using is FIPS 140-2-certified, she will have met her goal. PCI compliance is used for credit cards, AES is not a certification, and GLBA is a U.S. act that requires financial institutions to secure their customers private information.

61. B. Rotating secrets limits the blast radius of exposed or compromised secrets. Extending their lifecycle does the opposite and means they can have a longer lifecycle in the hands of attackers. Replacing secrets with tokens won't meet the needs of most service environments. While certificate revocation lists (CRLs) exist, secret expiration lists do not.

62. B. Olivia is conducting functional testing that seeks to test whether software meets business requirements. This does not specify a load or stress test scenario.

63. C. SMS factors are considered the least secure of these options because of SIM swapping and VoIP-based attacks on SMS messages.

64. C. Review of the source code is static testing and does not meet Ben's needs. The other answers all include dynamic testing options.

65. B. CAPTCHA-based security systems help to reduce the impact of bots by requiring human interaction. While there are ways to work around CAPTCHAs, Yariv knows that they require additional work from attackers and will help reduce the overall load from bots. SQL injection and XSS are not mentioned in the question, and requiring logins without additional protections will not help.

66. D. When Emily logs in using her Google credentials, Google acts as the identity provider and tells the third-party service provider that she has logged in using her user ID and passwords successfully. The service provider must then authorize her to use services. Nothing in the question indicates whether the service provider may be a storage provider.

67. D. Not all programs (or organizations) will require database access, or even use databases, and hashing is not a common requirement since the data will not be readable. Encryption at rest and in transit, as well as data masking, are all commonly employed to protect sensitive information.

68. C. SAML is an XML-based protocol, and Kristen knows that an XML firewall that is SAML-aware with appropriate rules for identity-based protection would be her best option. IDS systems cannot rate-limit even if they are SAML-aware. WAFs are designed for web applications rather than specifically for XML and SAML-based filtering, and a DAM is a database-specific tool.

69. C. Using SSO does not prevent the use of multifactor authentication. In fact, it often makes it easier since organizations can centralize their use of MFA.

70. D. Static testing reviews source code. Dynamic testing would test outcomes and performance.

71. B. Biometric readers are the least likely secondary factor to be supported by cloud vendors. Hardware and software tokens as well as SMS factors are commonly supported by cloud providers.

72. D. Once planning is done, organizations typically move into the Requirements Gathering phase to ensure that they know what the software they will build will do. Design, Build, Test, Deploy, and Maintain are common follow-up phases.

73. B. Waterfall phases each serve as the input for the next phase and move only in one direction.

74. B. Requirements are typically mapped to the software in the Design phase. Requirements will be created in the Define phase, validated in the Test phase, and of course the software will be run in production in the Operations phase.

75. D. Nonfunctional testing seeks to test to meet customer expectations and performance requirements, including how software behaves under abnormal conditions. Black box, or zero knowledge, testing attempts to replicate an attacker's experience; white box, or full knowledge, testing provides complete insight into an environment or tool, including access to source code and documentation, and functional testing is conducted based on business requirements.

76. D. Since there are a number of different open source licenses, Gabriel's best bet is to ensure that his organization reviews the licenses that apply to each software package or component they use. This can be complex and time-consuming, and organizations often limit the licenses they are willing to accept to reduce this burden.

77. B. Injection, distributed denial-of-service, cross-site scripting, on-path, and credential stuffing attacks are all commonly aimed at APIs. Malware attacks, however, are not a common API threat.

78. B. The SAFECode fundamental practices note that errors should be handled in a secure and graceful way. It recommends against providing too much information in errors and that unanticipated errors should be flagged to both users and administrators but with different levels of information appropriate to each group.

79. C. Jason should use a commercial certificate authority for any certificate used in production. This allows users to validate the certificate and the certificate chain to ensure trust.

80. B. A signature ensures that the file is both the correct file and that it has not been changed, and validates that it was provided by the signer. An SHA2 hash is the second-best option, although attackers might modify the hash on the site or modify the file before it is hashed. File size and version number are the least useful options.

81. A. Interactive application security testing (IAST) uses software instrumentation to validate performance and function and is typically conducted during the QA/Test phase of the

SDLC. SCA or software composition analysis reviews the components that make up an application. Interactive and structured DST were made up for this question.

82. A. Changing encryption algorithms if a problem is found with one that is currently in use is actually a best practice that SAFECode recommends. They call it "cryptographic agility" and note that you need to be able to transition to new mechanisms, libraries, and keys when needed. Defining what to protect, what mechanisms will be used, and how keys and certificates will be managed are all common best practices and are also recommended by SAFECode.

83. A. In a PaaS environment, the customer is responsible for the security of applications in the production environment. The service provider will be responsible for the underlying hardware and platform itself.

84. A. Abuse case testing will test how users could abuse the software, including the type of issues James is concerned about. White box, or full knowledge, testing and black box, or zero knowledge, testing both describe the amount of information that testers have about the environment, and use case testing validates how software is supposed to be used, not how it could be abused.

85. D. Active Directory, SAML, and vendor-native SSO options are all commonly supported, but LDAP is not a commonly supported SSO option for most cloud vendors.

86. A. In the Define phase, organizations work to determine the purpose of the software and what it needs to do to meet the needs of users. Design and Development stages then work to architect and build software that meets those requirements. Detect is not an SDLC phase.

87. C. Setting a nonprivileged user as the process owner will work in many cases. Setting the container owner as a nonprivileged user won't stop root from running it in a poor configuration. Limiting root login or requiring multifactor won't stop a process from running as root either.

88. A. Jessica should perform static testing to help her organization identify code quality issues by reviewing the source code for the application. Dynamic testing can identify functional issues but may not identify code quality or business logic flaws. Black box testing won't allow the access to the code she needs, and software composition analysis seeks to understand what components make up an application.

89. B. The STRIDE threat model does not deal with business continuity and disaster recovery (BC/DR) actions. All the other options are elements of STRIDE: escalation of privilege, repudiation, and spoofing.

90. D. API gateways are well suited to this type of architecture because they focus on service discovery and API security as well as rate-limiting and other security controls like authentication. XML firewalls and cloud application security brokers (CASBs) are both used for other purposes, and RPC gateways allow remote procedure calls to other networks and services.

91. A. The earlier security inputs are included in the project, the more efficient and less costly security controls are overall. The Define phase is the earliest part of the SDLC, and thus is when security staff should be included.

92. A. Tahir is conducting a nonfunctional test that checks for behavior under load and since the program is actually running, it is dynamic testing rather than static testing of source code.

93. B. Joanna is using a single sign-on (SSO) infrastructure to allow her to sign on in one location and to use those credentials in multiple locations with various service providers. RDP (Remote Desktop Protocol) is used for graphical access to Windows systems, OTP is a one-time password, and MFA is multifactor authentication.

94. A. Tampering impacts the integrity of data by modifying it.

95. C. OWASP, the Open Web Application Security Project, provides both cloud and web application security top 10 lists that are community sourced and which are well suited to awareness training. ASVS sets standards for application validation and security testing. CVE and NIST are not community-based web application security guides.

96. D. Interactive application security testing (IAST) would be most likely to occur during the Testing phase of the SDLC.

97. C. Using automated creation tools for passphrases will prevent staff members from reusing passwords or falling into habits that result in easily guessed passphrases and passwords. Using a word list, shared passphrases, or simply adding complexity will not meet Malika's needs.

98. A. SAML (Security Assertion Markup Language) is commonly used to enable identity federation. FIPS 140-2 is a U.S. government encryption mechanism standard, XML may be needed but is a very broad standard for extensible markup languages, and FIM is federated identity management, a generic term describing the overall concept, not a technology or technological capability.

99. C. Replicating production for QA testing, then promoting from QA to production once testing is complete, is a common design practice in application development environments. Adding software going through QA to production environments or allowing users to use QA systems instead of production can lead to a negative user experience, and creating a QA environment that doesn't match production may invalidate testing.

100. A. ASVS uses a three-level code validation assurance level model, with level 3 requiring critical applications to meet in-depth validation and testing requirements.

Chapter 5: Domain 5: Cloud Security Operations

1. C. A service-level agreement (SLA) defines service-level targets and the responsibilities of the IT service provider and customer. An OLA (operational level agreement) is an internal agreement between the IT service provider and another part of the same organization and supports the service provider's delivery of the service. Service acceptance criteria (SAC) are the criteria used to determine whether a service meets its quality and functionality goals. Finally, a service-level requirement (SLR) defines the requirements of a service from the customer's perspective.

2. C. Proactive customer communications is key to managing expectations. Reactive communications are often used for data breach notification, regulatory compliance, and problem management.

3. C. Juanita knows that the major cloud vendors provide their own customized versions of Linux that often include additional agents and tools to help them work better with the provider's infrastructure. She should verify that this is the case, but it is the most likely scenario for a freshly built system as described.

4. A. When managing systems at scale in the cloud, Ben knows that the best option is often to use the cloud IaaS vendor's tools, particularly because they are typically designed to handle both operating systems that may have special features to work in the vendor's environment and applications.

5. D. Jason knows that cloud service providers typically do not allow direct or third-party audits of their systems and services but that they do provide audit results to customers.

6. A. A cloud hardware security module (HSM) is used to create, store, and manage secrets.

7. B. Charles knows that his situation calls for an infrastructure as code design, which uses code and configuration files or variables to allow rapid deployment using scripts and automated tools. A CI/CD pipeline will often leverage infrastructure as code and automation tools, but it doesn't directly meet this need. APIs (application programming interfaces) are used to access data from services, and check-in/checkout design was made up for this question.

8. A. From a service continuity management perspective, the number of business processes with continuity agreements is the only relevant answer from this list. Understanding the number of business practices that have continuity planning in place and assessing which gaps in coverage are critical is a common practice to improve service continuity.

9. B. Agile and DevOps are well suited to rapid release cycles, with continuous integration and continuous delivery processes. Waterfall and spiral both tend to take longer periods of time for each release, and RAD is not as widely adopted and not as release focused.

10. B. Assessing results occurs at the end of the seven-step process, helping provide feedback into the next cycle's vision determination phase.

11. A. Maintenance mode migrates virtual machines to other hosts or waits until they are powered down to allow for hardware or other maintenance. Tim knows that he'll need to ensure all VMs are migrated or shut down and that he can then perform maintenance.

12. A. Kathleen should look for a security information and event management (SIEM) tool. They're used to centralized log collection, analysis, and detection capabilities and often have automated methods of finding issues and alerting on them. An IPS (intrusion prevention system) is used to detect and stop attacks, a CASB (cloud application security broker) is used to control and manage access to cloud services, and MITRE is a U.S. government–funded research organization with a heavy focus on security work.

13. B. TLS (Transport Layer Security) is an encryption protocol used to secure data in transit. VLANs are used to logically separate network segments, DNSSEC is intended to provide security to domain name system requests, and DHCP provides IP addresses and other network configuration information to systems automatically.

14. C. Blocking inbound connections to port 22, the default SSH port will stop attackers and third parties from outside of the network from accessing SSH as long as it hasn't been changed to another port. TCP 3389 is associated with RDP.

15. B. A configuration management database (CMDB) is frequently used in mature standards-based configuration management environments where it stores both configuration management and information about relationships between configuration items (CIs). CRMs are customer relationship management tools and aren't part of the CCSP exam. A change catalog was made up for this question.

16. B. Maria knows that PaaS environments are patched by the vendor and that she does not need to perform patching of the software or cloud service. She may, however, have to decide when to adopt patches or versions—although she won't be able to delay adopting new versions forever!

17. C. The ITIL subprocesses for availability management are designing services for availability, availability testing, and availability monitoring and reporting. Even if you're not familiar with ITIL, thinking about a standards-based approach to availability might help you— design, testing, and monitoring are all logical steps in a process like this.

18. B. Vendors are the least likely to have contractual or regulatory requirements that mean that they must be notified. Vendors often have to tell their customers about breaches, but customers typically do not need to tell their vendors!

19. A. Megan's next step once she has an inventory is to create a baseline. With that in hand she can establish a CMB, deploy new assets configured to meet the baseline, and document deviations that the CMB approves if needed.

20. B. Guest operating system virtualization tools add additional functionality like use of GPUs, shared clipboards, and drag and drop between guest operating systems, shared folders, and similar features that require additional integration between the guest OS and the underlying hypervisor and hardware.

21. D. The security review objective focuses on whether security practices and procedures align to risk tolerance for the organization and includes verification and testing like an SOC 2 Type 2 audit does. Design, testing, and management of incidents involve the topics they describe.

22. B. Ensuring that the code itself is secure in an automated process requires a tool that can be run as part of the process. That means that the only option from the list that is viable is an automated review of code. Manual static code review isn't a good fit for a CI/CD pipeline in most cases due to speed requirements. WAFs and IPSs can help protect the application, but again, they don't test the code or make the application itself more secure.

23. B. Since IaaS provides the customer with access to and control over some of the network, they must take responsibility for network-based risks. The IaaS provider provides services and infrastructure, and thus must take responsibility for some of the network-based risks as well. Third-party incident responders do not play a role in risk responsibility in this model.

24. B. Configuration management typically starts with baselining. While policies and documentation are important, creating a baseline allows organizations to understand what they have and what state it is in, a critical part of the change management practice.

25. D. Network latency is the critical factor when transaction volume is key. Bandwidth is less critical for small transactions, even when there are thousands of them. Routes may influence all of these options but aren't as critical as the impact they have on the traffic.

26. A. Azure's best practices suggest creating disk snapshots for both the VM's operating system and data disks, safely storing the snapshots, then comparing hashes between the images and the originals. Comparing the hashes of a snapshot to a copy won't validate it against the original, VMs can't be exported as hashes, and disk images aren't signed in a way that makes sense for this type of forensic use. If you'd like to read the full practice document for more detail, you can find it at `https://docs.microsoft.com/en-us/azure/architecture/example-scenario/forensics`.

27. A. Businesses typically don't manage customer capacity. Instead, they would assess their own capacity, known as business capacity management.

28. B. Data breach regulations typically focus on customer notification. Nick should work with legal counsel to ensure that his organization is compliant with any notification requirements for his industry and location.

29. B. Valerie should carefully document the chain of custody for the disk images so that they can be considered valid for potential legal action. Legal hold is the process for preserving data for legal action, not for documenting actions taken with disk images and other forensic artifacts. Seizure is a type of acquisition but isn't mentioned here, and disposal would occur after the potential legal case.

30. C. Tagging is a critical part of instance scheduling, but even more so for large numbers of instances. It allows schedules to be easily applied to all instances with the proper tags. Since Asha wants to use her cloud provider's scheduling, a third party does not meet her requirements. Auto-scheduling was made up for this question, and disabling unused instances helps with spend but doesn't help more than tagging would for scheduling.

31. C. Adding new hardware to increase performance is not an element of hardening. Hardening is the process of provisioning a specific element (in this case, a host) against attack. Audits don't protect against attacks; they only detect and direct responses to attacks.

32. A. Automated patching systems can cause disruptions if a bad patch is released or if there is an installation problem that is not detected. That means that a human is often in the loop for patching, or that patches are installed in nonproduction environments first where they can be validated prior to further installations. Automated systems typically do have abilities to report on patches that fail installation and on systems that do not have patches in place, and it is a desirable feature to speed patching and patch accuracy via automation.

33. B. The management systems control the entirety of the virtual environment and are therefore extremely valuable and need to be protected accordingly. When possible, isolating those management systems, both physically and virtually, is optimum.

34. B. ITIL v4 categorizes deployment management as part of release management.

35. C. Carlos knows that virtual machines use virtualized processors and that temperature and voltages can't be tracked for virtual CPUs. He can track load, and most operating systems have a built-in method for doing so. If voltages and temperature are an ongoing concern, he will need to monitor them at the underlying operating system, hardware, or hypervisor level.

36. C. Megan is a process owner and is responsible for the fit to purpose for the continual service improvement effort. Continual service improvement managers (CSI managers) improve ITSM processes and services. Process architects ensure that processes work together and support each other effectively, and customers consume or purchase services.

37. D. Felicia wants to perform firewall-like rules-based filtering, which is a function of network security groups. Honeypots are used to capture and observe attacker behaviors, and IDSs and IPSs are used to detect and, in the case of IPSs, potentially prevent attacks based on behaviors and signatures.

38. B. Risk can't be entirely prevented, but it can be drastically reduced. Hardware redundancy, local sharing and balancing, and failure mode design are all common practices when designing redundancy into cloud datacenters.

39. A. Cloud providers who are PCI-compliant will typically provide an attestation of compliance upon request. This type of documentation is important for regulators as part of compliance validation. SOC audits don't specifically test PCI compliance, and most vendors will not allow customers to conduct PCI assessments of their underlying infrastructure.

40. A. IaaS vendors typically allow customers to scan their own internal systems but may recommend that certain types of instances with lower resources are not scanned to avoid disruption. While vendors may provide scanning tools, they typically don't require customers to use them in an IaaS environment. Since external scans can inadvertently impact other customers, external scanning is typically prohibited or limited, and scheduling a time and date may be required for more advanced or specialized testing.

41. B. Using load balancing to drain load from existing systems and then replacing them with new, patched instances is a common best practice for cloud-hosted service environment patching. Manual and scripted patching can cause outages, as could re-IPing as systems are swapped over.

42. B. Disabling logging would prevent administrators from diagnosing problems. Transferring users, preventing new connections, and notifying customers are all common practices when entering maintenance mode.

43. C. A virtual trusted platform module (vTPM) is the only solution that will meet Jack's needs. HSMs (hardware security modules) are used to create, store, and manage secrets, including cryptographic keys and certificates, but aren't used for boot security. Cloud TPM was made up for this question, but hardware and cloud HSMs do exist.

44. D. Yarif is running a Type 2 hypervisor, which is defined as a hypervisor that runs on top of an operating system rather than on bare metal like a Type 1 hypervisor. Classic and advanced hypervisors are not commonly used terms.

45. C. While ITIL focuses on identification, containment, resolution, and maintenance, the overall goal is restore service as soon as possible after an incident. It does not focus on third-party responders. Problem escalations to incidents are part of identification but aren't the main goal, nor is identifying incidents to allow response.

46. A. Incidents are defined in ITIL as interruptions of normal service, including reductions in the quality of services that may violate an SLA. Problem management resolves the cause of problems, while incident response restores services to normal levels.

47. D. All problems are potential causes of incidents, but not all problems result in incidents.

48. D. The number of individuals impacted is of interest to customers and management but is not a useful KPI for availability.

49. C. Information security policies—particularly what ITIL calls "underpinning information security policies"—are the basis of security management in ITIL.

50. C. In a continuous integration/continuous delivery pipeline, automated testing is conducted and the code must pass testing before code is released. Human intervention or approval is not typically required for CI/CD pipelines.

51. B. Snapshots are the most common means of capturing disk images from virtual machines in IaaS environments. Using forensic image acquisition tools can be challenging in cloud environments due to a lack of access to the underlying hardware. DBAN is a wiping tool, and file copy utilities often don't provide a complete forensically sound copy, although they may be the only option in some cases.

52. C. These are examples of infrastructure-as-code tools. While Agile pipelines may use Terraform, they would do so as part of an infrastructure as code strategy. They aren't specifically used for incident response or legal hold strategies but could be leveraged for both, once again as part of an infrastructure as code solution.

53. A. ISO 20000-1 describes service management. ISO 27001 describes an information security management system. ITIL is not an ISO standard, nor is COBIT—in fact, they're their own standards.

54. B. A security information and event manager (SIEM) is the ideal tool for this purpose. A network operations center (NOC) and an IPS (intrusion prevention system) won't centralize logs and incident information, and DLP (data loss prevention) is intended to stop data from leaving an organization.

55. B. Unlike an IDS, an IPS needs to be placed in-line with traffic. This means that an IPS can block legitimate traffic if it is improperly identified or if the IPS fails in a closed state. An IDS cannot fail open or closed, as it is not in-line. Both IDSs and IPSs can use signature and behavior-based detection.

56. C. Turning on flow logging can provide the visibility Amanda wants. Flows show which IP address contacted another IP address, the source and destination ports, and the volume of data. None of the other types of logging listed will be as useful for this task.

57. A. AI features in SIEM devices are often used to analyze and learn network traffic patterns, then use log correlation and threat intelligence features to identify unexpected and potentially malicious behavior while leveraging learning capabilities. Log correlation and threat intelligence alone will not do this, and reporting is needed afterward.

58. A. A typical DHCP response will provide a default gateway, a subnet mask, DNS server information, and an IP address for the host to use. It does not assign MAC addresses to systems—that's a hardware-level setting, and it doesn't define a default route, just a default gateway, nor does it provide firewall rule definitions.

59. D. Using secure boot, disabling cut and paste between VMs and the console and removing unnecessary hardware are all common security practices. Since the virtual machine console is equivalent to direct access to the system, use of the console should be limited to only critical actions and the virtualization management platform should be used for the majority of actions.

60. A. Honeypots are used to capture attack traffic for study but aren't used to stop attacks. Firewalls, security groups, and IPSs are all used to stop attacks by preventing malicious traffic from entering a network.

61. A. Using alternate CPU architectures isn't a common high availability technique. Using multiple vendors, having SLAs in place, and using self-hosted failover capabilities are all methods that can achieve this goal.

62. A. Susan's outage points to a need for availability management. Susan may invest in redundant systems, additional monitoring, or other practices and design elements that can ensure her organization's website will be more resilient and thus more available.

63. A. The only data that Li is likely to be able to obtain for forensic investigation is log files. Disk images, VM snapshots, and network packet capture data require lower-level access to systems and the network than an SaaS provider will normally make available.

64. B. Service capacity management measures performance and checks it against requirements set in SLAs and service-level requirements. Business capacity management involves interpreting business needs into requirements for services and architecture. Component capacity management focuses on the actual components of an infrastructure. Finally, contract capacity management is not an ISO/IEC 20000-1 configuration management subprocess.

65. D. An SOC, or security operations center, can be physical or virtual, and typically consists of a team that monitors for security events on an ongoing basis. An SOC team is likely to use a SIEM (security information and event management) tool. NAS is network attached storage, and SCCM is the name for Microsoft's now-outmoded Systems Center Configuration Manager, now branded as Endpoint Configuration Manager.

66. C. Hui's organization is using a cloud orchestration technology to automate tasks in their cloud environment. That may include scheduling, but it covers a much broader set of tasks than just scheduling. Maintenance mode is used to remove running systems from a VM cluster to allow for hardware or software upgrades. Abstraction is a term that describes a means of hiding the details of a system, often as a way of making management or other tasks simpler.

67. B. Megan is using an artificial intelligence (AI)-based tool that learns from the data it is exposed to and improves its capabilities. An IPS looks for malicious or unwanted network traffic and can block it. Log analysis may be involved in Megan's tasks, but the problem describes far more than log analysis, and forensic data capture is done as part of investigations.

68. A. Jim has deployed a honeypot, a system designed to capture attacker tools and techniques to allow for analysis. Honeynets are networks set up in a similar manner to detect network attacks and attack techniques. Darknets are unused IP ranges that are instrumented to look for unexpected traffic indicating probes by potential attackers. Bastion hosts are used to provide secure access from a lower security zone to a higher security zone.

69. D. Olivia knows that once the data or artifacts have been identified, preservation is the next step. Even if you're not familiar with digital forensics techniques, you can consider the flow for a likely forensic capture process. Analysis, documentation, and presentation can't be done until data is captured!

70. D. IaC can cause errors to spread quickly. It actually helps increase consistency by removing opportunities for human error, it is easily updated, and it increases speed in most cases.

71. A. The benefits of any clustered environment come at the cost of higher prices. Keith should expect to spend more money, but gain performance, availability and reliability, and capacity depending on his configuration and design choices.

72. A. ITIL's configuration identification subprocess includes identifying and specifying the attributes for each configuration item type and subcomponent and the relationships between each CI or subcomponent and others in the organization. Configuration control focuses on managing changes in the configuration management system. Configuration verification and audit is a single subprocess and validates that configurations match what is expected.

73. A. The only metric among those listed that is typically available to customers in an infrastructure as a service environment is CPU utilization to help track usage.

74. C. CIs (configuration items) are the components or services that are managed as part of a configuration management effort. Configuration models are used to evaluate changes and causes of incidents. Configuration records are the records that describe configuration item relationships and settings. Service assets include a range of things that allow organizations to deliver services including third party vendor services.

75. D. While bandwidth, compute, and storage usage are all typically measured and billed, latency is usually not directly charged for. Instead, providers are likely to provide a distinct low-latency service if they charge for latency-related items.

76. A. Customers are typically unable to obtain forensic data from the underlying infrastructure as a service environment. Memory for the instance, disk volumes, and logs are all common cloud forensic artifacts.

77. D. SaaS providers are unlikely to allow third parties to scan their production services. While Selah could just scan her provider anyway, this is often prohibited in contracts that customers sign with their provider. Instead, Selah should ask the vendor about their patching and scanning practices to determine if they are appropriate to her organization's risk tolerance and to see if documentation or attestation of practices like an SOC audit is available.

78. C. If backups aren't working properly, or cannot be restored, checking all of the other actions described won't be of use.

79. B. A number of ISO standards related to forensics exist, including 27037, 27041, 27043, and 27050-1. ISO 27001 covers the best practice standards for information security management, and 27002 describes security controls. The ISO 9000 series covers quality management.

80. D. Security operations centers typically do not provide eDiscovery services. They do take on threat and intelligence monitoring, incident response and recovery, threat and vulnerability management, and data protection tasks, among many others.

81. B. Ryan's best option is to use GitHub's APIs to download the repository and then to store it in a secure location. Relying on GitHub's own backup practices leaves GitHub in control of the code and Ryan vulnerable to outages, and reliance on third-party sites doesn't give Ryan control of the backups either.

82. A. ISO/IEC 20000-1 focuses on business capacity management, service capacity management, and component capacity management.

83. D. Release and deployment plans focus on creating and deploying releases. Lifecycle management is handled under other sections of the ISO standard and not within RDM plans.

84. A. ISO/IEC 20000-1 requires that organizations establish, approve, and communicate their information security policy. If you're not familiar with ISO/IEC 20000-1 or similar standards, review the list of answers for unlikely answers—like requirements for third-party review. Using a standardized template can help to narrow down answers for questions like these.

85. B. Distributed resource scheduling in VMWare moves virtual machines from heavily loaded hosts to those with more resources available to help balance the load across the cluster. Automatic instance management and instance segregation were made up for this question, and round-robin load balancing is a form of load balancing where requests are distributed to each server in a cluster as they come in based on a list.

86. D. The amount of data stored on a drive isn't considered a hardware monitoring item. Powered-on time, temperature, and drive health are all elements of hardware monitoring.

87. C. The missing fourth item should be agreement sign-off and service activation, including service-level agreements and service acceptance criteria. Pricing is not part of ITIL v4 service management processes.

88. D. Michelle should select a virtual client that allows her to run her application in a cloud-hosted environment. This will allow the application to run in a secure location while still allowing her to access it from lower-trust devices.

89. B. While maintaining a library of software licenses is important, it is not part of hardening practices.

90. B. In ITIL the recovery plan includes detailed plans for returning systems and services to a working state and can also include recovering data to a known consistent state. The business continuity strategy sets the strategy for business functions. IT service continuity plans focus on how to ensure continuity during specified disasters for services and systems. Disaster recovery invocation guidelines explain how and when to invoke the DR procedures.

91. B. For many organizations the best option to select when facing cloud forensic investigations is to engage a third party. In this case, without an internal expert and as a small company, Jason's best bet is third-party experts.

92. A. A facility's geographic location influences both the requirements for things like HVAC as well as environmental threats like extreme weather. Proximity to population centers may have secondary influence on utilities or staffing, and both cost and security requirements may influence the design, but the larger impact is from its geographic location.

93. C. Change management practices and baselines need to include methods for handling deviations in reasonable ways. That means Rick should ensure that the policy includes an assignment of tasks, including deviation notification and documentation.

94. D. The production activities will make full use of pooled resources, so they will not be isolated unless the customer is paying for that specific characteristic of service. Provisioning, management, and access to storage should all be isolated to ensure security of those functions.

95. B. User interaction with the cloud is not described in this phrase. Ping, power, and pipe refers to connectivity, power, and facility space with services like HVAC.

96. A. For the purposes described in the question, a Tier 1 datacenter should suffice; it is the cheapest, and you need it only for occasional backup purposes (as opposed to constant access). The details of location and market are irrelevant and just distractors.

97. C. The most effective way for Isaac to acquire meaningful BC/DR capabilities is to move to a cloud-hosted datacenter. This means that his organization doesn't have to make major investments in their datacenter to add capabilities. Of course, staying with the current datacenter doesn't meet his needs already!

98. A. Creating and maintaining proper chain of custody documentation provides nonrepudiation for the process, ensuring that the handling will survive scrutiny at a later date. Data tampering by investigators could still occur but would be identified in a properly documented chain. Chain of custody might be required by law enforcement, but it won't help a company engage with them, and plausible deniability is not a forensic concept.

99. B. VLANs (virtual local area networks) are logical overlays used to segregate network devices. DHCP (Dynamic Host Control Protocol) provides a means of giving systems IP addresses and other important network information automatically when requested. VPNs (virtual private networks) are used to create secure channels between networks, typically over untrusted networks, and STP (Spanning Tree Protocol) is used to prevent loops in networks.

100. C. Backup power does not have to be delivered by batteries; it can be fed to the datacenter through redundant utility lines or from a generator.

Chapter 6: Domain 6: Legal, Risk, and Compliance

1. D. Vendor lock-in occurs when the customer is dissuaded from leaving a provider, even when that is the best decision for the customer.

These contract terms can be described as favorable only from the provider's perspective; option D is preferable to option A for describing this situation.

There was no description of negotiation included in the question; option B is incorrect.

IaaS is a service model and doesn't really apply to anything in this context; option C is incorrect.

2. C. ISO 27050 is an industry standard that provides guidance for eDiscovery programs. ISO 27001 and ISO 27002 provide industry standard control objectives and control suggestions for cybersecurity. ISO 27701 provides industry standard guidance for information privacy programs.

3. C. The entity that uses the data on behalf of the owner/controller is a data processor. The data subject is the person who the personally identifiable information (PII) describes. The entity that collects or creates the PII is the data owner or controller. Entities that regulate the use of PII are regulators.

4. C. In order to deliver credible, believable expert testimony, it's important that your personnel have more than an amateur's understanding and familiarity with any forensic tools they use to perform analysis. Formal training and certification are excellent methods for creating credibility.

    Scripting testimony is usually frowned on by the court; coaching witnesses how to perform and what to expect in court is all right, but it does not lead to credibility. Option A is incorrect.

    Your expert witnesses are not allowed to withhold any evidence from their testimony if it is pertinent to the case, even if that evidence aids the other side. Option B is incorrect.

    You should pay your employees for their time, regardless of whether they're performing on the job site or in a courtroom, but this has nothing to do with enhancing credibility. Option D is incorrect.

5. C. Deploying a firewall is a risk mitigation strategy designed to reduce the likelihood or impact of the risk. If Prisha suggested that the organization simply continue to function as-is, that would be risk acceptance. Risk transference would shift the risk to a third-party, such as an insurance provider. Rejection, or denial of the risk, is not a valid strategy, even though it occurs!

6. C. Nora is an employee of the organization, so her work is clearly internal in nature. External work is performed by independent third parties. Nora is an auditor and she is testing the effectiveness of controls, so her work is within the scope of a formal audit, rather than an informal assessment. Therefore, this project should be described as an internal audit.

7. C. Carla is assigned as the manager of her organization's privacy program. This assignment is an example of the GAPP principle of Management. She is communicating about a change in privacy practices to her customers, which is an example of Notice. She is also offering those customers the opportunity to opt out of the use of their data. This is an example of the principle of Choice and Consent. It is important to note that consent does not need to be explicit and done on an opt-in basis. Opt-out, implicit consent also satisfies this principle. The principle of Access says that individuals should be able to review and update their personal information. There is no description of Access in this scenario.

8. A. SOX is only applicable to publicly traded corporations, not all companies. HIPAA may be applicable to the data you work with as a medical student, if you work with patient data. Your payment and personal data are governed by PCI DSS. FERPA protects your personal student information.

9. D. In a risk acceptance strategy, the organization decides that taking no action is the most beneficial route to managing a risk.

10. A. The Gramm–Leach–Bliley Act (GLBA) contains provisions regulating the privacy of customer financial information. It applies specifically to financial institutions.

11. A. The proper course of action when records are not available is to write a statement of scope limitation that describes the issue and the impact on the audit. Bill could have avoided this by performing an alternative test of the same control objective, but the scenario says this is not possible.

12. B. The General Data Protection Regulation prohibits entities within a country that has no nationwide privacy law from gathering or processing privacy data belonging to EU citizens. Entities can be allowed to do so if the following conditions are met:

(1) Their own country has nationwide laws that comply with the EU laws.

(2) The entity creates contractual language that complies with the EU laws and has that language approved by each EU country from which the entity wishes to gather citizen data.

(3) The entity voluntarily subscribes to its own nation's Privacy Shield program (assuming that program is found acceptable by the EU authorities).

There is no process for the entity to appeal to the EU for permission to do so, however.

13. B. Qualitative tools are often used in business impact assessment to capture the impact on intangible factors such as customer confidence, employee morale, and reputation.

14. D. The ISO 27001 certification is for the information security management system (ISMS), the organization's entire security program.

The SAS 70 and SSAE 18 are audit standards for service providers and include some review of security controls but not a cohesive program (and the SAS 70 is outdated); options A and B are not correct.

The SOC reports are how SSAE 18 audits are conducted; option C is incorrect.

15. A. An IT security audit is not intended to locate financial fraud; it may, however, lead to such revelations unintentionally. There are specific other audits that exist for this purpose. All the other options are incorrect because they are intended goals for IT security audits.

16. C. It is entirely appropriate to engage stakeholders during the audit process. While the CEO may be demanding information in a rude manner, that does not mean that they are not an important stakeholder. The audit team should carefully engage the CEO and keep them engaged throughout the audit process. The matter only needs to be referred to other authorities if the CEO makes improper requests.

17. C. The Statement on Standards for Attestation Engagements (SSAE) 18 is the current AICPA (American Institute of Certified Public Accountants) audit standard.

ISO 27001 is an international audit standard.

The Sarbanes–Oxley Act (SOX) is a U.S. law pertaining to publicly traded corporations.

There is no such thing as the IEC 43770 standard.

18. B. With rare exceptions, digital forensics does not include creation of data (other than the forensic reports regarding the analysis of data). While this could arguably be considered an aspect of digital forensics as well, the other options are more suited to describing digital forensics, so this is the best negative answer.

19. B. This is the definition of a gap analysis.

SOC reports are specific kinds of audits; option A is incorrect.

The scoping statement is a pre-audit function that aids both the organization and the auditor to determine what, specifically, will be audited. Option C is incorrect.

Federal guidelines are government recommendations on how something should be done. Option D is incorrect.

20. B. Belinda is obligated to gain assurance that the cloud provider has appropriate controls in place. It is unlikely that she will gain permission to audit those controls herself and, even if she gained this permission, that would result in excessive and unnecessary costs. She should instead ask the cloud provider for the report of an independent audit. SOC 1 audits are designed specifically to test the controls covering customer financial statements and would be the appropriate audit type in this scenario. SOC 2 audits cover cybersecurity controls more broadly and would be unnecessary.

21. D. Tony would see the best results by combining elements of quantitative and qualitative risk assessment. Quantitative risk assessment excels at analyzing financial risk, while qualitative risk assessment is a good tool for intangible risks. Combining the two techniques provides a well-rounded risk picture.

22. D. ISO 27018 describes privacy requirements for cloud providers, including an annual audit mandate.

Option A is incorrect because NIST SP 800-37 describes the Risk Management Framework and is not an international privacy standard.

The Personal Information Protection and Electronic Documents Act is a Canadian law relating to data privacy. Option B is incorrect.

Option C is incorrect because the PCI DSS is specifically for merchants who accept credit cards, not cloud providers (while cloud providers may process credit cards, and therefore must follow PCI DSS, option D is preferable, and a better answer).

23. A. Most state data breach notification laws are modeled after California's data breach notification law, which covers Social Security number, driver's license number, state identification card number, credit/debit card numbers, and bank account numbers (in conjunction with a PIN or password). California's breach notification law also protects some items not commonly found in other state laws, including medical records and health insurance information. These laws are separate and distinct from privacy laws, such as the California Consumer Privacy Act (CCPA), which regulates the handling of personal information more broadly.

24. A. When the cloud customer can ensure that their data will not be ported to a proprietary data format or system, the customer has a better assurance of not being constrained to a given provider; a platform-agnostic data set is more portable and less subject to vendor lock-in.

Availability may be an aspect of portability; the ease and speed at which the customer can access their own data can influence how readily the data might be moved to another provider. However, this is less influential than the format and structure of the data; option A is preferable to option B.

Storage space has little to do with vendor lock-in; option C is incorrect.

A list of OSs the provider offers might be influential for the customer's decision of which provider to select, but it is not typically a constraining factor that would restrict portability. Option D is incorrect.

25. B. The contract usually stipulates what kind of financial penalties are imposed when the provider fails to meet the SLAs (for instance, waiver for payment of a given service term). This is a huge motivating element for the provider.

Regulatory oversight usually affects the customer, not the provider; option A is incorrect.

The performance details are often included in the SLA but aren't the motivating factor; option C is incorrect.

In a perfect world, option D would be the correct answer; B is a better answer to this question, however.

26. D. A quantitative analysis of all of the risks facing an organization and their potential impact is best described as the organization's risk profile. Risk appetite, or risk tolerance, is the amount of risk that an organization is willing to accept. Risk appetite is a conceptual target, whereas risk profile is an assessment of the actual situation. Risk controls are used to manage risks to an acceptable level.

27. B. ISO/IEC 27018 addresses the privacy aspects of cloud computing for consumers and was the first international set of privacy controls in the cloud.

28. A. A litigation hold notice is required to prevent possible destruction of pertinent evidence that may be used in the case. An audit scoping letter outlines the parameters for an audit engagement. A memorandum of agreement documents a relationship between two organizations. A statement of work describes the work that will be performed by a contractor. None of these are used in response to the threat of a lawsuit.

29. C. Personally identifiable information (PII) includes data that can be used to distinguish or trace that person's identity and also includes information like their medical, educational, financial, and employment information. PHI is a form of PII that includes personal health information, EDI is electronic data interchange, and proprietary data is used to maintain an organization's competitive advantage.

30. B. Vendor viability is the risk that a vendor will not be able to continue operations and that a vendor shutdown will adversely impact customers. Vendor lock-in occurs when the costs of switching to a different vendor are prohibitively high. Vendor lockout occurs when a vendor prevents a customer from gaining access to their information. Vendor diversity is the use of multiple vendors to meet the same need to protect against vendor viability and reliability issues.

31. C. Risk mitigation strategies attempt to lower the probability and/or impact of a risk occurring. Intrusion prevention systems attempt to reduce the probability of a successful attack and are, therefore, examples of risk mitigation.

32. C. Sampling should be done randomly to avoid human bias. Sampling is an effective process if it is done on a truly random sample of sufficient size to provide effective coverage of the userbase. It is infeasible for a single person to review every single record. In an organization of 50,000 users with a 24 percent annual turnover, it is likely that at least 1,000 of those records have changed in the last month. This is still too many records to review. Asking account administrators to select the records to review is a conflict of interest, as they are the group being audited.

33. A. SLAs do not normally address issues of data confidentiality. Those provisions are normally included in a nondisclosure agreement (NDA).

34. B. The most appropriate standard to use as a baseline when evaluating vendors is to determine whether the vendor's security controls meet the organization's own standards. Compliance with laws and regulations should be included in that requirement and are a necessary, but not sufficient, condition for working with the vendor. Vendor compliance with their own policies also fits into the category of necessary, but not sufficient, controls, as the vendor's policy may be weaker than the organization's own requirements. The elimination of all identified security risks is an impossible requirement for a potential vendor to meet.

35. D. HAL Systems decided to stop offering the service because of the risk. This is an example of a risk avoidance strategy. The company altered its operations in a manner that eliminates the risk of NTP misuse. A risk mitigation strategy would continue offering the service but do so in a more secure manner. A risk acceptance strategy would continue offering the service as is. A risk transference strategy would shift some of the risk to a third party.

36. B. SSAE 18 is an audit standard for service organization controls (SOC) audits. These audits are conducted by independent, external audit firms.

37. D. Installing a device that will block attacks is an attempt to lower risk by reducing the likelihood of a successful application attack.

38. A. SSAE-18 does not assert specific controls. Instead, it reviews the use and application of controls in an audited organization. It is an attestation standard, used for external audits, and forms part of the underlying framework for SOC 1, 2, and 3 reports.

39. B. The Communications Assistance to Law Enforcement Act (CALEA) requires that all communications carriers make wiretaps possible for law enforcement officials who have an appropriate court order.

40. A. The Federal Information Security Management Act (FISMA) specifically applies to government contractors. The Government Information Security Reform Act (GISRA) was the precursor to FISMA and expired in November 2002. HIPAA and PCI DSS apply to healthcare and credit card information, respectively.

41. D. Privacy impact assessments (PIA) are used to review the appropriateness of all PII use by an organization. Business impact assessments (BIA) consider risks more broadly and are used in risk assessment processes. Business process assessments (BPA) are used to evaluate the efficiency of an organization's processes and identify opportunities for improvement. PPA is not an assessment type.

42. C. It is possible that Kevin could use any one of these documents. We should zero in on the portion of the question where it indicates that these are best practices. This implies that the advice is not mandatory and, therefore, would not go into a policy or standard. The fact that the advice is general in nature means that it likely is not well suited to the step-by-step nature of a procedure. A guideline would be the perfect place to document these best practices.

43. B. An organization's information security management system (ISMS) is a broad program covering all aspects of cybersecurity. This would include uses of customer data, network firewall protections, endpoint security, and many other control types. It would not cover the accuracy of the organization's financial statements, which would be within the scope of the financial audit. It would, however, include an evaluation of the cybersecurity controls affecting financial systems and statements.

44. D. An affidavit is only a form of formal testimony presented to the court. All the other options are enforceable governmental requests.

45. D. The Payment Card Industry Data Security Standard (PCI DSS) is a set of cybersecurity controls required for organizations that process credit card data. It is not a risk management standard and there is no information in this scenario that describes credit card processing. ISO 31000, NIST 800-37, and the Control Objectives for Information Technology (COBIT) are all relevant risk management standards.

46. A. The United States does not have a comprehensive national privacy law. Instead, it has a patchwork of industry-specific and subject-specific legislation. France and Germany are both members of the European Union and are subject to the comprehensive General Data Protection Regulation (GDPR). Canada has a comprehensive law titled the Personal Information Protection and Electronic Documents Act (PIPEDA).

47. A. ISAE 3402 provides international guidance on the assessment of service providers and is the appropriate standard to use in this situation. SSAE 18 is the equivalent document for assessments performed within the United States. SSAE 16 is an outdated version of that standard and has been superseded by SSAE 18. ISAE 3410 covers greenhouse gas emission statements and is completely irrelevant to this scenario.

48. C. The Sarbanes–Oxley Act (SOX) was enacted in response to the 2000 accounting scandal that caused the bankruptcy of Enron. At that time, top executives laid the claim that they were unaware of the accounting practices that led to the company's demise. SOX not only forces executives to oversee all accounting practices, but holds them accountable should such activity occurs again.

49. A. The most serious complication introduced by geographic expansion is the applicability of different laws and regulations from multiple jurisdictions. While datacenters in different countries may have different electric standards, this is not a major issue, as datacenter equipment is available for different electricity standards. There is no indication that Joe would expand into regions that lack sufficient internet connectivity or bandwidth, and there is no reason that Joe's organization would not be able to use the same operating systems in different regions.

50. C. The right to be forgotten, also known as the right to erasure, guarantees the data subject the ability to have their information removed from processing or use. It may be tied to consent given for data processing; if a subject revokes consent for processing, the data controller may need to take additional steps, including erasure.

51. B. The data controller makes the determination of purpose and scope of privacy-related data sets. The other options are the names of other privacy-related roles.

52. A. Because RAM is inherently volatile, and virtual resources are simulated only for limited time periods, virtual RAM is probably the most volatile data store.

Hardware RAM is probably as volatile as virtual RAM, but the virtualization aspect of option A may make it a more suitable answer for this particular question.

Log data and drive storage should both be durable and not volatile at all, so options C and D are incorrect.

53. C. The European Union provides standard contractual clauses that may be used to facilitate data transfer. That would be the best choice in a case where two different companies are sharing data. If the data were being shared internally within a company, binding corporate rules would also be an option. The EU/U.S. Privacy Shield was a safe harbor agreement that would previously have allowed the transfer but is no longer valid.

54. A. In an SaaS model, the customer has little insight into event logs and traffic analysis useful for evidentiary purposes. The customer will largely be reliant on the cloud provider to locate, collect, and deliver this information for eDiscovery.

Regulators do not take part in eDiscovery option B is incorrect.

In this situation, your company is the cloud customer and will not have a great deal of access to event logs, which may be a crucial element of eDiscovery options C and D are incorrect.

55. B. Ben should encrypt the data to provide an additional layer of protection as a compensating control. The organization has already made a policy exception, so he should not react by objecting to the exception or removing the data without authorization. Purchasing insurance may transfer some of the risk but is not a mitigating control.

56. B. While all of these areas may be indirectly touched by a GAPP assessment, the assessment is primarily focused on privacy, as GAPP is the Generally Accepted Privacy Principles.

57. C. Brad should first perform a gap analysis to identify any areas where his organization is not compliant with the new regulation. This gap analysis can serve as the roadmap for remediation efforts. The business impact analysis (BIA) is performed as part of a risk assessment process. Privacy impact analyses (PIA) focus primarily on privacy matters. Baseline development is done to identify common configuration standards.

58. B. A health and fitness application developer would not necessarily be collecting or processing healthcare data, and the terms of HIPAA do not apply to this category of business. HIPAA regulates three types of entities—healthcare providers, health information clearinghouses, and health insurance plans—as well as the business associates of any of those covered entities.

59. A. A master services agreement (MSA) is an umbrella document that governs many different projects conducted by the same service provider. Each one of those projects is then described within a statement of work (SOW). A business partnership agreement (BPA) is used to define the terms of a joint venture between two organizations. A memorandum of understanding (MOU) is an informal document describing the relationship between two organizations or business units of the same organization.

60. C. The CCM cross-references many industry standards, laws, and guidelines.

61. A. The annualized loss expectancy (ALE) is the amount of damage that the organization expects to occur each year as the result of a given risk. The annualized rate of occurrence (ARO) is the number of times the organization expects the risk to occur each year. The single loss expectancy (SLE) is the amount of damage that the organization expects to occur each time the risk materializes. The exposure factor (EF) is the percentage of the asset that will be damaged each time the risk materializes.

62. B. In general, companies should be aware of the breach laws in any location where they do business. U.S. states have a diverse collection of breach laws and requirements, meaning that in this case, Greg's company may need to review many different breach laws to determine which they may need to comply with if they conduct business in the state or with the state's residents.

63. A. This is an example of due care. Due care is that you're taking the same care that an ordinary, reasonable person would take under the same circumstances. So, when you're making day-to-day security decisions, you're making the same decisions that a reasonable security professional would take.

Due diligence, like due care, is all about doing the right things, but due diligence is all about prior planning. When we perform due diligence, we're putting all of the governance structures, processes, and frameworks in place to make sure that we are meeting our obligations.

Liability is the measure of responsibility an entity has for providing due care. Reciprocity is a legal arrangement where the benefits granted by the government to citizens of a country should be returned by that other country to the citizens of the first government.

64. B. The Payment Card Industry Data Security Standard (PCI DSS) governs the storage, processing, and transmission of credit card information. The Health Information Technology for Economic and Clinical Health (HITECH) Act extends the provisions of HIPAA regarding the protection of health information. The North American Electric Reliability Corporation (NERC)'s Critical Infrastructure Protection (CIP) program outlines compliance requirements for firms involved in the maintenance of the electric grid.

65. C. Installing a firewall reduces the likelihood of the risk materializing and is, therefore, a risk mitigation action. Risk avoidance would shut down the web services completely to avoid the associated risk. Risk acceptance would take no action and continue operations as is. Risk transference includes actions that shift some of the financial burden of a risk from one organization to another. Purchasing insurance is the most common example of risk transference.

66. C. The North American Electric Reliability Corporation's Critical Infrastructure Program (NERC/CIP) provides security standards for electric utilities and other elements of critical infrastructure. The Health Insurance Portability and Accountability Act (HIPAA) and the Health Information Technology for Electronic and Clinical Health (HITECH) Act govern personal health information. The Payment Card Industry Data Security Standard (PCI DSS) governs credit and debit card records.

67. B. The application of a consistent security standard at the time a virtual machine (or a physical machine, for that matter) is built is called baselining. The standard configuration is known as a baseline.

68. D. The custodian is usually that specific entity in charge of maintaining and securing the privacy-related data on a daily basis, as an element of the data's use.

The compliance officer might be considered a representative of the data controller (your company), or perhaps the data steward, depending on how much actual responsibility and interaction with the data you have on a regular basis. Option A is not as accurate as option D.

The cloud provider (and anyone working for the provider) would be considered the data processor under most privacy regulations; option B is incorrect.

Your company is the data controller, the legal entity ultimately responsible for the data. Option C is incorrect.

69. B. The most definitive source of guidance when conducting an audit is the standard under which the audit is being conducted. Auditors may consult other sources for guidance when interpreting standards, but the standard remains the definitive reference.

70. B. The Doctrine of Proper Law is used when a dispute occurs over which jurisdiction will hear a case. Tort law refers to civil liability suits. Common law refers to laws regarding marriage, and criminal law refers to violations of state or federal criminal code.

71. A. Supply chain management can help ensure the security of hardware, software, and services that an organization acquires. Chris should focus on each step that his laptops take from the original equipment manufacturer to delivery.

72. B. If the vendor operates with reasonable security procedures, it is unlikely that the devices will be tampered with at the vendor's site. Similarly, if Greg's organization has reasonable security procedures, tampering at his site is also unlikely. Misconfiguration by an administrator is always possible, but this is a post-installation risk and not a supply chain risk. It is possible that devices will be intercepted and tampered with while in transit from the vendor to Greg's organization.

73. A. The correct answer is the SOC 1 report, which is designed to assess the controls primarily revolving around financial reporting, formerly found in the SAS 70. The SOC 2 is a report that provides information related to one or more of the AICPA five security principles.

74. C. Internal audit teams perform a variety of audits and assessments that are mainly used by internal customers. It is quite common for these teams to investigate employee malfeasance. Internal auditors are generally not used when the customer is external. Examples include providing audited financial statements (where the investing public is the customer), certifying against an international standard (where the certification requires an independent audit), and complying with PCI DSS or other regulatory requirements that demand an independent assessment.

75. D. The Health Insurance Portability and Accountability Act (HIPAA) is a U.S. federal law governing the privacy of protected health information. The California Consumer Privacy Act (CCPA) is a California state law. The General Data Protection Regulation is European Union law. The Payment Card Industry Data Security Standard (PCI DSS) is a private contractual relationship and is not a law.

76. C. SOC 2 audits cover the confidentiality, integrity, and availability of information and are intended for internal audiences only because they contain sensitive information. SOC 2 audits should only be shared with customers under a nondisclosure agreement. SOC 3 audits cover the same controls as SOC 2 audits but are intended for a general audience. SOC 1 audits cover only the internal controls related to financial statements and reporting. SOC 4 audits do not exist.

77. A. The data custodian role is assigned to an individual who is responsible for implementing the security controls defined by policy and senior management. The data owner does bear ultimate responsibility for these tasks, but the data owner is typically a senior leader who delegates operational responsibility to a data custodian.

78. D. A quantitative assessment employs a set of methods or rules much like a qualitative assessment, with the difference being the use of absolute numerical values. So instead of High, Medium, and Low, values such as 1, 2, and 3 are used respectively.

79. D. The Federal Risk and Authorization Management Program (FedRAMP) provides a list of prescreened cloud service providers authorized to work with U.S. government agencies. FIPS 140-2 is a security standard for cryptographic modules. ISO 27017 is a standard for evaluating the security of cloud service providers but does not offer a list of prescreened providers. NIST 800-53 is a standard covering security and privacy controls for information systems.

80. A. Digital forensics procedures outline the process of collecting evidence in a manner that it may be used in court with reliability. eDiscovery may use forensic procedures, but it is specifically intended to ensure compliance with litigation hold obligations and is not used to collect evidence for security incidents. Common law is a set of legal principles derived from historic precedent. ISO 27001 is a standard providing guidance on cybersecurity and privacy controls.

81. A. Due diligence includes all of the prior planning done to create an environment where due care can succeed. This includes creating governance structures and frameworks.

82. D. The replacement cost technique values assets at the price it would take to replace them on the current market and is the most appropriate technique to use when looking to cover your costs. The original cost technique uses the purchase price of equipment. The depreciated value technique takes the original cost and reduces it over the expected life of the equipment. Estimation simply makes an informed guess of the asset value.

83. B. If your cloud vendor goes out of business, any legal and contractual terms you have with them will be essentially useless. Therefore, you should not rely upon contractual terms, service-level agreements (SLAs), or litigation to resolve this issue. Escrow places a copy of the code in the hands of an independent third party who will release it to customers if the vendor goes out of business.

84. B. A qualitative assessment is a set of methods or rules for assessing risk based on non-mathematical or categories or levels. One that uses those mathematical categories or levels is called a quantitative assessment. There is no such thing as a hybrid assessment, and an SOC 2 is an accounting report regarding control effectiveness.

85. A. Cloud vendor contracts typically provide customers with the right to either perform audits or receive the results of independent audits. They also normally include termination provisions and the right of the customer to access their own data. Cloud providers generally do not grant customers the right to access their facilities in order to ensure the security of data belonging to other customers.

86. B. ISO 27002 is an international standard focused on information security and titled "Information technology—Security techniques—Code of practice for information security management." The Information Technology Infrastructure Library (ITIL) does contain security management practices, but it is not the sole focus of the document, and the ITIL security section is derived from ISO 27002. The Capability Maturity Model (CMM) is focused on software development, and the Project Management Body of Knowledge (PMBOK®) Guide focuses on project management.

87. C. Cloud services operate under a shared responsibility model. Depending on the nature of the cloud service and the terms of the contract, security responsibilities will be split between the customer and the service provider.

88. D. The data steward is an individual who has been delegated responsibility by a data owner for particular categories of information. Data custodians are those responsible for handling and protecting information, such as IT professionals. Data processors are third-party organizations that handle information on behalf of an organization.

89. D. Ron's company is a data processor in this instance, as it is receiving records from the European firm. The European firm is the data controller in this case, as they bear responsibility for the data. The individuals described in the records are the data subjects. Data owners are tasked with making decisions about data such as who receives access to it and how it is used.

90. A, C. Supply chain risks occur when the adversary is interfering with the delivery of goods or services from a supplier to the customer. This might involve tampering with hardware before the customer receives it or using social engineering to compromise a vendor employee. Hacking into a web server run in an IaaS environment is not a supply chain risk because the web server is already under the control of the customer. Using a botnet to conduct a denial-of-service attack does not involve any supply chain elements.

91. C. The exposure factor is the percentage of the facility that risk managers expect will be damaged if a risk materializes. It is calculated by dividing the amount of damage by the asset value. In this case, that is $5 million in damage divided by the $10 million facility value, or 50 percent.

92. B. The annualized rate of occurrence is the number of times that risk analysts expect a risk to happen in any given year. In this case, the analysts expect tornadoes once every 200 years, or 0.005 times per year.

93. A. The annualized loss expectancy is calculated by multiplying the single loss expectancy (SLE) by the annualized rate of occurrence (ARO). In this case, the SLE is $5,000,000, and the ARO is 0.005. Multiplying these numbers together gives you the ALE of $25,000.

94. C. Risk transference involves shifting the impact of a potential risk from the organization incurring the risk to another organization. Insurance is a common example of risk transference.

95. A. The risk assessment team should pay the most immediate attention to those risks that appear in quadrant I. These are the risks with a high probability of occurring and a high impact on the organization if they do occur.

96. A. Guidelines provide advice based on best practices developed throughout industry and organizations, but they are not compulsory. Compliance with guidelines is optional.

97. C. Most privacy laws include a breach reporting requirement. These provisions exist in the Gramm–Leach–Bliley Act (GLBA), the Health Information Technology for Economic and Clinical Health (HITECH) amendments to the Health Insurance Portability and Accountability Act (HIPAA), and the General Data Protection Regulation (GDPR). The Family Educational Rights and Privacy Act (FERPA) does not contain breach reporting requirements.

98. D. Service-level agreements (SLAs) generally include operational metrics, such as network performance, compute capacity, and help desk response times. They would generally not set standards for the number of security incidents because that metric would incentivize the service provider to cover up security incidents rather than openly share information.

99. D. The Service Organizations Control audit program includes business continuity controls in an SOC 2, but not SOC 1, audit. Although FISMA and PCI DSS may audit business continuity, they would not apply to an email service used by a hospital.

100. B. The SLA should contain elements of the contract that can be subject to discrete, objective, repeatable, numeric metrics. Jurisdiction is usually dictated by location instead, which should be included in the contract but is probably not useful to include in the SLA. All the other options are excellent examples of items that can and should be included in the SLA.

Chapter 7: Practice Test 1

1. C. Tier 1 and 2 datacenters are not required to have sufficient redundant components to remain operational during equipment maintenance. This is a requirement of both Tier 3 and Tier 4 datacenters. Therefore, the lowest acceptable tier would be Tier 3.

2. B. In an infrastructure as a service (IaaS) model, the provider is only responsible for provisioning the devices and computing/storage capacity; the customer is responsible for everything else, including the security of the applications.

    All the other answers are incorrect because those individuals/organizations do not accept responsibility for securing cloud-based applications.

3. C. Software composition analysis (SCA) is designed to identify open source libraries and other dependencies in software used inside of an organization. It often detects dependencies that developers may not have been aware of during software development. Static application security testing (SAST), dynamic application security testing (DAST), and interactive application security testing (IAST) are all techniques used to identify security flaws in code created by developers and may not necessarily detect the use of dependent packages.

4. C. Network intrusion detection systems (NIDSs) work specifically at watching for anomalous or malicious system activity at the network level and provide alerts and/or reports on such activity. They do not provide any type of blocking activity or remediation by themselves.

5. A. Hypervisor access should be strictly limited in order to preserve tenant isolation in the multitenant environment. For this reason, customers should never be given direct access to the hypervisor itself. Any configuration changes necessary on a hypervisor should be made by employees of the IaaS provider itself.

6. A. In the public cloud computing model, the vendor builds a single platform that is shared among many different customers. This is also known as the shared tenancy model.

7. C. This is the definition of federation. PKI is used to establish trust between parties across an untrusted medium, portability is the characteristic describing the likelihood of being able to move data away from one cloud provider to another, and repudiation is when a party to a transaction can deny having taken part in that transaction.

8. A. All of these technologies have some capability to assist with this task, but the question is asking about the one that is best suited for this purpose. Data loss prevention (DLP) systems are specifically designed to detect and prevent unauthorized exfiltration of sensitive information. Cloud access security brokers (CASBs) are designed to consistently enforce security policies across cloud providers. Intrusion prevention systems (IPSs) are designed to identify and block malicious activity on the network or on a system. Next-generation firewalls (NGFWs) are designed to block unauthorized network connections.

9. C. While off-site storage is a cloud service offering, it is not intrinsic to the definition of cloud computing. The core characteristics of cloud computing do include broad network access, metered service, and on-demand self-service.

10. D. During a tabletop exercise, team members come together and walk through a scenario without making any changes to information systems. The checklist review is the least disruptive type of disaster recovery test. During a checklist review, team members each review the contents of their disaster recovery checklists on their own and suggest any necessary changes. During a parallel test, the team actually activates the disaster recovery site for testing, but the primary site remains operational. During a full interruption test, the team takes down the primary site and confirms that the disaster recovery site is capable of handling regular operations. The full interruption test is the most thorough test but also the most disruptive.

11. C. This is a very difficult question because it references some similar ISO standards. We can immediately eliminate ISO 27701 as an option because that standard references privacy controls, rather than the security controls that Tonya is evaluating. The remaining three standards all cover security controls. However, ISO 27017 is specifically focused on cloud provider security controls and would be the standard best suited to Tonya's needs. ISO 27001 and 27002 are more general-purpose standards covering security controls at any type of organization.

12. A. Tokenization replaces sensitive data elements with a unique identifier. These records may be reidentified using a lookup table in a database. If this lookup table was compromised, then the data is not secure. If the lookup table remains secure, the privacy of the data remains intact. Tokenization does not use cryptographic keys, which are used in encryption. Tokenization also does not use hash functions, which are used in hashing.

13. B. Using different vendors for multiple systems of the same type adds resiliency; if one product has an inherent manufacturing flaw, the other should not, if it comes from a different producer. The other suggestions are all good practices for building a datacenter, but they do not offer redundancy or resiliency.

14. D. EAL4 indicates that a system has been methodically designed, tested, and reviewed. EAL3 indicates that a system has been methodically tested and checked. EAL2 indicates that a system has been structurally tested. EAL1 indicates that a system has been functionally tested.

15. A. A honeypot consists of a computer, data, or a network site that appears to be part of a network and seems to contain information or a resource of value to attackers but is actually isolated and monitored. Although a honeypot is generally run in a sandbox, they are not the same thing.

16. D. Transport Layer Security (TLS) is the most common way to implement the Hypertext Transfer Protocol Secure (HTTPS), which provides encryption between a web server and a client. Secure Sockets Layer (SSL) was previously used for this purpose but is now considered outdated and insecure. Internet Protocol Secure (IPsec) is used to create encryption network connections between a remote user and a network or between two networks but is not commonly used for web applications. Domain Name Systems Security Extensions (DNSSEC) is used to provide authenticated name resolution.

17. B. SOC 2 audits cover the confidentiality, integrity, and availability of information and are intended for internal audiences only because they contain sensitive information. SOC 2 audits should only be shared with customers under a nondisclosure agreement. SOC 3 audits cover the same controls as SOC 2 audits but are intended for a general audience. SOC 1 audits cover only the internal controls related to financial statements and reporting. SOC 4 audits do not exist.

18. D. Adam might be required by law, regulation, or contract to notify any number of stakeholder groups. Contracts with customers and partners may include notification clauses. Regulators may have jurisdiction over this breach depending on the location and subject matter, and their regulations may require prompt notification of a potential breach.

19. C. API gateways typically offer features that include rate limiting, access control, and logging. They do not normally perform content filtering. This capability is often performed by web application firewalls (WAFs) that operate in conjunction with an API gateway.

20. A. The most accurate source of location information is data obtained from the Global Positioning System (GPS). GPS provides precise pinpoint location data. IP addresses may be loosely correlated with physical location, but this data is notoriously inaccurate. MAC addresses are tied to a particular piece of hardware and are not tied to a physical location. User attestation depends on users providing accurate and truthful responses.

21. A. A hardware security module (HSM) is designed specifically to safely store and manage encryption keys. These devices are considered more secure than storing keys in software since the encryption techniques can be much stronger.

22. B. In a typical TLS handshake, the client sends the message (called ClientHello) that initiates the negotiation of the session.

All the other options are incorrect.

23. A. In the infrastructure as a service (IaaS) model, the customer is responsible for everything up from the hardware layer.

In platform as a service (PaaS) and software as a service (SaaS), this will be performed by the provider; options B and C are incorrect.

Function as a service (FaaS) is a subcategory of PaaS and, therefore, D is also an incorrect answer.

24. D. The exposure factor is the percentage of the facility that risk managers expect will be damaged if a risk materializes. It is calculated by dividing the amount of damage by the asset value. In this case, that is $750,000 in damage divided by the $2 million facility value, or 37.5 percent.

25. C. The annualized rate of occurrence is the number of times each year that risk analysts expect a risk to happen. In this case, the analysts expect fires will occur once every 50 years, or 0.02 times per year.

26. A. The annualized loss expectancy is calculated by multiplying the single loss expectancy (SLE) by the annualized rate of occurrence (ARO). In this case, the SLE is $750,000, and the ARO is 0.02. Multiplying these numbers together gives you the ALE of $15,000.

27. B. The most difficult challenge when working with many different cloud providers is working through the eDiscovery procedures offered by each relevant provider. Most providers today provide eDiscovery capabilities and are willing to cooperate with litigation-related requests. The cloud does not change the complexity of identifying relevant records, which is normally done by keyword search, or determining when eDiscovery is necessary, which is normally made by legal counsel.

28. C. Encryption secures data at rest and in transit. The provisioning capability of IRM systems focuses on providing rights to individuals based on roles and job functions. Tagging and data labeling are used to ensure that data is handled appropriately based on rules.

29. A. Threat modeling is the idea of identifying specific points of vulnerability and then implementing countermeasures to protect or thwart those points from successful exploitation. All the other answers are incorrect variants.

30. B. Situations where humidity is too high may result in the buildup of moisture and corrosion of equipment. If humidity falls too low, it may result in static electricity issues. Humidity issues generally do not contribute to fires or physical access control failures.

31. D. Data loss prevention systems do use pattern matching, metadata, and content strings to identify the presence of sensitive information.

Tokenization is a technology that replaces sensitive data elements with alternative values that are not sensitive. This action may be taken in response to the presence of sensitive information, but it is not used to detect sensitive information.

32. A. SHA3 is a hash function that replaces data with values that can be referenced without exposing the actual data. Anonymization focuses on removing data that can be associated with specific users or individuals, masking uses alternate characters to conceal data, and shuffling switches data around while retaining actual data for testing.

33. D. SOC 3 reports are intended for public disclosure. SOC 1 and SOC 2 reports are intended only for use within a company or with trusted partners.

34. B. All management functions should take place on a highly secure, isolated network called the management plane.

The toolset may be available via remote access but is not in any way to be considered public-facing; option A is incorrect.

Resource pooling contradicts the use of dedicated storage areas for each customer; option C is incorrect.

Usually, virtualization management will be a responsibility of the provider because it is a crucial element for all customers; option D is incorrect.

35. B. With platform as a service (PaaS), the cloud provider will administer both the hardware and the OS, but you will be in charge of managing the applications and data. There is less likelihood of vendor lock-in with PaaS than software as a service (SaaS), because your data will not be put into a proprietary format (option B is preferable to option C).

With infrastructure as a service (IaaS), your company will still retain a great deal of the administrative responsibility, so PaaS is a better option; option B is preferable to A.

Security as a service (SECaaS) is a specialized service offering for managed cybersecurity services and would not meet the general-purpose computing needs described in this scenario.

36. B. While all aspects of cloud computing are necessary to provide a true cloud service, this type of business flexibility is possible because of rapid (close to instant) elasticity, the means to scale your usage up and down as needed.

All the other options are facets of cloud computing but are not as pertinent to the question.

37. B. Data owners hold overall responsibility for data that they own and are typically responsible for classification decisions. Data custodians are responsible for the data, ensuring access control, proper storage, and other operational controls. Data processors are often third parties who process the data as part of a business process, and data users are end users who use the data for their job.

38. B. Cross-site scripting attacks execute code on a remote user's system. SQL injection vulnerabilities allow an attacker to send commands through a web application to the database supporting that application. Cross-site request forgery and server-side request forgery attacks seek to exploit trust relationships by tricking systems into authorizing unauthorized activity.

39. C. Many security solutions, particularly DLP and similar tools, require a "learning curve" as they become accustomed to new data sets/configurations in order to discriminate between false positives and actual data loss. One week is not enough time to get an accurate determination of the efficacy of these products, and waiting to gather more data over time is a good idea.

The origin of the products probably does not matter in any significant way; options A and B are incorrect.

Hastily migrating out of the current cloud environment (whether to another cloud provider or back on-premises) is reactionary and could prove expensive. Option D is incorrect.

40. A. While any stakeholder may request information about service outages, customers have the greatest stake in outages and are most likely to demand timely communication about outages and their resolution.

41. D. The logical design phase is the part of the SDLC in which all functional features of the system chosen for development in analysis are described independently of any computer platform.

42. D. While it's likely the participating organizations will be subject to other federal regulations, HIPAA covers electronic patient information, so it will definitely be applicable in this case.

FERPA applies to educational institutions, so option A is incorrect.

FMLA dictates how employers give vacation time to employees, so option B is not correct.

PCI DSS is a contractual, not regulatory, standard, so option C is incorrect.

43. D. This is an excellent description of the hybrid model, where the customer owns elements of the infrastructure (the on-premises traditional environment) and the cloud provider owns other elements (the cloud environment used for the temporary additional demand).

All the other options are cloud deployment models but do not suit this particular case.

44. C. REST calls web resources by using uniform resource identifiers (URIs).

Extensible Markup Language (XML) may be used for REST, but it is not a requirement as it is in Simple Object Access Protocol (SOAP). Option A is incorrect.

Security Assertion Markup Language (SAML) is a form of XML used in passing identity assertions; option B is incorrect.

Transport Layer Security (TLS) is a secure virtual private network (VPN) mechanism, not an element of SOAP. Option D is incorrect.

45. A. The Information Technology Infrastructure Library (ITIL) is a set of practices that focus on aligning IT services with business needs.

46. B. Virtual server instances use block storage to provide disk volumes. These are typically mounted as drives on the server instance. Object and archival storage cannot be mounted as a drive. Ephemeral storage is not preserved when a server is shut down, so it is not appropriate for important long-term data.

47. C. A master services agreement (MSA) is an umbrella document that governs many different projects conducted by the same service provider. Each one of those projects is then described within a statement of work (SOW). A business partnership agreement (BPA) is used to define the terms of a joint venture between two organizations. A memorandum of understanding (MOU) is an informal document describing the relationship between two organizations or business units of the same organization.

48. C. The fact that many various customers (including some that may be competitive with, or even hostile to, each other) will be utilizing the cloud environment concurrently means that isolating each is of the utmost importance in the cloud environment.

DDoS is an availability threat, not something to do with confidentiality, so isolation does not serve much purpose in reducing it. Option A is incorrect.

Unencrypted message traffic is not the prevailing general reason for the need for isolation; it might be one specific, particular aspect of a confidentiality concern, but option C is preferable to B.

Insider threat is not countered by isolation in the same way that isolation protects against threats due to multitenancy; option C is preferable to D.

49. A. The identity provider would hold all of the identities and generate a token for known users. The relying party (RP) would be the service provider and would consume the tokens. All other answers are incorrect.

50. C. All of these options are methods of applying encryption to sensitive data. However, the question asked specifically about stored data and, of the choices listed here, only volume encryption affects stored data, or data at rest. Transport Layer Security (TLS), virtual private networks (VPNs), and IP Security (IPsec) only protect data in transit over a network.

51. D. Inert gas systems use no water and are unlikely to damage sensitive electronic equipment, even if discharged. Wet pipe, dry pipe, and preaction systems all use water and may damage or destroy electronic equipment if activated or damaged.

52. A. Portability is the term used to describe the ease with which a customer can move from one cloud provider to another; the higher the portability, the less chance for vendor lock-in.

Interoperability describes how systems work together (or don't); because the question did not mention the use of your own company's systems, interoperability does not seem to be a major concern in this case. Option B is incorrect.

Resiliency is how well an environment can withstand duress. While this is of obvious importance to all organizations in the cloud, it is usually seen as a defense against availability concerns, while the question has more to do with portability; option A is still preferable to option C.

Nothing in the question suggests a need for the company to retain some form of governance; option D is incorrect.

53. A. FIPS 140-2 is a detailed federal government standard for cryptographic modules, including HSMs, and is likely to contain detailed technical requirements. The Payment Card Industry Data Security Standard (PCI DSS) may reference the use of HSMs but does not contain detailed technical requirements. ISO 27017 similarly provides a high-level description of cloud provider security controls but does not contain detailed technical requirements. The Common Criteria outline a process for certifying secure information systems but do not contain detailed technical requirements.

54. B. Audits don't really provide any perceptible effect on user experience.

All the other options are good reasons for performing audits.

55. A. As a cloud customer, the organization is not responsible for making up-front infrastructure purchases, which are capital expenditures.

Cloud customers do, however, make continual operational expenditures for IT resources in the form of their payments to cloud providers. Option B is incorrect.

Modern business is driven by data as much as any other input, regardless of sector or industry; this does not change whether the organization operates in the cloud or in the traditional IT environment. Option C is incorrect.

The cloud does not obviate the need to satisfy customers. Option D is incorrect.

56. D. To be used in a secure manner, certificates must take advantage of a hash function that is not prone to collisions. The MD2, MD4, MD5, and SHA-1 algorithms all have demonstrated weaknesses and would trigger a vulnerability. The SHA-256 algorithm is still considered secure.

57. A. This vulnerability should not prevent users from accessing the site, but it will cause their browsers to display a warning that the site is not secure.

58. B. This error is a vulnerability in the certificate itself and may only be corrected by requesting a new certificate from the certificate authority (CA) that uses a secure hash algorithm in the certificate signature.

59. C. RAID uses additional hard drives to protect the server against the failure of a single device. Load balancing and server clustering do add robustness but require the addition of a server. Scheduled backups protect against data loss but do not provide immediate access to data in the event of a hard drive failure.

60. C. Mean time to repair (MTTR) is the time required to repair a device that has failed or is in need of repair. The term *mean* indicates the average time as opposed to the actual or past experiences.

61. B. Static application security testing (SAST) differs from dynamic application security testing (DAST) in that it looks at source code and binaries to see if it can detect problems before the code is loaded into memory and run.

62. C. Relational databases organize data into tables, which is a highly structured format. Therefore, relational databases should be expected to contain structured data.

63. A. DNSSEC is basically DNS with added security benefits. These benefits include providing origin authority and data integrity guarantees when queries are answered. DNSSEC also provides authenticated denial of existence when domain names do not exist. DNSSEC does not provide confidentiality, so it does not offer payload encryption.

64. C. The recipient of a message encrypted using an asymmetric encryption algorithm decrypts that message using their own private key. Therefore, Alice should use her own private key to decrypt the message that Bob encrypted using Alice's public key. Bob would not use his own private key to encrypt the message because then anyone (not just Alice) would be able to decrypt the message with his public key.

65. D. In an elevation of privilege attack, the attacker transforms a limited user account into an account with greater privileges, powers, and/or access to the system. Spoofing attacks falsify an identity, while repudiation attacks attempt to deny accountability for an action. Tampering attacks attempt to violate the integrity of information or resources.

66. C. A Type 2 hypervisor is one in which an operating system is installed onto the hardware with the hypervisor being installed on top of the OS. These types of hypervisors are thought to be more vulnerable to attack since the attack surface is larger, therefore providing more opportunities for intrusions.

67. C. FedRAMP is a government-wide program that provides for a standardized approach to security assessments, authorization, and continuous monitoring of cloud products and services. FedRAMP certification can be quite costly and difficult to achieve but is required if you want to host a U.S. government agency or subcontractor.

68. D. Senior management is always responsible for determining the risk appetite of any organization, regardless of where and how it operates.

Neither the cloud provider, nor the ISP, nor federal regulators determine the risk appetite of your organization. Options A, B, and C are incorrect.

69. D. Sending invoices to clients is an act of transferring data and is, therefore, an example of the Share phase of the cloud data lifecycle.

70. D. Carla should use a digital signature to provide nonrepudiation. Anyone later wishing to verify the integrity and authenticity of the data may validate the digital signature. Digital signatures combine the use of cryptographic hash functions and encryption, but neither of those technologies on their own provides nonrepudiation. Multifactor authentication provides strong access control, but does not provide nonrepudiation.

71. B. Because you will be creating proprietary software, you will probably be most concerned with how it will function across many platforms, in a virtualized environment, and in an environment that you do not own or operate. Interoperability describes how well a system relates to other systems.

Portability is always a concern for cloud customers, as it is an indication of how likely the customer is to be subject to the risk of vendor lock-in. However, because you are using your own proprietary software and not that of another company, this is not a major issue in this case. Option A is incorrect.

Resiliency is how well an environment can withstand duress. Although this is of obvious importance to all organizations, it is usually seen as a defense against availability concerns; the question has more to do with interoperability, and thus option B is still preferable to option C.

Nothing in the question suggests a need for the company to retain some form of governance; option D is incorrect.

72. B. Content-based discovery includes two subcategories: string matching and pattern matching. This is an example of pattern matching, where Luis's tool is looking for data elements that fit a common pattern. There is no indication that Luis is looking at labels or metadata or, in fact, that these elements even exist. Classification-based discovery is not a type of data discovery technique.

73. B. SAML 2.0 is currently the standard used to pass security assertions across the internet. REST and SOAP are ways of presenting data and executing operations on the internet, and HTML is a way of displaying web pages.

74. A. The purpose of an uninterruptible power supply (UPS) is to provide power to systems for a short period of time. They provide immediate backup power from a battery that should be quickly replaced by long-term backup power from a generator or similar source. For this reason, you should only expect the UPS to last for about 10 minutes.

75. A. Degaussing refers to the practice of using strong magnets for scrambling data on magnetic media such as hard drives and tapes. Although scrubbing generally can scramble data as well as degaussing, it does not use magnets.

76. A. It is appropriate to set a lifecycle policy that follows the standard use case. This would mean archiving data after 90 days and then deleting data after five years to minimize costs. Gary can handle any litigation holds that arise as exceptions to this standard policy, as litigation holds typically affect only a small portion of data.

77. B. Gary should take the action required to comply with the litigation hold notice, but he may do so as narrowly as possible to minimize costs. In this case, the data affected is from March 2022, so he should take action to ensure that this data is not deleted. The data may still be archived. He does not need to take any action on data from other time periods unless the litigation hold notice is expanded.

78. A. The data subject is the person who the personally identifiable information (PII) describes. The entity that collects or creates the PII is the data owner or controller. The entity that uses the data on behalf of the owner/controller is a data processor. Entities that regulate the use of PII are regulators.

79. D. Sandboxing is often used for testing untested applications or carving out resources that cannot then touch other parts of the same system as part of a security strategy to isolate those operations. Therefore, isolating or cordoning off the compute environment is needed.

80. A. The CSA CCM will aid you in selecting and implementing appropriate controls for various regulatory frameworks. The CCM does not aid in collecting log files; that is the function of a security information and event management (SIEM), search engine marketing (SEM), or security information management (SIM) tool. The CCM will not help ensure that the baseline is applied to systems; automated configuration tools are available for that purpose (although this answer might be interpreted as desirable; the CCM will help you select appropriate controls for your baseline, but it won't check to see if those are applied). Contract terms are not enforced by the CCM; the service-level agreement (SLA) should be the mechanism for that task.

81. A. Both ISO 31000 and National Institute of Standards and Technology (NIST) 800-37 are risk management frameworks.

Control Objectives for Information and Related Technology (COBIT) is ISACA's framework for managing IT and IT controls, largely from a process and governance perspective. Though it includes elements of risk management, NIST 800-37 is still closer in nature to ISO 31000, so option A is preferable to B.

ITIL (Information Technology Infrastructure Library) is a framework mostly focused on service delivery as opposed to risk management; option C is incorrect.

The General Data Protection Regulation (GDPR) is a European Union law regarding privacy information, not risk management; option D is incorrect.

82. C. Trusted platform modules (TPMs) are chips inside a computer that perform a variety of security functions, including managing full-disk encryption keys. Hardware security modules (HSMs) are more sophisticated (and expensive) devices used to manage encryption keys across an enterprise. Public key infrastructure (PKI) is a system of issuing and maintaining encryption keys for use among many individuals and organizations. Intrusion prevention systems (IPSs) monitor for and block malicious activity on a system or network.

83. B. Testing the product in a runtime context is dynamic testing.

Because this is being done in runtime, it is neither code review nor static testing; options A and C are incorrect.

Using a small pool of specified individuals is not truly open source, which would involve releasing the game to the public. Option D is incorrect.

84. C. The due care principle states that an individual should react in a situation using the same level of care that would be expected from any reasonable person. It is a very broad standard. The due diligence principle is a more specific component of due care that states that an individual assigned a responsibility should exercise due care to complete it accurately and in a timely manner.

85. D. Of the answers given, option D is the most important. It is vital that any datacenter facility be close to sound facility resources such as power, water, and connectivity.

86. C. Archival storage typically has long retrieval times and provides the most inexpensive method for storing data. Other storage classes, including block storage, general-purpose object storage, and raw storage, have higher pricing.

87. B. There is no indication that any changes were made to the service or supporting infrastructure, so the change management process would not likely be impacted. This situation is an incident and should be handled using the incident management process. It is also an availability failure and possibly a violation of a service-level agreement, so the availability management and service-level management processes are also involved.

88. A. These are technical controls, automated systems that perform security functions.

    An argument could be made that there is an administrative component to these controls as well: the firewall rules, the DLP data discovery strategy, etc.—these are expressed in the form of a list or set of criteria, which might be viewed as an administrative control. However, the system itself (which is what the question asked) is still a technical control. Option A is preferable to option B.

    Because these devices/systems do not deter physical intrusion but rather logical intrusion, they are not considered physical controls.

    "Competing" is not a control type.

89. C. The protection of intellectual property is a greater concern during a divestiture, where a subsidiary is being spun off into a separate organization, than an acquisition, where one firm has purchased another. Acquisition concerns include consolidating security functions and policies as well as integrating security tools.

90. B. Vendor lockout occurs when a cloud provider ceases operations and customers are unable to access their data. Vendor lock-in is the result of a lack of portability, for any number of reasons. Masking redacts certain digits or text from sensitive information to make it less sensitive. Tokenization replaces sensitive data elements with placeholder values.

91. C. Data classification decisions are typically made based on the sensitivity, criticality, and/or jurisdictions involved. These decisions are not typically made based directly on the age of the data. If age does factor into a decision, it is because the age would lower the sensitivity and/or criticality of the data.

92. C. Default credentials are the bane of security everywhere. This is definitely the correct answer because it should *not* be part of the baseline build.

    All the other options are actual baselining functions.

93. D. When data is subject to a litigation hold, data custodians must suspend any mechanisms that may delete or modify affected data. For this reason, Richard should set the retention period to indefinite for as long as the litigation hold remains in place.

94. C. Virtualization toolsets help map storage; support improved networking, video output, sound, or input capabilities; or otherwise improve the experience and functionality for virtualized operating systems. They are commonly used in virtualized environments and provide a secure connection between the technologies.

95. A. There are two possible techniques for revoking a digital certificate: updating the certificate's status using the Online Certificate Status Protocol (OCSP) and adding the certificate to a Certificate Revocation List (CRL). Of these, OCSP provides faster updates and is the preferred method. It is not possible to change the public or private keys associated with an existing digital certificate.

96. D. This is a community cloud, because various parties own different elements of it for a common purpose. A private cloud would typically be owned by a single entity, hosted at a cloud provider datacenter. A public cloud would be open to anyone and everyone. Hybrid cloud environments mix together elements of public and private cloud computing.

97. D. Capacity management ensures that IT resources are sufficient to meet current and future business demands. Availability management improves the resiliency of IT services to ensure their ability to meet customer needs. Service-level management ensures that the IT organization is fulfilling its obligations to internal and external customers. Configuration management entails documenting the approved settings for systems and software, which helps establish baselines within the organization.

98. B. The cloud data lifecycle is: Create, Store, Use, Share, Archive, Destroy.

99. D. Ephemeral storage is temporary storage associated with a server instance. It will be deleted if the server is terminated, but it will not be deleted if the server is simply stopped or rebooted. Stopping a server allows it to be restarted at a later time, which requires access to the ephemeral storage. Terminating a server completely deletes it and the ephemeral storage.

100. C. Tokenization is an approved alternative to encryption for complying with Payment Card Industry (PCI) requirements.

Obfuscation and masking don't really serve the purpose because they obscure data, making it unreadable; storing payment information that is unreadable does not aid in the efficiency of future transactions. Moreover, neither technique meets PCI requirements. Options A and B are incorrect.

Hashing does not serve the purpose because it is a one-way conversion of data; there is no way to retrieve payment information for future transactions once it has been hashed. Option D is incorrect.

101. B. RAID technology provides fault tolerance for hard drive failures and is an example of a business continuity action. Restoring from backup tapes, relocating to a cold site, and restarting business operations are all disaster recovery actions.

102. C. GLBA mandates requirements for securing personal account information in the financial and insurance industries; Bob's company provides financial services, so he will definitely have to comply with GLBA. If Bob's company is publicly traded, he may have to comply with SOX, but we don't know enough about Bob's company from the question to choose that answer. HIPAA is a requirement only for medical providers and their business associates. PCI DSS may apply to Bob's organization if they process credit card transactions, but PCI DSS is a private regulation and not a law.

103. A. Interview videos are typically stored as unstructured data. They are commonly simple binary objects maintained on disk. Sales transactions, customer contact information, and website visitor logs are all normally highly formatted data stored in a spreadsheet, database, or structured log file.

104. D. The Advanced Encryption Standard (AES) is currently used to encrypt and protect U.S. government sensitive and secret data. There are variants, but the most common is 256-bit, which is virtually impossible to break today.

105. D. Risk acceptance occurs when an organization determines that the costs involved in pursuing other risk management strategies are not justified and they choose not to pursue any action.

106. B. Linda should choose a warm site. This approach balances cost and recovery time. Cold sites take a very long time to activate, measured in weeks or months. Hot sites activate immediately but are quite expensive. Mutual assistance agreements depend on the support of another organization.

107. A. Purchasing insurance is a way to transfer risk to another entity. Risk avoidance actions change business processes to eliminate a risk. Risk mitigation activities reduce the likelihood or impact of a risk occurring. Risk acceptance takes no action to control the risk other than acknowledging its presence.

108. C. A cross-site scripting attack (XSS) occurs when an application receives untrusted data and then sends it to a web browser without proper validation, allowing an attacker to execute scripts in the user's browser, hijack sessions, or engage in other malicious behavior.

109. D. FIPS 140-2 is the federal standard for the accreditation and distinguishing of secure and well-architected cryptographic modules produced by private sector vendors who see to or are in the process of having their solutions and services certified by the U.S. government departments and regulated industries that collect, store, transfer, or share data that is deemed to be sensitive but not classified.

ISO 27036 provides standards for supply chain management. ISO 27050 provides standards for electronic discovery efforts. The Control Objectives for Information Technology (COBIT) provide a generalized management framework for IT organizations. None of these documents provide a standard for accrediting cryptographic technologies.

110. C. JavaScript Object Notation (JSON) and the Extensible Markup Language (XML) are data formats commonly used with semi-structured data, and MongoDB is a database platform commonly used to store JSON-formatted data. The Structured Query Language (SQL) is used to access relational databases, which contain highly structured data.

111. B. A SYN flood is where a TCP connection attempt is made and then cut short just prior to completion, thereby leaving a server waiting for a response. If enough of these connection attempts are made, a "flood" occurs, causing the end unit to consume resources to the point that either services and/or the system itself become unavailable for use. The other options have no connection with a flood of any kind.

112. C. Chain of custody refers to the process of never letting a piece of evidence out of one's control without proper signatory transfers indicating the who, what, when, and where it occurs so that the courts can ensure that the evidence could not have been tampered with.

113. C. Chris should conduct his investigation, but there is a pressing business need to keep the website online. The most reasonable course of action would be to take a snapshot of the affected system and use the snapshot for the investigation, maintaining website operations. There is no reason to believe that the web server or application has any vulnerability, so the use of the site for fraudulent activity doesn't merit shutting down the site.

114. A. In TLS, the parties will establish a shared secret, or symmetric key, for the duration of the session. All the other options are incorrect because they are not the form of cryptography used for the session key in a TLS session.

115. D. Secure sanitization is not included in all (or even many) SDLC models.

The other options are typical SDLC steps.

116. B. The hypervisor is responsible for coordinating access to physical hardware and enforcing isolation between different virtual machines running on the same physical platform.

117. A. Because the cloud provider owns and operates the cloud datacenter, the provider will craft and promulgate the governance that determines the control selection and usage. This is another risk the cloud customer must consider when migrating into the cloud; the customer's governance will no longer have direct precedence over the environment where the customer's data is located.

Both the cloud customer and the regulator(s) may have specific control mandates that might require the customer to deploy additional security controls (at the customer side, within the data, as agents on the user devices or on the provider side, or in application programming interfaces [APIs] as allowed by the service model or contract), so options B and C are also partially true, but A is a better answer as it is more general.

Option D is untrue because the end user does not determine which controls are selected for the cloud datacenter and how they are deployed. That is the responsibility of the cloud provider.

118. D. SAFEcode provides a global forum for software developers and technology leaders to come together in an effort to improve application security practices. ATASM, PASTA, and DREAD are all threat modeling frameworks.

119. B. The residual risk is the level of risk that remains after controls have been applied to mitigate risks. Inherent risk is the original risk that existed prior to the controls. Control risk is new risk introduced by the addition of controls to the environment. Mitigated risk is the risk that has been addressed by existing controls.

120. D. The order of volatility specifies the likelihood that data will be erased imminently. Investigators should collect the most volatile evidence first. The contents of RAM are highly volatile and are the most volatile data source listed here. This is followed by files stored on a server hard drive, files stored in archival storage, and the contents of firmware.

121. C. The Agile Manifesto specifically advocates for getting sample systems into the hands of the users as soon as possible in order to ensure that development is meeting customer needs. The Manifesto refutes all other elements of programming that slow down this effort, including an excessive focus on documentation and planning.

122. B. A platform as a service (PaaS) environment will likely provide the best option for testing the game; the provider will offer various OS platforms for the game to run on, giving your company the opportunity to reach as many customers (using various platforms) as possible, raising your potential for market penetration.

Although infrastructure as a service (IaaS) is not a terrible option and would give your team additional control of the entire test, it would also require the team to duplicate many different platforms and OSs, requiring a much greater level of effort and additional expertise at what would likely be a much greater cost. Option B is preferable to option A.

A software as a service (SaaS) model will not allow your team to install and run the game; option C is incorrect.

Function as a service (FaaS) is a subcategory of PaaS computing, but it does not allow for the running of full applications, such as video games. Instead, it is designed for executing small portions of code, making option D incorrect.

123. B. SOAP uses an XML-based approach to interoperability, allowing systems to interact more easily.

SOAP is not particularly lightweight; in fact, it is kind of cumbersome. Option A is not true.

SOAP is not especially more secure than DCOM or CORBA; option C is incorrect.

SOAP is newer than the other technologies; however, that is not the reason it is preferable in a web context. Option B is still preferable to D.

124. A. Business impact analysis (BIA) determines the impact on a business from the loss of support or availability of any resource. It also establishes the escalation of that loss over time, identifies the minimum resources needed to recover, and prioritizes the recovery of processes and supporting systems.

125. A. A private cloud is an infrastructure provisioned for exclusive use by a single organization consisting of multiple customers (e.g., business units) and may be owned, managed, or operated by the organization, a third party, or some combination of both and may exist on- or off-premises.

Chapter 8: Practice Test 2

1. C. HA, or high availability, mode uses a heartbeat to detect when systems fail. If the heartbeat stops, the virtual machines from that node are restarted on other hosts.

2. A. Will knows that containers should package a single application per container. Installs should be configured to meet the needs of the application, and default tools should be removed if not needed. Tagging is critical to allow easy control of containers.

3. B. ISO/IEC 27017 is a security standard that was specifically designed for cloud service providers. ISO/IEC:20000:1 and PCI DSS are broader standards, and the EU's General Data Protection Regulation is not cloud-specific, either.

4. A. Since Helen operates an e-commerce site, she is likely to accept credit cards and will need to ensure PCI compliance—a standard required by contract, not by regulation. FedRAMP is a U.S. federal program that focuses on security assessment, monitoring, and other elements related to cloud services. COBIT is a framework that defines practices for the management of IT, much like ITIL.

5. D. Tools like Amazon's Patch Manager use patch baselines to determine which patches will be installed or not installed and when they will be installed and can also scan to determine patch status. This fits both Ilya's need for flexibility and the organization's preference for buy versus build type tools.

6. C. Yasmine is conducting nonfunctional testing. This can be somewhat confusing, and it can help to remember that functional testing focuses on the business requirements of the software, not its performance or customer expectations of experience. There isn't enough information to call this black box (zero knowledge) testing or white box (full knowledge) testing.

7. B. Encrypting logs using customer-managed keys is a best practice to ensure logs are not accessible to third parties. Adam should make sure that his organization controls and manages their keys securely. Allowing the vendor to control the keys means that third parties, including law enforcement or attackers who breach the provider's security, could gain access to his organization's logs, and not encrypting logs means they are not protected at rest.

8. C. SMS delivered codes are considered the least secure because of attacks against SMS, including SIM-swapping and cloning attacks as well as Voice over IP telephony exploits. Hardware- and software-based code generation are considered more secure and thus more desirable.

9. C. Email and web pages both have structural elements but are not strictly defined and can contain unstructured data. This means that they are examples of semi-structured data.

10. B. Geofencing allows organizations to designate specific locations to allow or deny operations from. This will allow Felix to set the organization's facilities as acceptable access locations while denying access from other locations. Zero trust focuses on continuous authorization and authentication, traffic inspection looks at traffic to identify unwanted or unexpected traffic, and network security groups work much like firewalls to allow or deny traffic based on rules.

11. A. Valerie knows that a region-wide outage could result in a need to operate in another region until services are restored. While this can be a significant undertaking, it may be necessary in a true disaster scenario. While she could look at another cloud provider, the amount of new work required to move from one provider to another is significant. Simply choosing another availability zone or deploying more resources in the same zone or region will not meet her needs because they would all be impacted if the region was down.

12. A. Casey knows that she won't have access to hardware-level monitoring for her new environment. That means that CPU and disk utilization are both things she will still be able to monitor but that fan speeds, system temperatures, and system voltages will not be something she is responsible for or able to access.

13. A. In PaaS environments, customers control the applications they build and the data in the environment. Everything else is the responsibility of the platform vendor.

14. C. Uninterruptible power supply (UPS) systems use batteries or other mechanisms to provide power during brownouts when power sags. A generator takes time to come up to speed and doesn't handle short disruptions easily. Purchasing power from two different providers may

help, but if brownouts are still occurring, the UPS is a better solution. Power distribution units (PDUs) are used to get power to servers and systems and to control and monitor it, but they don't have an impact on brownouts or power losses.

15. A. Infrastructure as a service solutions allow customers to build and manage their own infrastructure using resources provided by the service provider. PaaS provides customers with a platform to build their applications on, and SaaS provides software as a service. CaaS sometimes stands for containers as a service but is not a broadly adopted cloud term.

16. D. Susan's organization is using anonymization to remove identifiable information from the customer data. Randomization would randomize the data, removing its linkages to other elements while retaining formatting and content to allow for testing. Data masking removes elements of data from view, often using asterisks or other characters to replace the information. Hashing uses hashes to create data elements that can still be referenced without the original data being accessible.

17. B. SOC 2 audits cover security controls and Type 1 audits cover a point in time. SOC 1 audits cover financial controls, and Type 2 audits cover a period of time.

18. D. In an IaaS environment the customer will be responsible for web servers and other services provided. DNS logs, billing records, and API logs are all likely to be under the control of the service provider.

19. D. ITIL defines an availability manager as the individual responsible for defining, analyzing, planning, measuring, and improving availability of IT services. This key role is the process owner for availability management in ITIL.

20. C. Wayne's architects have a specific role defined by his organization. That means that a custom role with appropriate rights is the best option for the cloud architects. Cloud vendor best practices and built-in roles are available as starting points, but organizations typically go beyond those roles as they define their own needs. Finally, MFA isn't used to map roles.

21. B. Policies need to be written to work with organizational culture or they are likely to fail. That means writing a policy and expecting culture to change is not a common principle. In fact, it is a terrible idea!

22. A. Lucca knows that privacy issues are legal issues, not technical issues. Data breaches, system outages, and denial-of-service attacks all target systems and technical infrastructure.

23. B. Type 2 hypervisors are run on top of an existing operating system. Type 1 hypervisors are installed on bare-metal systems, essentially as their own operating system. Neither requires being run in the cloud, and Type 2 hypervisors can often be run inside of other hypervisor environments, although it may not always work as well as intended.

24. A. Amazon's S3 is an example of object storage. Block storage works like a traditional local drive, although the disks are typically virtual, whereas network file storage allows you to connect to a drive across a network. Native storage is not a common cloud storage type.

25. A. Privacy impact assessments focus on the what, why, and how of personally identifiable information, including legal and policy requirements, risks, and controls. It does not specifically seek to identify the cost of privacy controls or efforts.

26. A. Including labels in the files in a way that allows them to easily follow the files is the most effective option for Mike. While labels could be modified or removed, normal usage will not result in their loss. Filenames are often changed, a second file can easily be forgotten or removed, and cryptographic wrappers introduce overhead and are also likely to be decrypted and forgotten.

27. C. Regulations often have a required time frame for notification built into the law. It may set a time period or simply be tagged as requiring a reasonable time frame, but regulations are the most likely to require this. Customers and partners may have contractual requirements for notification rather than being required by law, and law enforcement notification is often at the option of the organization.

28. C. Modern design principles call for automation for monitoring whenever possible. The scope and scale of cloud deployments as well as the volume of logs and other monitoring information mean that manual efforts are unlikely to be successful. Instead, manual efforts should be reserved for escalation and oversight whenever possible. Meeting compliance requirements, using layered security, and automating deployment of sensitive tasks are all in Google's Cloud Architecture Framework's security principles found at `https://cloud.google.com/architecture/framework/security/security-principles`.

29. B. Common phases in waterfall-based SDLCs include Requirements Gathering, Analysis, Design, Implementation, Testing, Deployment, and Maintenance. Reverse engineering is not a typical SDLC phase.

30. B. Michelle should verify that her cloud provider provides a cloud HSM (hardware security module) capability. A cloud HSM will allow her to generate, store, and manage cryptographic keys and other secrets securely in the cloud.

31. C. In most IaaS environments, computation time is virtualized and allocated based on performance. That performance is billed based on time, but allocation isn't based on time. Customers may be able to pay for dedicated CPUs or cores; however, this is not the most common model for allocation, and it carries additional expense.

32. D. Gurvinder should ensure that his organization finds a vendor that will guarantee a service-level agreement (SLA) that meets the organization's needs. A QSA is a PCI assessment professional, an NDA (nondisclosure agreement) is used to protect sensitive data shared between organizations or individuals, and an MSA (master services agreement) defines how organizations will work together.

33. C. Confidential computing is a technology that protects data in use, even while being processed thanks to the use of protected CPU enclaves.

34. A. Susan should deploy an IDS (intrusion detection system). IDS deployments are designed to see traffic and identify issues without stopping it. An IPS is placed in-line to detect and potentially stop attacks. Firewalls and network security groups use rules rather than detection.

35. D. ISO/IEC 20000-1 points to service catalog items, including descriptions of the service, service-level definitions and objectives, contact points, support information, dependencies on other services, and security details. It doesn't include risk ratings—those are typically maintained outside of a service catalog as part of an organization's risk management discipline.

36. A. STRIDE stands for Spoofing, Tampering, Repudiation, Information Disclosure, Denial of Service, and Elevation of Privilege.

37. C. Google Workspace is an example of a software as a service environment where Google provides the software and all of the underlying support and infrastructure is run by Google. Brian's organization simply provides users with access to workspace, unlike a platform as a service model where they would have to develop applications inside of the platform. An infrastructure as a service model would involve running systems and infrastructure, and DaaS frequently means desktop as a service.

38. B. Software composition analysis is the process of determining what open source components make up a software package. Static testing looks at source code, interactive security testing looks at code for vulnerabilities while it is being interacted with by a human or automated tester, and fuzzing sends unexpected input to software to see where it may fail or respond in unexpected ways.

39. C. Partnership agreements often have breach notification clauses built into them. Chris should use the breach notification language in their partnership agreement to guide his communications with the partner organization. That organization may choose to share additional information but is unlikely to detail customers, systems, partners, or services unless required to by the agreement.

40. C. Residual risk is the risk that remains after controls are implemented. Inherent risk is the original level of risk that exists before controls. Opportunity risk and controlled risk were both made up for this question.

41. B. Virtualization is the key building block technology that allows multiple systems to run on the same hardware. Selling fractions of systems allows cloud providers to efficiently use their resources as part of the cloud business model.

42. A. Using TLS for all communications can help protect data in motion. AES is often used for data at rest. Using UDP or requiring a three-way handshake like TCP does not add security for data in transit.

43. D. Rick should look for proper indemnification language that ensures that the vendors take responsibility for problems or issues that they cause. An operational level agreement (OLA) is an internal agreement on service levels, a SLA is a service-level agreement, and service-level management won't meet Rick's needs either.

44. C. An SOC 3 report is intended for general audiences, and Type 2 reports provide information about controls over time. SOC 1 covers financial practices, SOC 2 looks at security controls but is intended for internal audiences, and SOC 4 doesn't exist.

45. B. FIPS 140-2 is a U.S. government encryption standard, and vendors often ensure that their hardware and software is FIPS 140-2-certified. EBCDIC is an 8-bit encoding scheme used on IBM mainframes that was a rival to ASCII for character encoding, and the remaining answers were made up.

46. A. DevOps in a continuous integration/continuous delivery environment emphasizes automation of security processes to allow consistent, speedy delivery. Major releases, testing in production instead of before release, and static code review are all likely to slow down a CI/CD pipeline.

47. B. Michelle knows that eDiscovery can be more complex in a cloud environment and that her organization may need to invest extra time and effort in preparing for eDiscovery in the cloud if they anticipate lawsuits to be an ongoing issue or event. While cybersecurity risks, data security, and copyright infringement could be involved, eDiscovery is the primary risk listed here.

48. C. In ephemeral environments IP addresses are frequently reused, and usernames aren't directly associated with systems in most cases. That means that tags are the most important item to capture to ensure that each system can be logged appropriately.

49. A. Justin knows that tagging early in the data lifecycle can help data loss prevention (DLP) systems by making it easier to detect sensitive data that may be in transit or at risk of being exposed. Data lifecycle management is helpful but not as critical for this specific purpose as DLP. IDS detection can use tags to identify data in motion but can't stop it, meaning that it will be less effective for stopping data breaches than a DLP. Honeypots are not used to capture tags; they're focused on acquiring tools and technique information from malicious actors.

50. A. Cloud identity providers commonly support SAML and OpenID. LDAP is more commonly used for on-site directory purposes. RDP (Remote Desktop Protocol) is a Windows remote access protocol, and FedID was made up for this question.

51. A. SOC 2 Type 2 reports cover security controls and practices over a period of time, while Type 1 reports cover a point in time. Hyun knows that SOC 1 reports cover financial practices and aren't appropriate for his security needs.

52. C. Kayla knows that multiple systems with a load balancer can handle availability issues more easily. If a system fails to respond, the load balancer can remove it from the pool and send an alert. She also knows that this can result in better performance and the ability to scale more easily to meet higher demands. Confidentiality, the number of vulnerabilities, and shorter patching windows are not results of this type of design.

53. C. Rene knows that business continuity focuses on continuing to operate during a disaster. That means that deploying instances to multiple availability zones is a reasonable business continuity choice. Planning for region failure or provider failure and ensuring staff aren't all in the same location are common disaster recovery practices.

54. B. OWASP recommends the use of dynamic secrets to limit the blast radius of compromised applications and secrets. A dynamic secret is requested and generated dynamically when an application starts, meaning that attackers who recover secrets from a running application and then use them or attempt to obtain them from source code will not succeed.

55. A. Jim is likely using ephemeral block storage that is treated like an actual disk would be. Ephemeral storage exists only as long as the instance does. Long-term storage is used for backups and other long-term needs, object storage uses APIs and treats each file as a unique object rather than as traditional files in a filesystem, and container storage is not a type of storage.

56. B. Lisa knows that packet capture on a shared management backplane is prohibited by cloud providers. She'll need to use built-in logging mechanisms and configuration review to understand what occurred in her environment.

57. D. The process of matching fields in one database to another is called data mapping. Data migration can involve any of a number of processes for moving data, data mining is a term used to describe pulling insights and information from data sets, and data consolidation might involve moving data to a central repository or location.

58. A. Wayne should look for systems that support AES-256 encryption at rest as well as customer-provided keys to ensure that his data remains safe while resident on his cloud provider's infrastructure. MD5 and SHA-1 are both hashing algorithms, not encryption algorithms, and CRC is a means of validating that data is intact.

59. C. Sandboxing technologies are very frequently used for testing malicious software. If you'd like to give it a try, Cuckoo Sandbox is an automated malware analysis tool that you can experiment with. Sandboxes are not used to build redundant infrastructure, for rapid application development, or for FIPS testing.

60. A. Sharing responsibility with a cloud provider can make the registered entity's job easier—but also increases the risk of unauthorized disclosure, makes the control structure more complex, and makes it harder to ensure confidentiality of encrypted data.

61. A. Static code analysis, the process of reviewing the source code, is the most likely way for Jason to identify business logic issues. Vulnerability scanning won't identify business logic issues, and the likelihood of dynamic testing identifying them is much lower than for static inspection. Software composition analysis focuses on identifying open source components in software, not on business logic.

62. A. Creating a snapshot will preserve both the memory state and the data associated with an instance. Making separate copies of any mounted volumes will support the investigation and capture any data that is not part of the instance itself. Shutting down the instance will lose memory state, and most cloud providers do not provide a forensic response team for customers.

63. C. Creating and using baselines helps ensure that systems and services meet an organization's desired configurations as they are deployed. Multifactor authentication and vulnerability scanning are both useful practices, but they don't help in this scenario. Default settings are one of the most common misconfigurations—using them instead of intentionally choosing settings is a root cause for misconfiguration issues!

64. B. A statement of work (SOW) describes the work that an organization will perform under the relationship defined by a master service agreement. An SLA is a service-level agreement, an NDA is a nondisclosure agreement, and a SOP is a standard operating procedure. None of these define what an organization will do as part of an MSA.

65. D. Christina is using federation, where an identity provider authenticates identities it is responsible for while service providers like Christina authorize users who have been authenticated to perform actions and to use rights inside of their service. This could involve client/server designs, but the question does not define this, and while Christina is acting as a service provider, the relationship itself is a federation relationship. Collaboration is not used to describe this type of identity architecture.

66. B. Software composition analysis is the process of identifying the open source components and packages that make up a tool or product. Naomi should perform software composition analysis to understand components and packages she may need to update or that could create additional risks in her environment. Static testing—either automatic or manual—would require reviewing source code, which would involve high levels of effort without meeting the high-level goal of understanding the risks of the components as components. IAST (interactive application security testing) is useful for validating running software but does not meet Naomi's needs.

67. B. Selah knows that there is multiple common open source licensing, including Apache and BSD licenses, the GNU public license (GPL), and others. Selah needs to understand the licenses that apply to the software she uses, particularly if she wants to distribute any software for commercial use. The cost of licensing, length of license period, and changes in the license are not common concerns for open source software due to the way that open source licenses are normally written.

68. D. The company is using single sign-on, a technology that allows users to sign on once and then remain signed in while using multiple services and systems. Each system or service may provide its own authorization to logged-in users. Federation relies on an identity provider, which authenticates users who can then use services from service providers; since Eric is operating inside of a single company, and no identity provider is mentioned, this is not federation. MFA (multifactor authentication) is not mentioned, and IAM is the general discipline of identity and access management.

69. B. ITIL defines three subprocesses for configuration management: configuration identification, configuration control, configuration verification and audit. If you encounter a question like this and aren't familiar with details of ITIL or other standards, consider which options are least likely to make sense in the scenario.

70. B. Conducting a gap analysis requires a baseline or configuration standard to validate against. Chuck knows that he'll need to build a baseline, then test against it. An OLA is an operational-level agreement used for internal service provider metrics services. A disaster recovery and business continuity plan is not typically required for a gap analysis, but not having one would likely be considered a gap, and an ITIL-based CI is useful for documentation but not a requirement here, either.

71. C. Annie knows that while automated testing is useful, it has limitations and will miss issues that a human can identify. That means that she'll focus on manual QA testing if she needs more insight into the software. Fuzzing tests software by providing unexpected inputs, which won't meet Annie's QA needs, and software composition analysis determines what open source components are part of a software package.

72. A. In federated environments identity providers will provide browsers or other clients with a token to pass to the service provider that supports the user's identity assertion. A password or session ID is not passed, and a URL may be passed but without a password.

73. C. Theresa is describing a recovery point objective, or the amount of data that can be lost after recovery from a disaster. A recovery time objective defines how long systems can be offline. Neither snapshot windows nor snapshot durations are commonly used terms.

74. D. The rate of risk occurrence per day is unlikely to provide useful context for the risk management program. The number of risks that have been identified and the number of risks that have occurred over a longer period of time can be useful, and the cost of the program itself is an important metric to track.

75. B. Storage capacity management is most frequently associated with managing costs in IaaS environments. It can also be a concern in both SaaS and PaaS environments, particularly if usage doesn't match typical customer models. Performance, continuity, and security are not major drivers of capacity tracking tools.

76. C. Lisa knows that one of the most difficult challenges in many modern organizations is to determine the full scope of the organization's cloud usage and environment. Even in organizations that have tight controls, additional services are often found when auditors assess actual usage.

77. A. MFA tokens are hardware devices and aren't stored in cloud secrets management tools. API keys, passwords, and certificates are all commonly stored in secrets repositories.

78. B. Gary's primary threat model with a remote workforce will be laptops and mobile devices. Using a DLP client on those devices will allow monitoring where the data is being used, accessed, and likely shared.

79. A. Tagging data when it is created ensures that it will be tagged from the beginning of its lifecycle. Additional tags may be added during the Use, Share, and Archive phases if they are needed.

80. B. Serverless environments are built around microservices meaning that identity and access management (IAM) focuses on very specific and directed rights for each role or service. Serverless allows organizations to ignore patching the underlying infrastructure, ephemeral infrastructure makes it hard for attackers to compromise and retain access to serverless deployments, and serverless relies on instrumentation for visibility.

81. D. Nick is using tenant partitioning by separating his customers into separate buckets. That means he can design around customers never having access to shared storage space, hopefully increasing the security of his design. This doesn't aggregate storage—in fact, it separates it. Using multiple buckets isn't virtualization or containerization, either.

82. A. Automated testing can frequently identify SQL injection, cross-site scripting, and component issues, but business logic risks are harder to identify without understanding of both business processes and how the code itself works. Katie may need additional review for critical code by humans in the process if she has recurring issues with business logic flaws.

83. A. Thulani is recording the chain of custody for the forensic artifacts. A chain of custody can be extremely important to prove that data was not tampered with, particularly in legal cases or police investigations.

84. A. The EU's GDPR includes a wide range of privacy requirements. U.S. law is far less consistent and does not directly align to EU requirements. This means that Derek knows that the difference in privacy law in different jurisdictions can be a significant compliance challenge.

85. B. Enabling password complexity requirements has largely been replaced by use of SSH keys and multifactor authentication. Changing the SSH port number and limiting which users can log in are also both common practices.

86. D. ISO/IEC 22301:2019 defines business continuity management. ISO 27001 is a standard on how to manage information security, ISO 28000 specifies security management systems, and there is no ISO 853-1.

87. D. DHCP (Dynamic Host Configuration Protocol) operates on UDP port 67 for the server and UDP port 68 for clients.

88. B. Sara's usage matches a hybrid cloud environment, where she provides some of the infrastructure and the rest is provided by third-party cloud providers. Private cloud is run by the organization, multicloud involves multiple vendors, and community clouds are created by groups with a common interest or objective that want to operate a cloud.

89. C. Isabelle knows that cloud providers commonly make APIs accessible for access to their logging and other facilities. She can take advantage of the API access to get the data she needs, but she will need to carefully document the process, queries, and other details to ensure her data is forensically sound.

90. A. Data in cloud environments should be encrypted at rest and then cryptographically shredded when it is no longer needed to ensure that the data is not recoverable.

91. A. Infrastructure as code strategies leverage code to design, build, and deploy infrastructure, allowing for quick changes at scale and the ability to redeploy or perform other maintenance easily and quickly. Containerization-based strategies focus on containers. While it may rely on code, containerization alone doesn't meet the description of what Mark is doing. Software as a cloud and dynamic scaling architecture were made up for this question.

92. D. A dedicated hardware security module (HSM) is the most secure option for organizations that have the money and security requirements to support it. A dedicated HSM provides a hardware that is dedicated to the customer, rather than the shared environment provided by a cloud HSM. A TPM (trusted platform module) is used to store cryptographic keys used for hardware and system boot time security and isn't used to store and manage general-use secret keys.

93. A. Ashley is conducting abuse case testing, which focuses on testing software like an attacker. IAST involves instrumenting applications to monitor them while they are running for any security issues. User acceptance testing is done in partnership with users to determine if the software meets their needs and functional requirements, and static testing reviews source code.

94. A. ISO 27001 defines a broad range of security controls and is a widely accepted international standard. SOC 1 is an audit standard for financial operations, GDPR is a data protection regulation for the EU, and HIPAA is a U.S. law covering healthcare and insurance providers.

95. B. An ITIL-based change management process typically starts with the creation of the RFC. It is then reviewed, then approved or denied, and then planning and implementation occur as well as an after-deployment review.

96. D. Gina's organization is using tokenization. They may choose to use a form of hashing for the tokenization process, but there is not enough information in the question to determine that. Masking would replace some data with alternate characters, avoiding revealing the entire data element. Anonymization seeks to remove any directly identifiable data like names, addresses, or similar information.

97. B. The requirement to retain data related to a lawsuit, investigation, or for other legal reasons is called a legal hold.

98. B. When certificates are revoked, they are placed on a certificate revocation list. Users and systems that use the certificate can check the CRL for that certificate authority to determine what certificates have been revoked. Certificates can still encrypt data, messages are not sent out to all users, and the expiration date is not changed for the certificate since it is included in the certificate itself.

99. A. Data stored in a database is considered structured data. Since there is a defined format, structured data is typically the easiest to perform data discovery on.

100. D. Since Patricia wants to have a system learn a baseline, then watch for new malicious behaviors while integrating the ability to learn, AI is her best option. AI-based systems can learn from data over time. A SIEM may include AI, but that is not specified here, making AI a better answer. A WAF (web application firewall) and an IDS (intrusion detection system) won't do what Patricia needs.

101. B. Kathleen knows that engaging external counsel with appropriate expertise with the laws of the country that her organization is moving into will result in the best answers. OWASP and NIST don't provide guidance on international law, and reviewing laws internally without expert counsel is typically not as likely to result in appropriate decision-making.

102. D. Business, legal, and regulatory requirements are all common drivers for data retention policies. Data integrity is important but typically doesn't drive data retention policies. Instead, data integrity is likely to drive technical implementation requirements that help to ensure data integrity is maintained over the data's lifecycle.

103. A. Parker should look for an API gateway that can help to rate limit and control API access by his organization's customers. API gateways often act as load balancers and firewalls as well, and API engine isn't a term typically used in this context.

104. B. Ron should be concerned about vendor lock-in due to the investment his organization has in the specific tools available in his vendor's environment. While this allows Ron's team to more fully take advantage of the features of the IaaS environment, it would take significant new investment to move to another cloud vendor since a large amount of the work would need to be redone. Interoperability is a concern when working between two or more clouds or services. Code escrow places source code with a third party in case the developer goes out of business, and API contention is not a commonly used term.

105. C. Rick's company is using data dispersion, the concept of storing data in more than one location to reduce the chance of a major loss event. Data cloning is not a commonly used term in this context. Data modeling is used to identify elements of data for efforts like database creation.

106. A. Using software composition analysis is a key first step when using open source tools, as it allows organizations to understand which components are part of their systems and services. After that, performing relevant updates and keeping track of what components may not be receiving updates is critical. Penetration testing and static code review may be helpful, but they aren't typical solutions in this scenario.

107. A. Megan is a data owner. Data custodians are responsible for transport, storage, and implementation of business rules for data. Data processors use data for business efforts, and data stewards are responsible for data governance tasks based on business rules.

108. A. Many open source packages do not have commercial or paid support or vendors to assess. This makes assessing the risk of open source packages and tools more difficult from a vendor risk perspective. Open source software is actually easier to conduct static code review of than many commercial products since the code is available. Open source software vendors do sell support contracts, and risk information is available via the same sources as other vulnerability information.

109. B. Henry knows that traditional forensic copy techniques won't work but that a snapshot will provide the same information that the officer is used to working with. Thus, Henry needs to explain what is possible and how it can be used. The forensic copy process may be faster or slower depending on the cloud systems and process; the forensic copy can be verified, particularly if the system is paused; and cloud providers do allow forensic copies of customer-owned and -managed systems.

110. D. Audits fall under security review, where security measures and processes are validated and checked for regular testing. Design and incident management doesn't include this, and security testing ensures that security mechanisms are validated.

111. C. In IaaS environments, network connectivity is determined by instance type and sizing, and thus how much customers will pay for the capabilities they need. Changing to a more capable instance type is the most common way to do this, although providers may also provide the ability to increase network bandwidth as an independent setting. Changing network interface cards or operating system settings won't accomplish Diana's task.

112. D. The final stage of the cloud secure data lifecycle is to destroy the data.

113. B. Sarbanes–Oxley has language requiring that fraud is reported, including data breaches, and that reporting must be included in quarterly and annual reports.

114. D. Agile processes gather information from users, customers, and documentation. Reverse-engineering software to obtain requirements is not a common requirements-gathering process.

115. B. The OWASP Top 10 provides a regularly updated list of the most common pitfalls and problems with application development and is a commonly used basis for training in many organizations. MITRE's ATT&CK framework is used to document adversary tactics and techniques, and both the SANS Blue Book and NIST's CMBD were made up for this question.

116. C. Cloud service brokers aggregate services, provide integration services, and otherwise help their customers work with cloud service providers. Regulators enforce the law, and cloud stewards were made up for this question.

117. A. The CVE (Common Vulnerabilities and Exploits) rating system provides an industry standard to describe, rank, and track vulnerabilities. None of the other items listed are vulnerability ranking systems.

118. D. The EU's General Data Protection Regulation (GDPR) would directly impact the organization's data gathering and handling practices in France. ISO/IEC 27018 and GAPP are both standards that the organization might choose to adopt, and FERPA is a U.S. higher education privacy regulation.

119. C. Fiona knows that capturing snapshots is the most frequent means of creating backups for guest operating systems. Copying the underlying guest OS disks and using backup clients are both sometimes used, but snapshots of the guest OS from the guest itself is not.

120. B. Olivia knows that cloud providers typically don't allow customers to audit them, but that many provide audit artifacts upon request. She should request the audit information she needs and may even find that the provider already makes it available as part of an audit artifact service.

121. A. ITIL describes release closure as what occurs after verifying that logs and the management system are up-to-date with updated information. Deployment and build happen before this, and documentation is not an ITIL subprocess for releases.

122. A. Type 1, or bare-metal, hypervisors are used to host most cloud IaaS services. Running Type 2 hypervisors on top of existing operating systems is typically less efficient and adds operational and management overhead. There are only two types of hypervisors, meaning Types 3 and 4 don't exist.

123. C. Sean should rent space in an existing Tier 3 datacenter facility. If Sean was operating at a large scale instead of having outgrown a converted closet, building or buying a datacenter might make sense.

124. C. Customers are typically not allowed into cloud service providers datacenter facilities. This helps to reduce risk of access to customer data due to physical access. Inexpensive power, environmental risks, and redundant design are all common concerns for cloud datacenter design.

125. B. Maria's organization is using a masking technique to hide most of the credit card number. Leaving the last four numbers un-masked is a technique intended to allow validation of card numbers. Hashing was the result in a fixed length string of letters and numbers as part of a one-way function. Randomization might be used to mix up real data for a sample data set, and de-identification removes personally identifiable data like addresses, Social Security numbers, or names.

Index

versioning, 38, 70, 196, 216
virtual client, 102, 231
virtual environment, 92, 226
virtual local area network (VLAN), 52, 104, 202, 204, 224, 232
virtual machine (VM)
    configuration management (CM) tool requirements within, 64, 213
    maintenance mode for, 87, 224
    monitoring of, 92, 226
    movement of, 2, 176
    security for, 53, 96, 203, 228
virtual private network (VPN), 136–137, 202, 204, 211, 232, 251
virtual trusted platform module (vTPM), 94, 227
virtualization, 59, 158, 207–208, 263
virtualization management toolset, 132, 248
virtualization platforms, 5, 178
virtualization toolset, 144, 255

virtualized servers, 4, 177
VMWare, 101, 231
volume-based storage, 36, 190, 195, 198

W

warm sites, 60, 146, 187, 208, 257
waterfall methodology, 78, 156, 220, 262
web application firewall (WAF), 70, 74, 216, 218
web-based payroll system, 180
website, 51, 53, 97, 202, 204, 228
white box (full knowledge) testing methodology, 68, 215, 220

Z

zero-trust network architecture, 3, 176, 260
zero-wiping, 189

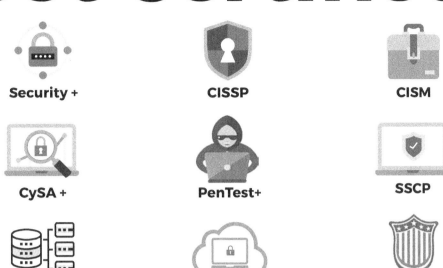

Online Test Bank

Register to gain one year of FREE access after activation to the online interactive test bank to help you study for your (ISC)² Certified Cloud Security Professional (CCSP) certification exam—included with your purchase of this book! All of the chapter questions and the practice tests in this book are included in the online test bank so you can practice in a timed and graded setting.

Register and Access the Online Test Bank

To register your book and get access to the online test bank, follow these steps:

1. Go to www.wiley.com/go/sybextestprep. You'll see the "**How to Register Your Book for Online Access**" instructions.
2. Click "here to register" and then select your book from the list.
3. Complete the required registration information, including answering the security verification to prove book ownership. You will be emailed a pin code.
4. Follow the directions in the email or go to www.wiley.com/go/sybextestprep.
5. Find your book on that page and click the "Register or Login" link with it. Then enter the pin code you received and click the "Activate PIN" button.
6. On the Create an Account or Login page, enter your username and password, and click Login or, if you don't have an account already, create a new account.
7. At this point, you should be in the test bank site with your new test bank listed at the top of the page. If you do not see it there, please refresh the page or log out and log back in.